Healthy, Active and Outside!

Running an outdoor programme
in the early years

Janice Filer

Routledge
Taylor & Francis Group

LONDON AND NEW YORK

First published 2008
by Routledge
2 Park Square, Milton Park, Abingdon, Oxon OX14 4RN

Simultaneously published in the USA and Canada
by Routledge
270 Madison Ave, New York, NY 10016

Routledge is an imprint of the Taylor & Francis Group, an informa business

© 2008 Janice Filer

Typeset in Times New Roman by
GreenGate Publishing Services, Tonbridge, Kent

Printed and bound in Great Britain by
Antony Rowe Ltd, Chippenham

British Library Cataloguing in Publication Data
A catalogue record for this book is available from the British Library

Library of Congress Cataloging-in-Publication Data
Filer, Janice.
  Healthy, active and outside! : running an outdoor programme in the
early years / Janice Filer.
      p. cm.
  ISBN 978-0-415-43652-6 (pbk) -- ISBN 978-0-203-93309-1 (ebk) 1.
Outdoor education. 2. Outdoor recreation for children. 3. Play
environments. 4. Adventure education. I. Title.
  LB1047.F55 2008
  371.3'84--dc22
2007046455

ISBN 978–0–415–43652–6 (pbk)
ISBN 978–0–203–93309–1 (ebk)

Contents

Illustrations

Tables

Acknowledgements

Firstly, thanks to all the children and families I have worked with during the programme for permission to share their stories and to use their photographs; for their willingness to take part and the commitment they have shown to the project despite their day-to-day struggles to cope with difficult lives – I have so much admiration for all of them. I am especially indebted to them for their support of the programme and the time they have given to share the enjoyment of a happy, healthy, active outdoor lifestyle; for their continued interest and attempts to understand that there is method in my so-called madness – not often do parents see their child's teacher sitting in the middle of the woods in the pouring rain trying to light a fire to keep everyone warm, or sliding down muddy wet banks during a game of chase!

My thanks to the stakeholders of the projects who continued to provide funding – Bridging the Gap, On Track, the Children's Fund and the Bristol Behaviour Support Service – and for the confidence they have shown in my work.

My thanks to the school, Badock's Wood, in which the programme takes place, particularly the Early Years Department, who trusted me to work on a regular basis with the children in their care; to the loyal group of crèche workers who have supported and stayed with me every step of the way; to the Learning Support Assistant, Lin Collier, who has spent more time outdoors with me than she has inside, and for the understanding she has shown when life gets tough.

My thanks to the lecturers at Bristol University, Dr Christopher Riddoch and Dr Angela Page, who encouraged me to carry out research on this project during my time there as a part-time student.

I would also like to thank the head teacher of Bluebell Valley Nursery, Pat Heaslip, who had faith in my instinctive teaching style and allowed me to open up my doors for play to flow freely in and out regardless of the weather or time of day. She encouraged me to take full advantage of the 'awe and wonder' aspect of education found only in the natural world outside the classroom and of the children's desire to gain first-hand knowledge and understanding of the world around them. I am indebted to her quiet encouragement which allowed me to find my own way through the fence at the back of the school grounds and to take the children with me in my quest to find an alternative, fully inclusive way of teaching wholly outside, in the beautiful bluebell woods surrounding the school, long before it became fashionable once again to take children outdoors. And no, I still do not conform: I do not wear shoes or 'proper' teaching clothes; you don't need them outdoors in the woods – there's no one of importance there to see you!

Finally, and most importantly of all, thanks to my family, all of whom have taken an interest and supported my work – Paul, Jo, Kass, Josh, Sam, Lauren and Jakob for their patience and understanding of my outdoor escapades, volunteering to help in a myriad of ways, from video-recording the programme, lighting safe fires, supervising children and always acting as fine role models in demonstrations of good practice, attitude and behaviour. To my five healthy, active children much love and thanks for the many long, joyful hours we have spent playing together outside. For showing me the importance of outdoor play and giving me the inspiration to write this book. For the lifelong passion you have given me for the outdoor way of life by generously sharing childhood activities, paddling through streams, watching wildlife, seeds grow, clouds scudding across the sky, wind blowing through trees, experiencing the sheer joy of running down hills or through overgrown meadows – essential sustenance to feed the spirit. All this has enabled the magic of childhood never to fade from my life and hopefully yours too. To their generosity and ability to share it all with other people's children even when they have such full, independent lives of their own. Lastly, thanks especially to my own parents, who always stayed outdoors with me as a child long after everyone else had gone inside.

Abbreviations

CD	Creative Development
CLL	Communication, Language and Literacy
ELG	Early Learning Goals
EPPE	Effective Provision of Pre-School Education
ESD	Education for Sustainable Development
EYFS	Early Years Foundation Stage
HAO	Healthy, Active and Outside
INSET	In-Service Education and Training
KUW	Knowledge and Understanding of the World
LA	Local Authority
LEA	Local Education Authority
LTL	Learning Through Landscapes
NGB	National Governing Body
NOS	National Occupational Standards
NVQ	National Vocational Qualification
PD	Physical Development
PSED	Personal, Social and Emotional Development
PSRN	Problem Solving, Reasoning and Numeracy
TOPS	Top Outdoor Programmes

1 Introduction

The emphasis on physical expression in this programme gives children the opportunity to learn and succeed in a holistic child-centred way. The Healthy, Active and Outside (HAO) programme is unique and distinctive and presents exciting opportunities to stimulate decision making with regard to developing the outdoor environment into a space to improve knowledge and understanding of outdoor education. It has the potential to contribute towards the development of the whole child, including social interaction, communication and relationship building for all children, whatever their ability, at the same time as interpreting the curriculum guidance creatively to engage all children. However, this cannot be achieved without some understanding about play itself. Equally important is the need to develop a shared understanding of the outside area's potential use for all outdoor play and the need to create opportunities for risk taking at the same time as offering children opportunities to be alone or to be with others, to be active or to be still, and much more. Throughout the book the terms 'setting' or 'school' are used to denote any education establishment for young children and the term 'parent' is used to denote parents, carers and guardians. In case studies all names have been changed to protect the children's identities.

It is hoped this book will inspire practitioners to assess the potential of their outdoor space and the feasibility of making the necessary improvements to implement the programme explained in it. Following the advice in this book will help unlock the potential of your grounds by increasing awareness among staff of the potential of outdoor learning and give them the confidence and knowledge to exploit the full value of the outdoors for all children in their setting.

The first chapter of this book gives background information about the author and the history of the outdoor programme. It describes the reasons for writing the book and gives a brief overview of the themes running throughout it. In addition, it examines the importance for young children of being active and getting outdoors and includes information about young children's mental health in relation to the need for being active and getting outside to experience fresh air, daylight and the natural outdoor space. Finally, there is a section on how to use this book.

There is a growing awareness that children need to get outdoors more as there are serious concerns about children's activity levels and rising associated behavioural, mental and physical health problems. With structured, technology-driven lives it is easier for children to stay indoors playing on computers or at PlayStation games, or watching DVDs, videos and television, than to socialise with other children in a healthy, active way outdoors in the fresh air. With childhood obesity at the top of the political agenda, much emphasis is placed on getting children healthy by encouraging them to be more active. Children are entitled to learn in the way that best suits them, and as playing outdoors is an integral part of their natural growth and development, that often means taking the curriculum outdoors with them. Bronowski (1975) describes the experiential approach to learning:

> We see it every time a child learns to couple hand and tool together...to fly a kite or play a penny whistle. With the practical action there goes another, namely finding pleasure in the action for its own sake in the skill that one perfects, and perfects by being pleased with it. This at the bottom is responsible for every work of art and science too: our poetic delight in what human beings do because they can do it. The most exciting thing about that is that the poetic use in the end has truly profound results.
>
> (Bronowski, 1975: 116)

This book provides a guide on how to set up a physically active outdoor programme in any early years setting that can be adapted to suit any timescale from one or two days to a whole term or year's work. The programme presents many opportunities for engaging and motivating children, young people and staff in considering a whole site and whole organisation approach to teaching and learning outdoors. The main focus is to convince practitioners of the value of outdoor play – to show them how to get young children outside to take part in healthy, outdoor physical activities that provide them with positive fun experiences which will enhance their general learning and development; and in addition, to encourage children to become healthier by improving their fitness alongside feeling the sheer joy of just being outside. At last there is government investment and corporate involvement and support for school grounds. Today, supporting the health and full development of every child and providing opportunities for enjoyment and personal learning have become a concern for many businesses, including ones not directly involved in producing sports or play equipment.

Background information about the author

The author, Dr Janice Filer, is an early years specialist currently working for the Bristol Behaviour Support Service. This book is the result of over 30 years' continual experience in the field of outdoor physical education and movement for children from 0 to 18 years of age which began long before it became fashionable once again to focus on outdoor learning. It draws upon the findings of a research project that focuses on running an outdoor activity programme for children in the Foundation Stage of education from 2000 until the present day. As a result of the programme's efficacy and success in a multi-agency project called 'Bridging the Gap', the author was commissioned by the Children's Fund to continue the work. The programme continues to include an element of research which focuses on listening to young children's views and experiences of the outdoor space.

History of the outdoor programme

The outdoor programme is the central focus of an action research study which began as a pilot study in a Bristol nursery school in 1991. It was originally set up to make a case to the local authority for learning outside the classroom and to provide an understanding of the unique contribution that outdoor experiences can make to young children's lives. The programme was developed by the teacher in the project, who held the post of coordinator for the environment and outdoor play in the nursery school from 1989 to 1999. The outdoor environment created there enabled children to learn and develop through outdoor experiential activities and was the pilot for the longer-term project. This programme evolved over time and is now known as the 'Healthy, Active and Outside (HAO) programme', developed as an early intervention for the multidisciplinary project Bridging the Gap from 1999. The programme was taken on by On Track in 2002 and is funded by the Children's Fund until 2008. In 2005 the outdoor programme was runner-up in a national challenge to find the best outdoor project in a competition organised by Learning Through Landscape and the early years journal *Nursery World*.

In addition, this book sets out to demonstrate good practice which will inspire other settings and motivate them to develop their own outdoor play. It is aimed at the diverse workforce that now exists in the Early Years Foundation Stage of education and childcare and takes into consideration the four overarching themes of the framework:

1   the unique child
2   positive relationships
3   the environment
4   learning and development.

It provides an example of an active outdoor programme to help settings develop accessible and affordable solutions to using the outside space that will enable them to take on board the strategy for children 'Choice for parents, the best start for children' and the 2006 Children Act, and meet many of the 'Standards for Learning Development and Care for Children from Birth to Five' set out in the statutory framework for the Early Years Foundation Stage (EYFS) (DfES, 2007; formerly the Curriculum Guidance for the Foundation Stage, National Standards for Under Eights Day Care and Childminding, Every Child Matters and Change for Children documents).

The activities in the programme are designed for children from approximately 3 to 5 years of age but with a little imagination, they can be adapted for any age! All activities in this book are designed to include children at every stage, from the initial audit of the existing site through to making surveys, planning, designing and creating the environment, flyers, invitations, planting, digging, growing and cooking, playing and demonstrating to others what has been achieved through all the stages of the programme, to reflection and full engagement in the final celebrations. The activities are designed to include as many or as few of the other adults involved in the setting as necessary, from parents, staff, other children to volunteers and visitors from the local community, depending on how individual settings decide to use them.

This practical book will guide you through the process of changing and developing the outdoor environment of your setting to maximise its learning potential and to get children outside in the fresh air to enjoy experiential physical activities. It is full of ideas and strategies to enhance the area outside the setting in order to make the most of the grounds and will enable you to recognise the true value that the outdoors can have on a child's life and educational development.

The content includes real-life examples, case studies and examples from the programme that illustrate the process of setting up an outdoor programme. It also includes explanations of the core values that highlight the importance and benefits of outdoor play and step-by-step photocopiable activity sheets that guide you through each stage of the activity to encourage the participation of the children taking part.

Once children start formal education they can spend as much as 25 per cent of their time outside in the grounds, making friends, playing games, meeting challenges, taking risks, facing new experiences and learning about their own abilities and the world around them. The grounds around a setting are the one space that all children have access to, and, as such, are a valuable resource for teaching all aspects of the early years curriculum. The programme demonstrates how practitioners can promote and enhance the development of those grounds in order to use and value the outdoor play area in diverse and innovative ways.

Outdoor play in the early years

Outdoor play is no longer just about physical development; it is now given the equal status to indoor play it deserves in terms of the planned experiences that are provided for young children. The outside area offers a rich, multi-sensory environment that is meaningful and stimulating for all young children, providing them with 'real' experiences that help embed their early learning, at the same time fulfilling the requirements of the EYFS curriculum framework. Young children are by nature experiential learners and playing out is an integral part of their growth and development. Most children find the outdoors exciting, engaging and fun and are eager to be outside and ready to learn from the 'real' play experiences they have outdoors. The outdoors offers young children the essential experiences that are vital to all areas of their well-being, health and development. Outdoors is where most children would rather be and there is no excuse for them not to be there because any indoor learning can be supported and extended by applying it to the 'real' situations that children encounter when they play outdoors.

Being outside gives children first-hand contact with weather, seasons and the natural world and it encourages all aspects of children's development because it has such a positive impact on their mental health and sense of well-being. Playing outside in open spaces offers children opportunities for doing things in different ways and on different scales to indoors. Outdoor environments give children freedom to explore and use all their senses, and encourage them to be physically active and exuberant and to let off steam.

Why outdoors?

It is still sometimes assumed that outdoor education requires some form of 'trip' out of school and with increasing bureaucratic requirements for off-site visits it can seem daunting for practitioners to organise. The school grounds offer a comparable alternative for outdoor learning as this is the one place in a setting that can be used for any subject, at short notice and for little or no cost. Whether your grounds are large and varied or small and barren, they represent a rich resource that offers many educational benefits.

The outdoors should no longer just be thought of as a place for adventure activities or field work because it is widely accepted that all subjects can benefit from taking place outdoors, and this book includes some cross-curricular ideas for getting started. For those practitioners used to the comfort of their classrooms, even going into the outdoor grounds can seem daunting but if they listen to children and take the lead from them there is no alternative, as the outside is where the majority of children would rather be. Using the grounds for teaching and learning provides access to resources not available in a classroom. There are many more opportunities outdoors to use different teaching styles which enhance children's self-esteem and self-confidence and develop stronger relationships between staff and pupils (Titman, 1999). Using the outdoors as a teaching and learning environment sits well with the current early years philosophy as at least 90 per cent of the learning outdoors is a hands-on experience. Studies have shown that the retention rate for learning by doing is 75 per cent – compared to 5 per cent for listening. It is hoped that this book will provide strong support for learning outside the classroom for all young children because giving them the opportunity to get outdoors to learn in the experiential way offered in this programme will make a significant contribution to raising their achievement.

The 'Learning outside the Classroom' manifesto

The 'Learning outside the Classroom' manifesto provides the foundation of the programme and it states:

> We believe that every young person should experience the world beyond the classroom as an essential part of learning and personal development, whatever their age or ability or circumstance.
>
> (DfES, 2006b)

The manifesto provides a powerful impetus for implementing the programme in any early years setting and highlights the importance of learning about real issues in real places amongst real people so there is no longer the excuse that children should be inside learning. Children will only value the world they live in if they can experience it first-hand. The programme impacts on children's self-esteem, achievement and behaviour and raises their expectations and aspirations through innovative teaching and learning. Motivation is enhanced, impacting upon raising standards of achievement. By focusing on sustainable development of the grounds and the modelling of good practice found in the programme, settings that follow its guidelines will be able to promote positive behaviours which will transfer to the local community. Children who take part in the programme will grow and develop sound in the knowledge of how to make a positive contribution to society.

The programme is designed to take place in a range of outdoor environments depending on what space is available. The grounds of many schools and settings provide rich, multifaceted learning resources which offer opportunities for formal and informal learning and play. The programme can take place in the local environment (with permission) because in every community there is a wealth of opportunity for outdoor learning within walking distance of the setting which can be used to enrich all areas of the curriculum. The programme is designed to be used in a flexible way and can take place at any time that suits the individual setting – within the normal session times, before or after school, during weekends or the holidays, depending on need.

Anyone can be involved in the programme and by working together all young children can benefit from getting outside in the fresh air to take part. It is particularly beneficial for young children whose circumstances make it difficult for them to participate. All that is needed is an open mind, flexibility, the will to make it happen and creativity in the way the programme is adapted. Everyone can enjoy playing outside, and watching young children learn through real outdoor experiences shows that the outdoor environment reaches children in ways that the indoor cannot. High-quality outdoor play will inspire children to develop a healthy appetite for an active outdoor lifestyle which will serve them well into adulthood.

Whatever the weather, the outdoors provides young children of all ages and abilities with endless opportunities for discovery, involvement and challenge. A first-hand knowledge of the world around them, opportunities to be spontaneous and get involved in imaginative play, movement and sensory experiences are all enhanced by getting outside.

This book is full of strategies and ideas for effective practice and gives useful advice on how to set up an outdoor programme which will help support practitioners in providing a broad and balanced curriculum for the young children they work with, across all areas of learning. It provides information and ideas to enable the practitioner to create an outdoor environment to inspire quality learning experiences and an inclusive, enriched curriculum for all young children. The ideas and resources in this book have been tried out in real settings by the author and as such they are accessible, practical and designed to help the practitioner make the most of the outdoor space at the same time as maximising learning experiences. The book aims to inspire its reader to feel motivated to set up an outside learning environment for young children, based on advice and practical ideas on how to go about it with confidence and the knowledge that the research behind the programme proves that it really works in practice.

The programme is based upon the philosophy of the Forest Schools developed in Denmark in the early 1980s, where children are allowed free exploration of the outdoor environment as an integral part of their early education. The first programme took place once a week for 30 sessions and children were withdrawn from their usual school curriculum to attend. It took place wholly outdoors in three 10-week blocks to fit into the school terms, throughout the changing seasons, whatever the weather. Children between the ages of 3 and 6 years were encouraged to develop personal and social skills through the mastery of small, achievable tasks and through the exploration of the outdoor environment; they were also encouraged to grow in confidence and self-esteem.

Children learn to respect their environment, to abide by rules and standards of behaviour, to work in teams and to respect one another. The benefits to the children are on many levels as they learn to appreciate what their bodies can do in the natural outside world. Although the programme is not particularly designed for children with special educational needs, many of the children attending the first programme needed additional support for emotional, behavioural or social difficulties they were experiencing at home, school or both. Many of the children were exhibiting challenging behaviour and were given the opportunity to develop control over their behaviour and improve their concentration, independence, social and physical skills through outdoor experiential activities. Safety outdoors is given priority as children learn about the boundaries within which they must work. The sense of freedom from being outdoors in a large open space instead of being cooped up in a classroom is well suited to children whose learning style demands that they need to learn in an active, 'hands-on' way.

The programme aims to teach children positive interaction skills, communication skills, problem-solving strategies, anger management and appropriate school behaviours, and to promote their self-esteem and general social competence through outdoor adventure and environmental activities. The outdoors offers specific opportunities for children to satisfy their sense of adventure. There is immense value in playing under an ever-changing sky in different weather conditions in the fresh air where there is natural light. Playing outdoors is a fundamental aspect of a child's learning experience. Having a safe outdoor play space to run around in freely and play with a range of both natural resources and manufactured play equipment is an essential part of early child development. A safe outdoor space to take part in active, healthy outdoor activities and practise physical skills alongside learning about the world around them and their place within it is an essential part of early childhood. Never before has it been so important to enable children to have an active, healthy outdoor lifestyle as it is today. With increasing obesity problems, use of technology and inactive lifestyles it is important to provide a stimulating outdoor environment where children can initiate, construct, pretend and create freely.

Figure 1.1 Exploring natural materials

Figure 1.2 The power of the hands-on approach to learning leads to full engagement

When children first venture outside, most outdoor play is physical but with time it will develop to become more imaginative, realistic and progressive. Often the learning that takes place outside the classroom is the most memorable of all experiences that help children make sense of the world around them by linking feelings with the learning that takes place. These early outdoor experiences have a strong influence on our values and the decisions we make and often stay with us well into adulthood, affecting everything we do regarding behaviour, work and our day-to-day lifestyles.

Learning outside the classroom is not just about what we learn but about the way that we learn, about how and where we learn. Direct experience is a powerful tool for raising achievement. The

Figure 1.3 Working together

hands-on experiential, holistic approach of the programme maximises the potential for learning as it involves a powerful combination of physical, visual and naturalistic ways of learning. Research shows that it is important to understand how the brain works and how different learning styles are used in the acquisition of knowledge. It also shows that children need to engage with the world around them through experiencing it first-hand. 'We have to understand that the world can only be grasped by action, not by contemplation. The hand is more important than the eye...The hand is the cutting edge of the mind' (Bronowski, 1975: 116).

The programme is based on this powerful approach to learning that is often called 'experiential' or 'authentic' learning. Throughout the programme children explore what they see, touch, hear, taste, smell and do. Good-quality learning outside the classroom will support what is going on inside the classroom as it will lead to a deeper understanding of the difficult concepts that span traditional subject boundaries, such as listening, problem solving and thinking, and the life skills of interpersonal communication, cooperation and team building.

Learning through play

Play is the language of children, and through pretending they learn to navigate between real and imaginary worlds while learning the differences between them. Creative outdoor play gives children the opportunity to use their imaginations, which helps to promote original thinking, flexibility, adaptability, empathy and the ability to generate multiple solutions to a problem. Play is the most important activity that children will take part in outside as it is a means through which they find stimulation, well-being and happiness in order to grow physically, emotionally and intellectually. The outdoor environment is well suited to meeting children's needs for all aspects of play and is the most relevant way of offering learning based upon first-hand experiences and individual interests.

Getting outdoors gives children the opportunity to take part in activities that extend their knowledge, understanding and skills and lay the foundations for future learning through a combination of free and structured play. Children will experience the wonderment and excitement of the outdoor environment whilst establishing a healthy attitude towards an active, outdoor lifestyle. The well-structured outdoor play activities suggested in Chapter 9, which utilise a wide range of existing resources to make the most of the outdoor environment, if they are selected with care for planned activities in each of the Early Years Foundation Stage (EYFS) learning areas, will give children the opportunity to meet challenges in a variety of ways. Children need free play to extend and deepen learning and in Chapter 6 there is a section which suggests practical ideas for setting up the outside for free play. Presenting and setting them up in a stimulating way will entice the children to make best use of them.

Children need to experience a variety of situations, and the outdoor space is as important as the indoor one. It needs to be neither too daunting nor too lacking in challenge, and to look attractive if it is going to stimulate the children. Most settings have some outdoor space which is suitable for children to run around in freely and use wheeled toys and small games equipment such as balls and beanbags. There should also be some safe way in which children can climb, swing, hang and balance. A grassy area will provide many opportunities for outdoor play where children can exert themselves as they run up and down and push, pull and carry portable loads. An undulating surface, preferably a grassy one with some natural features such as bushes, will provide children with exciting challenges.

Whatever the size, shape or surface of the outdoor play space, it can be made attractive and inviting by the way it is set up for the children to play. Any unsightly areas can be disguised, bare walls can be brightened up and stimulating markings can be drawn on the ground even if they are only temporary chalk marks. A large outdoor play space, well endowed with natural features, will stimulate activities such as running, jumping, balancing and climbing. With a little imagination and planning, even a small concrete yard can be set up to encourage good-quality outdoor play.

With supervision, all children need to know how to carry outdoor equipment and how to set it up safely to suit their own needs. As the children become more competent outdoors, wheeled toys can be extended to become part of imaginative play. Fixed climbing frames can be very versatile if they are not always used for climbing. Provide a variety of props to transform them into imaginative play bases such as dens, boats or rockets. Patches of garden can be designated for digging. Provide children with a range of items such as buckets, spades, old flowerpots, sieves, moulds and wooden planks to use outdoors. Access to water for dampening things down and for washing dirty hands and equipment provides many opportunities for extending outdoor play. Encourage investigative play by fixing up pulleys, water trays and planks of wood to make gradients. Outdoor resources need to be set up with care to avoid dangerous situations. Children need to help clear away messy activities so that they learn how to clear up after themselves. Keep a set of outdoor-only child-sized dustpans and brushes for this purpose.

The role of the adult

Once the children are involved in any outdoor activity, adults need to ensure that they show an interest in what they are doing by watching and giving sensitive assurance and encouragement to extend the children's play. Once children become familiar with the activities or equipment provided, the adult's role is to help them become more confident and controlled. An adult may need to intervene to prevent any dangerous activity from happening and explain why it was necessary to intervene. Some children need to have their energies redirected if they are placing themselves or other children at risk or are behaving in an unacceptable way, spoiling other children's play, showing off, not concentrating on a difficult movement, or being too noisy. In addition, the adult should compliment children or show delight in their accomplishments.

The role of the adult is one of sensitive, constructive intervention, showing an awareness of what the children are doing, respect for a child's need for privacy and a feeling for when to extend their understanding. The adult must always be careful not to take over an activity to the extent that a child loses interest. During outdoor play the adult will have an active role, as many outdoor activities require an adult to facilitate children's learning, whilst interacting with them in a physical way. The adult may be a passive observer, an interested listener, a leader of the activity or game or there to help the children move on from a plateau by using open-ended questions to make them think. Demonstrations are useful to illustrate and reinforce the task or activity but should be used with care so that children still have the confidence to find their own ways of doing things. By fully exploring the possibilities of outdoor play with children, the adult will realise that its potential for early learning is on equal par to any other type of play area.

Resources and storage

The main resource is the outdoor play space itself. This needs to be swept or washed down regularly. It needs to be well maintained and checked regularly to remove any dangerous hazards. All other outdoor props need to be collected together from a variety of sources. Reclaimed materials should be cleaned and made safe as young children are apt to put things into their mouths. Change the resources regularly to provide new experiences and challenges. It is important to have a set of resources which are used just outdoors. Duplicate indoor resources so that the children will not be disappointed when they want to play with them outside. The outdoor resources need to be collected together, cleaned and checked for safety at the end of each day. They need to be stored separately from the indoor resources so that there is no confusion. Outdoor resources should be stored safely in labelled containers, near the outdoor play space. Make a note of the number of resources put out and count them back in at the end of each day. Wash and store them ready for use again.

Organisation

Ideally the inside space should open directly onto the outdoor space so that children can have free access to it. For this to occur, the outdoor space needs to be constantly supervised. If this is not possible, you need to plan a time when you can take the whole group of children outdoors together. If there is another adult available for some of the time, small groups may be able to play outside. The children may be playing freely or they may be taking part in more structured activities. Group sizes will vary according to the activity. Children might be playing individually, in pairs, in small groups or taking part in a whole group activity. Care must be taken not to overcrowd the outdoor area with too many children or too many resources because children need room to run around and use their bodies in a more energetic way than they do indoors. Many outdoor activities invite bold body movements or involve the use of large-scale equipment. The type of equipment and materials provided for children to play outdoors will determine the range of activities which take place. Children will often make their own decisions about what equipment they need for their play, solving their own problems in their own way, but they need to be reminded of all safety issues, ground rules and boundaries each time they go outdoors as it is very easy for children to forget them once they become involved in play.

Young children should spend as much time outside in the fresh air as they spend indoors and need well-designed, well-organised, integrated indoor and outdoor environments which are available simultaneously. Being able to play outside is not an optional extra for young children; it should be part of every child's daily environment and life. The indoor and outdoor environment should offer experiences which are significantly different from each other but at the same time offer young children unique complementary experiences which allow them to play, learn or just be. Outdoor and indoor play should be offered simultaneously, with equal status and attention but in a joined-up way which supports young children's holistic development and all areas of the early years curriculum. The outside area must be considered on equal terms with the inside space and needs to be well thought out and organised for optimum use by both adults and children, and its design must support developmentally appropriate practice which is driven by the children's individual needs and interests.

Many children relate well to the learning experiences offered outdoors because the freedom of being outside enables them to move about without the restrictions often in place in the indoor area. Children can be more active, noisy or messy and use all their senses and their whole body in ways which are not possible inside. They can engage in the outdoor environment to explore, and make sense of life and the world around them, as well as expressing feelings freely and being creative. To make the most of the natural resources outdoors the early years curriculum should be offered through a wide variety of holistic experiences which range across the continuum from active to calm.

To encourage children's participation, independence, self-organisation and empowerment the adult plays a crucial role in achieving an effective learning environment by ensuring that outside provision is well organised, stimulating, play based and built upon children's interests in order to meet their individual needs. In order for high-quality outdoor play to take place, where children are involved and deeply engaged in activity, children need to know they have time not to be hurried so

Figure 1.4 Making a fence over a period of several weeks

that they can develop play ideas. These ideas need to be supported by sensitive adults who respect that some things need to be left in place for more than one session. The nature of some play sees children go in and out of playing over a period of time as they create scenarios and develop resources and play spaces as they are driven by the need to problem-solve on a big scale until the play idea has been exhausted. This play can go on for days or even weeks, depending on the interests of the children at the time, and needs uninterrupted time.

Concerns relating to outdoor teaching

Some of the concerns that practitioners unused to outdoor teaching might have include:

- distraction to others
- discipline
- peer reaction
- unpredictable weather.

To help practitioners new to working outdoors feel more confident, they need a progressive induction, starting with the opportunity to observe more experienced colleagues, followed by a period of team teaching. With agreed ground rules and a defined area that children know to come back to, it will not take long to convince them of the value of working outdoors.

Distraction to others

Some practitioners feel children playing outdoors will distract those still inside. This can be avoided by carefully choosing the location and setting clear guidelines before the children go out. Children should be taught that noise levels must be kept down to reasonable levels near the building but further away they can make more noise. Setting up zones for quiet play near the building and those inviting more exuberant physical play further afield will alleviate this problem.

Discipline

There are often concerns about how to cope with the discipline needed to work outside. Once children are used to going outside to learn, their behaviour is often better than it is inside as they are more self-motivated. This is particularly true for kinaesthetic learners (predominantly boys) because the physical movement that naturally accompanies outside activities will aid concentration.

Peer reaction

Some practitioners worry what their colleagues will think if they are regularly outdoors with children and are at times embarrassed that their colleagues will perceive their outdoor lessons as not 'proper' work, or that the children will look to be 'just playing about' to passers-by. These concerns will cease by the end of the academic year because the progress the children make will justify the decision to move outdoors for learning and remove any doubts that might have existed at first. You will be able to relax in the knowledge that not only has outdoor education yielded the desired results but the children have had the most enjoyable start to their formal education possible and it has been good for you too!

Case study

When I first joined a nursery school as a physical education specialist, being used to working outdoors on a daily basis I quite naturally and unthinkingly opened my doors from start to end of each session to give children free choice of equal access to the inside and outside. I never fully understood the complaints from colleagues that it was easy for me because my class never did any proper work as we were always outside. Fortunately, I had the backing of what I now know to be an insightful, forward-thinking head teacher who fully encouraged outdoor play. The children were much happier when allowed to follow their natural instincts to be outside in the open air to learn through play. I too felt happier to be outside with them as it suited my natural instinctive style at the time. Several years later, forced back inside the classroom by the different policies and routines introduced by a new head teacher who had difficulty in seeing the value of outdoor play at that time, the children, and I, their teacher, would stand waiting by the doors. Looking out until that magic time halfway through the morning after the so-called real learning had taken place, I was allowed to open my classroom to let them out to play. Since those days there has been a whole new movement that appreciates the value of outdoor play, so it is much easier to encourage outdoor learning and to foster a deeper understanding of the value of getting children outdoors for learning. Gradually, when other colleagues experience the benefits of getting outdoors for themselves, there will be a change in attitude. In settings where there is any real resistance it may be necessary to hold a staff meeting or In-Service Education and Training (INSET) day to raise the understanding and to create a meaningful policy to ensure that outdoor play happens for every child, not just the ones whose teachers enjoy it themselves.

Unpredictable weather

The notion that the weather is too bad to go outside is no longer a good enough excuse to stay indoors. Outdoor play should be available all year – there is no such thing as unsuitable weather, only unsuitable clothing! Unpredictable weather is often cited as a barrier to going outside. Interestingly, countries with less mild climates, such as Norway, have always had more outdoor teaching and learning than we do here in the UK. There are many ways to minimise the disruption from unpredictable or bad weather; for example:

- keep supplies of bad-weather clothing ready, such as waterproof jackets, leggings and Wellington boots;
- have contingency plans to relocate indoors if necessary;
- put together short-notice boxes to allow you to seize the opportunity to go out when the weather is fine, or when it snows or is frosty;
- build shelters in the grounds large enough for a whole class.

Figure 1.5 Building shelters to protect from the rain

Case study

As the programme is designed to take place entirely outdoors, the first consideration was to make sure that the children were suitably prepared and dressed to go outdoors in all weathers. This issue was discussed during the initial meeting with the parents as many of the children involved in the programme were too young to take on this responsibility for themselves. The leaders provided outdoor clothes for any children who might have forgotten them on the day or were from families who could not afford to wash extra muddy clothes or provide them for their children in the first place. The first year the outdoor programme took place was the coldest, wettest on record but due to the time constraints of the research design we could not wait for good weather. Most sessions were held in wet, rainy conditions and there were times when we were outdoors with very young children in what can only be described as blizzards! Children were always dry, safe and warm and thoroughly enjoyed what could only be described as slithering around in the mud during many of the activities. We put up temporary shelters at the start of every session, lit a campfire to keep warm, took soup and hot drinks, and had stocks of wet weather clothes, mittens and hats and spare dry, warm clothes waiting to be changed into when we got back indoors. By the end of the first programme, the children had experienced the changes of all the seasons during one of the wettest years on record whilst learning to stay within firm, consistent boundaries (see Figure 1.6). As a bonus, the children had great fun and were fully engaged in learning throughout the programme.

How to use this book

The chapters in this outdoor play book are organised into areas which will help you learn about the background of the programme (Chapter 1 – Introduction) and find out about the evidence to support the use of the programme (Chapter 2 – What the research tells us). There is a chapter that will show you how to go about creating a suitable outdoor environment (Chapter 3 – Creating the outdoor environment), a chapter that covers the important aspects of safety when setting up an outdoor programme (Chapter 4 – Safety for healthy outdoor learning), advice on taking the steps

Figure 1.6 Playing in the rain

to move outside (Chapter 5 – Moving outdoors) followed by many practical ideas about how to put the theory into practice (Chapter 6 – Theory into practice), and ways to assess children outdoors (Chapter 7 – Assessing children outdoors). The next chapter (Chapter 8 – Links with home) demonstrates how to involve parents in the whole process of setting up the outdoor programme, and is followed by a detailed explanation of the practical activities that can be used throughout the programme (Chapter 9 – The planned activities). Finally, the concluding chapter (Chapter 10 – Final goodbyes) shows how to bring the programme to a satisfactory conclusion.

The activities embedded in the chapters are designed to take place in a variety of outdoor play settings. All the outdoor play activities described in this book are directly linked to the six areas of learning in the EYFS framework (QCA, 2001). Many of them can be adapted for use in other areas, including the indoor space. They are planned to stimulate and develop young children's outdoor play experiences in a safe, enjoyable way. Each activity is based around a key learning objective. For each activity, advice is given about the size of the group, what resources are required, how to set up the activity and how to carry out the activity with the children. In addition, there are ideas to help you adapt the main activity to meet the needs of older/more experienced children or younger/less experienced children. Each activity includes extension ideas to follow up the activities, showing cross-curricular links where appropriate. There is also a section containing suggestions for questions to ask relating to the activity. Also embedded in the chapters of this book are photocopiable sheets which are cross-referenced and related to a specific activity detailed in other sections of the books, and which can be photocopied or adapted to suit the needs of the setting.

Figure 1.7 Sheltering from the rain

2 What the research tells us

Introduction

This chapter discusses the literature available to back up the reasons for running an outdoor programme as part of the early years curriculum provision and extended schools programmes. It highlights the problems some children have regarding the early transition from home to school and how this outdoor intervention tackles difficulties appropriately when they are developmental and before they have become embedded as habits. Case studies are used to demonstrate how the outdoor programme has helped individual children, families and schools.

The controversial issues of young children's development are of growing interest to many people and organisations. Although there is a wide variety of literature related to children and physical activities, respectively, there is very little written about very young children or to unite these areas. Research shows that children find lessons outdoors more relaxed, more interesting and easier to understand, and they also think their teachers are friendlier towards them. According to the research conducted into the Healthy, Active and Outside (HAO) programme, more than three-quarters of parents and teachers questioned believed that early outdoor programmes had had positive effects on children's overall attitudes to learning.

Key issues

There is major concern about the physical health of children in the UK. Much of this concern focuses around low levels of physical exercise. Children's play, especially outdoors, offers many opportunities for physical activity but this has never been systematically explored (Children's Play Council, 2002). There is growing public policy interest in children's play. Politicians and opinion formers are interested in exploring how good play opportunities can help improve quality of life and safety in neighbourhoods, tackle obesity and promote children's well-being, support children's development and build community cohesion. Alongside this, there is a growing view that good play experiences are not only an essential part of every childhood, but also a key public responsibility and an expression of our shared social obligations towards children.

There is a growing concern about children becoming more sedentary, spending progressively more time watching TV and electronic media, and that the majority of school activities are performed whilst seated (US Department of Health and Human Services, 2000). After looking at published studies on potential health risks of television viewing, Dr Aric Sigman, of the British Psychological Society, recommends that children under three should be banned from watching any TV, and older children, aged 3–5, should be restricted to viewing one hour a day of good-quality programmes. Children spend more time looking at screens than they do outside doing real things, which is detrimental to their health and well-being, particularly in the long term. He recommends that children should be outside experiencing real life and real things (Sigman, 2005). There is a growing concern about children spending more time indoors instead of playing outside (Reilly *et al.*, 1999) and the common opinion in most studies is that outdoor activities have a positive influence on children's health in general (Edgington, 2002; Jensen, 2000). Studies show how children's play in the natural environment stimulates their motor fitness and has a positive effect on their behaviour, emotions and their mental and physical well-being (Jensen, 2000). The natural environment affords possibilities and challenges for children to explore their own abilities through physical activity (Ouvry, 2000), and studies have shown that outdoor experiential education works well for all ages (Edgington, 2002; Ouvry, 2000).

Over the last 25 years, huge technological and cultural changes have transformed the lifestyle of people in the developed world – largely for the better. This has all happened so fast that we have failed to notice that the changes which benefit adults are not always so good for children. The influence of contemporary cultural change on children's development has led to a 'toxic cocktail' of side effects that is now damaging the social, emotional and cognitive development of a growing number of children, particularly their capacity to learn, with knock-on effects on their behaviour. One in six children in the developed world is now diagnosed as having 'developmental or behavioural problems' (Palmer, 2007).

Parents who buy electronic games or toy computers to boost learning for babies, toddlers or the very young are wasting their money. A government-funded study set up to examine the role of technology in the lives of three- and four-year-old children found that these high-tech devices are no more effective than traditional ways of learning but are more useful as aids to imaginative play (Plowman and Stephen, 2006). We need to replace on-screen interaction with real play and swap solitary computer game sessions for real games which are preferably outside, physical and fun. These days, when danger seems to lurk around every corner, we all wrap our children in cotton wool. But we must resolve to be less protective as children need to be out in the real world, exploring and interacting with it, and, more importantly, interacting with the people who live in it (Palmer, 2007).

Today's children have technological gadgets such as iPods, mobile phones and computers at their fingertips but despite a wealth of material possessions they seem to be missing out on the real riches of childhood. The freedom to explore outside is out of bounds for many children. According to research by Entertainment Rights, half of the parents interviewed felt that their children had no experiences of traditional childhood activities such as hopscotch, conkers and chasing activities. The freedom to play outside was seen as a thing of the past by nearly seven out of ten parents; so were activities such as hide-and-seek, building dens and climbing trees. More than half of the 4,000 parents who took part in the survey wished their children could enjoy a similar childhood to the one they had had.

The outdoor environment provides an innovative and creative learning and teaching setting, which can be very effective in providing good-quality learning experiences (Hayes, 1999). These experiences may develop children's self-confidence and offer unique opportunities for them to gain an understanding of the natural environment, reflect on what they discover, and learn their own physical limits in a safe setting (Filer, 1998). As many children find it hard to learn in a classroom, the outdoors may be a practical way for children to learn through other means of education.

Why the outdoors?

The importance of outdoor areas is stressed in the design guide published by Sure Start, *Building for Sure Start: A Client Guide. Integrated Provision for Under-Fives.* A well-designed outside environment with a range of opportunities and experiences is essential to healthy growth and development and can never be replicated inside a building, however well it is designed or resourced. It is generally accepted that the outside environment is an essential element of a good early years setting and its importance should be reflected in the quality of the space provided and in the skills and training of staff (DfES, 2004).

Early years specialists fear that outdoor environments are being overlooked because outdoor provision is no longer at the top of people's agendas with the increase in the development of children's centres. The senior development officer for Learning through Landscapes says, 'If you think of all the services that children's centres offer, the outdoors has a vital role in each of them which can't be replicated indoors' (White, 2004). In both the Foundation Stage curriculum document (DfES, 2000) and *Birth to Three Matters* (DfES, 2003b) there is an expectation that children will have access to the outdoors. Outdoor provision for young children is a necessity, not a luxury, particularly in the light of concerns about childhood obesity, inactivity levels and states of mental health.

There are many good reasons to incorporate physical activity and movement into the school curriculum. Movement increases heart rate and circulation and therefore arousal. Studies show increased performance following arousal activities (Tomporowski and Ellis, 1986). Increased arousal also narrows attention to target tasks (Easterbrook, 1959). Productive movement activities such as stretching increase oxygen levels to the brain and provide an opportunity for the eyes and musculo-skeletal system to relax (Henning *et al.*, 1997). Activity can also enhance spatial learning (Fordyce and Wehner, 1993). Certain kinds of movements can stimulate the release of the body's natural motivators. The chemical messengers called neurotransmitters play a primary role in our mind–body states and receptivity to learning. If the activity is compelling, adrenaline will be released. Quick energising activities increase energy levels, improve storage and retrieval of information and help learners feel good. Activity and its relationship to well-being are the focus of work by Goddard Blythe (2000) and Nuttall (1999). As we know, learning can happen in the sedentary fashion seen in the more usual classroom setting but the typical notion of keeping children in chairs for long periods of time may be misguided. The human body has walked, run, skipped or squatted for the last 50,000 years but it has not spent long periods of time sitting in chairs. Sitting in chairs for more than ten-minute intervals reduces our awareness of physical and emotional sensations and increases fatigue (Cranz, 1998). These problems reduce concentration and attention and ultimately result in discipline problems. In the usual classroom setting, children spend too much time sitting in chairs which do not offer enough flexibility to optimize learning (Rittel and Webber, 1973). What is so surprising is that this concept is not new. As far back as 1912 Dr Maria Montessori described the impact of chairs: 'Children were not disciplined, but annihilated' (Benton, 1986).

The programme is based on the notion that 'most seated learning activities can be accomplished in alternate positions such as standing, leaning, squatting, kneeling, walking or lying down' (Jensen, 2000: 31). The main emphasis is to incorporate active learning and movement activities. Flexibility is built into the programme so that the children have posture choices and the freedom to move as their mind–body state requires. As far back as the early 1950s it was proposed that children create and learn about the world through play (Piaget, 1952). It is through play that children explore their physical and emotional worlds, discover insights, and create hypotheses and experiments with their newly found knowledge. The programme gives children regular opportunities to learn through active play, and two of the many by-products of this play are adaptive learning and pleasure. Young children do not have a clearly defined transition stage from motor development to cognitive development. These developmental periods are so intertwined that each movement increases perception, which increases cognitive capabilities (Bushnell and Boudreau, 1993). Ultimately every movement a young child makes contributes to her/his cognitive map.

The National Curriculum (DfES, 2000) for physical education states that physical education should involve children in the continuous process of planning, performing and evaluating. The programme lends itself to teaching and learning styles which match this requirement. The programme is based on the intuitive notion that a child's work is his play (Piaget, 1952). All evidence points towards the encouragement of the more 'playground-type' interactions and movement activities, especially during the early childhood period. Interventions which use stimulating physical movements such as spinning, crawling, rolling, rocking or tumbling lead to subsequent significant gains in attention and reading (Palmer, 1980). Researchers have explored whether being mobile influences cognitive development, or understanding of the world, and it appears that being able to look at the world from different angles does improve other aspects of development (Karmiloff-Smith, 1994). However, some studies of interventions using physical activity as a base for learning suggest that there may be a strong influence prescribed by a particular teacher or practitioner and that the children may merely be benefiting from extra attention, which in itself can enhance learning (Khalsa, 1988; Sifft and Khalsa, 1991).

Sensory integration is another benefit of play. Some children have difficulty in registering and processing sensory information (Ayres, 1972). Their attention 'engine' runs out at an inappropriate level compared to other children in their class. These children may exhibit 'dysfunctional' focusing behaviours which help them remain at their preferred levels of arousal. In the normal classroom setting these children may rock in their chairs, fidget with things or bounce around, which is highly disruptive to the class as well as detrimental to the child's own learning. It is important to realise that these children are just doing what comes naturally to them and that they are not acting out or being impulsive, indolent, hypersensitive or generally difficult out of spite. They just cannot help themselves. The programme is ideal for children who display some form of dysfunctional focusing behaviour. Much of the fidgeting and moving around that happens indoors goes unnoticed outside as there is no pressure to keep such tight control by keeping children still on seats or on the floor.

Many children in schools today are laden down with problems and increasing trauma (Jensen, 2000); these heavy emotional issues either get addressed or impair learning. Children with either expressive barriers which cause them to shut down or significant emotional 'baggage' which causes them to act up benefit most from play-acting (Carmichael and Atchinson, 1997). Emotional adaptation can be more important to a child's success than cognitive skills (Goleman, 1995), which is another reason for using physical activities as a base for learning. Many of the children are in no state to learn and should have more movement incorporated into their lessons. Evidence suggests that exercise is the best overall mood regulator (Thayer, 1996). According to Thayer (1996), going for the brisk walks that were incorporated into the outdoor programme is the single best way a teacher can influence children's moods. Teachers who have children sitting on chairs for too long, at any age, are creating problems for themselves.

Another advantage of using the physical activity-based philosophy of the outdoor school programme is that it makes use of the 'binding' theory. This is a process where the brain links up information permanently, or binds one element to another. The teaching is done with enthusiasm, in a concrete, try-it-out way, followed by feedback usually through social rewards such as the thumbs up for success sign, cheers or smiles. This binding of cognition, emotion, meaning and context works because it makes use of the elements of implicit learning, which are feelings, movement and space. Content information alone is not enough to engage long-term memory, as the design of the human brain is such that it cannot continuously learn an unlimited amount of new information. Teachers need to forget the pressure to cover the material, slow down and incorporate physical activity into their lessons to give children the time for new learning to settle. All children need more movement breaks than they currently have in the normal classroom setting (Jensen, 2000), and young children in particular require more breaks from seat work (Bjorklund and Brown, 1998).

The mind–body state is important to learning and if the children are in a good state of both body and mind they will interpret what the teacher says in a more favourable way. Children will be able to learn more through movement activity, which we already know is the best way to manage learning states, and if we teach them how to manage their own states. The brain learns best through action and activity and maintains maximum efficiency when the organism is actively engaged in exploring physical sites and materials and asking questions to which it actually craves an answer (Gardner, 1999).

The programme study

This study of this HAO programme concentrated on several groups of children aged 3–5 years on the premise that providing experiential education through an outdoor environment would have many constructive benefits. The aim of the study was to adapt traditional teaching approaches to the outdoor programme to meet the needs of children in early years settings and to demonstrate the effectiveness of the adapted approach. There are data available on least ten outdoor programmes but because of financial and time constraints only the results of one programme have been written up, because the research in question was carried out by a practitioner for a doctoral degree. Analysis of the other programmes would provide a deeper understanding of how they work. However, the study still provides an interesting insight into the influence of the environment on young children's development.

The main areas of research are:

- attendance
- activity levels
- behaviour.

The results show that children who are able to go outside are more likely to have higher attendance levels than those confined to the indoors; they are more active and better behaved than the other children taking part in the study. In addition, the research shows how the environment impacts upon young children's development and clearly demonstrates that the children taking part in the outdoor programme are more physically active than the other children. They are more likely to be active when they play outside than when they play indoors even with similar curriculum content. Analysis of the observations of the children taking part in the programme revealed that there were more incidents of positive actions and behaviours than there were of negative ones. The evaluation also shows that the intensity of negative and aggressive behaviour was greater when the children were indoors than when they could play outside. Fewer incidents of aggressive behaviour were recorded outdoors than inside, indicating lower intensity levels of stress or distress for children when they are playing outside. There was a significant change in child behaviour as a result of participating in the programme. By the end of the programme all the children moved from the clinical to the normal range regarding emotional, behavioural or mental health difficulties. The findings show that all the children attending the outdoor programme have improved levels of perceived behaviour, physical activity and positive behaviour patterns compared to the control group of children. The possible factors affecting the changes in children's behaviour were also considered, and as an intervention that uses the children in its design, the programme has the potential to improve the health of children by increasing energy expenditure through the promotion of games involving physical activity. In addition, the findings show that the children's mental health had improved, particularly in the areas of raised self-esteem and confidence, which impacted positively upon their mental health states.

The study supports the efficacy of the programme and identifies many ways in which it can act as a facilitator to improve the lives of the children taking part in it. It shows that for the group of children studied, the environment can influence their development and that the programme is a valuable tool to scaffold and support this development. In addition, the results show that a well-designed outdoor model of education increases awareness of the outdoor environment in relation to children's development and play and that it could be adopted into mainstream school at a very low cost. The results are very encouraging, to say the least. Transferring the indoor curriculum to the outdoors through the programme is a clear example of research taking theory into practice, both to improve the learning environment and to give children the opportunity for the more active daily lifestyles needed to improve behaviour, lifestyle, and physical and mental health. It appears to show significant levels of success for those children with behaviour difficulties who struggle to cope with the more passive teaching and learning styles most frequently used in the indoor classroom.

Benefits of the programme

This investigation shows that there is potential for all children to gain benefits from attending an outdoor programme regardless of age, gender or social background. Success of the programme has occurred in a variety of ways. The uncommunicative appear to find the space, support and encouragement to give them the confidence to call out to friends as they explore the outside or tell about their experiences during the review of each session. The children who are continually in trouble for not sitting still find outlets for their so-called 'excess energy levels' as they freely explore the outside space, and the children who get into trouble for their behaviour are able to use their practical skills to help problem-solve. The child's image changes as they are seen in better light by others and their self-image improves as they grow in confidence and self-esteem.

Children who find it difficult to focus in the classroom become more engaged as they take part in activities that have real purpose to them, using real tools to build protective shelters from the wind, making food or helping to light fires to cook and keep warm. The passive or inactive child soon adapts to the physical element of the programme and is soon running around happily, slipping and sliding in the mud or carrying or pulling heavy objects up and down slopes. Even the more academic children can learn to be creative and more socially aware as they experience working together as a team. The learning that takes place is limited only by the children's own imagination and that of the adults who lead the programme.

3   Creating the outdoor environment

Introduction

Creating a safe, stimulating outdoor environment for children means that they will be given the opportunity to strengthen both their bodies and their minds at the same time as developing a sense of accomplishment and independence. This chapter begins with information about using the outside environment for a better quality of life, and on the importance of sustainability and of creating the right first impressions to the success of the programme. In addition, the process of setting up the outdoor programme is explained, as is how to engage people into the idea of trying something new. It shows them how to get young children outdoors to encourage them to become more active and used to the idea of a healthy active lifestyle. Finally there is a brief section on the importance of being an effective leader.

Using the outside environment for a better quality of life

The outdoor programme recognises the importance of sustainable development and the concepts documented in the UK Government publication *A Better Quality of Life* (Defra, 1999), which is the government strategy for sustainable development for the United Kingdom. Sustainable development is based on the idea of ensuring a better quality of life for everyone now and for generations to come. Consequently, in the UK and the world as a whole there are four concurring objectives, on the first three of which the programme bases its underlying philosophy regarding the use of the outdoor environment. These objectives are:

- social progress which recognises the needs of everyone
- effective protection of the environment
- prudent use of natural resources.

The strategy acknowledges that the Government cannot achieve sustainable development on its own and identifies actions that could be taken by business, local authorities, voluntary groups and individuals. There are key issues relating to quality of life that could be applied to the development of an outdoor programme for young children. The principles taken into consideration when developing the programme included:

- putting people at the centre
- taking a long-term perspective
- taking account of costs and benefits
- combating poverty and social exclusion
- respecting environmental limits
- using scientific knowledge
- transparency, information and participation.

The outdoor programme ensures that all who take part in it receive their entitlement to a balanced programme of environmental education alongside the planned physical activities.

Environmental education

According to the definition of environmental education drafted by the International Union for the Conservation of Nature at their Nevada conference (September 1979), the important elements of environmental education are identified in three strands:

- from the environment
- about the environment
- for the environment.

Education from the environment is where the environment is used as a familiar and relevant resource for educational purposes. In this way, a good deal of knowledge and understanding as well as the skills required will be developed by pupils.

Education about the environment should be with the purpose of developing knowledge and understanding about values and attitudes.

Education for the environment should lead to the inculcation of responsible actions in the environment, taken with an understanding of statutory and accepted codes of behaviour.

Underpinning the outdoor programme is the notion that environmental education is the process of recognising values and clarifying concepts in order to develop skills and attitudes necessary to understand and appreciate the interrelatedness amongst people, their culture, and their biological and physical surroundings. The theme of environmental education running parallel to the physical aspects of the programme gives children practice in decision making and helps them to formulate a code of behaviour about issues concerning environmental quality.

Challenges of developing the outdoors

There are many challenges that still face the practitioner who wants to find ways to promote the importance and value of the outdoor environment to all those involved in the setting. Often the programme facilitator has to convince the senior management team, other professionals, staff and parents of the value of the project. Sometimes the challenge lies in overcoming problems in accessing and using the outdoor environment due to the very design or organisation of the building itself. The children usually need very little convincing as many of them naturally choose to play outdoors when given the opportunity to do so. However, it is still a challenge to ensure that a shared outdoor space meets the needs of children of different ages and developmental stages. There is the challenge to make sure that the outdoor environment feels homely and safe enough to feel comfortable but at the same time provides an environment suitable for learning.

Planning the development of the outside

When creating an outside play space, in order to maximise the success of an outdoor programme the practitioner must take care to ensure that the changes made outside are:

- holistic
- participative
- sustainable.

Holistic

It is necessary to adopt a holistic process which considers the potential of the whole site where the needs of all the people, both children and adults, who use the outdoor site are considered. Look at how all areas of the curriculum can be enhanced alongside considering the physical, social and emotional needs of the children who will be using it.

Participative

A participative approach to developing the outdoor area should actively seek to include and involve all staff, children, parents and member of the community who use the outdoor space. Involve them in planning, decision making, helping with the practical work needed to develop the outside area, long-term maintenance and evaluation.

Sustainable

Ensure that the development process is sustainable both in principle and practice and that the project is both financially viable and practical in the long term. It is important to consider implications regarding maintenance of the outdoor project right from the start, from the very early stages of planning.

Figure 3.1 Working together to create the outdoor space

Figure 3.2 Spreading wood chips to make a dry base

It is important to consider the development of the outdoor space in terms of:

- where you are now
- where you want to be
- how to get there
- how to make changes.

To facilitate the development of the outdoor area certain questions need to be asked and points considered regarding these different perspectives at each stage of the ongoing cyclical process. It is important to consider:

Where you are now

Think about what already happens in your setting and where you are now regarding outdoor education and the physical features that make up the outside area. Find out how the outdoor area is currently used and how everyone in the setting already feels about outdoor play.

Where you want to be

Consider where you want to be by involving everyone in developing the plans for creating the outdoor environment you want in your setting. Think about what you want to be able to do outside, what the issues are and what your priorities are. Consider your vision for outdoor provision.

How to get there

Consider how you are going to get where you want to be in terms of outdoor provision by creating ideas and solutions together, by researching changes, designing your own changes and maybe even raising funds to help pay for them. At the same time think about who will do all the work and where all the materials needed to create the desired outdoor area will come from. Finally, think carefully about planning for maintenance and consider the sustainability of any new developments you want to make.

How to make changes

Make the necessary changes by involving everyone in each stage of the development and by planning small, achievable steps particularly for implementing plans for maintenance and sustainability. Finally, evaluate the impact of involving everyone and spend time celebrating the achievements.

Before you start, you need to have a thorough understanding of the physical outdoor environment and carry out an audit. Encourage everyone to get involved in gathering information to give an insight into how the outdoors is already being used. The process of developing an understanding of what you have already got in terms of physical resources can be turned into an enjoyable exercise for children, who can take part in activities such as helping to identify hazards or sunny or shady spots, or can record where the puddles gather after it has been raining. Determine the children's most and least favourite areas of the outside space and the way they already use it.

Make a list of the physical features that already exist, including plants and trees, pathways, surfaces, walls and raised areas so that you can maximise the use of the area once the programme begins. Involve the children as much as possible; for example, go around the outside area with a small group of children and let them take photographs so that they can discuss what they see regarding the features of the outdoor environment. Plot them on a basic map of the area.

Alongside the audit of the physical features of the outdoor site, it is a good idea to collect information about any legal, technical, financial and policy issues that might affect the running of an outdoor programme, particularly if you want to make any permanent changes to the site. You may need to know who owns the site, who else uses it and when, how much it is going to cost if you decide to make any changes, whose permission you might need to seek and who if anyone is already responsible for the maintenance.

If the site is part of the local authority area, it is easy to obtain a site plan from the relevant council department. If not, a plan of the outside area may need to be drawn up. It is possible to do this yourself and to encourage even the youngest of children to get involved in making plans of the outside area. A base plan can be used to map any existing features and resources, to determine areas for particular use or to plot any changes or improvements you might want to make.

A survey of what activities take place throughout the day, the different groups who already use the outside area, how they influence each other and how the outside area is already managed will help, as you do not want to create problems for the other users of the site. At this stage, start the analysis of the learning that already takes place outside: what activities take place, where and when? The practitioners using the site will already have information about this and will have an idea of the existing potential for supporting children's learning. At this stage it is a good time to start discussions with staff about any changes that would further develop and support outdoor learning, particularly if the outside space is used for 'playtimes' rather than curriculum activities. To help identify ideas linked to the potential use of the outdoor space or issues relating to the lack of use, it is useful to find out what prevents people from using the outside space. Set up a file to make a record of all these things as you go along as a reference for future planning. In addition, collect information about how the children already use the outside area and the activities (adult-led and child-initiated) they already engage in during outside play. Watch carefully to find out how they use the space, how their activities interact with each other and the areas the children choose for their play.

Through asking people about the outdoor space they will begin to think about their feelings about using it. It is surprising just how different people feel about going outside. There will be a variety of both positive and negative responses which will have to be considered when implementing the programme. Some aspects of it may have to be adapted to suit the needs of the people taking part, current users and the existing physical attributes of the outdoor environment in which the programme is going to take place.

After exploring feelings it may be necessary to start raising awareness of the importance of outdoor play. Once this has been achieved and all the information has been gathered, the next important step is to identify the needs of the group and/or setting and to plan the vision for the outside site.

As soon as the information-gathering process begins, priorities about the use of the outdoors will start to emerge as people will have many different views, needs and wants regarding its use. These will inform the design brief, from which a set of aims will be formulated which might include:

- to create new teaching and learning opportunities through further developing the use of the outside area;
- to use the process of change to create learning opportunities for children;
- to set up a Healthy, Active and Outside programme to enhance children's learning through outdoor play.

At this stage it is essential that questions are asked regarding what you want to do outdoors and exactly how you would like to use the outside space. Your vision for the use of the outside area will emerge from all the research, consultation and planning that has been taking place if you have followed the steps previously suggested in this chapter. The vision you have for the outside will define the shape and size of the different outdoor spaces and will show you where you need to have major features such as shelters, pathways and seating areas. The plan will identify existing or potential use of the area and any improvements that need to be made to maximise its use. Plotting the use of zoned areas on the vision plan or map to show what activities take place and where will help avoid the potential clash of incompatible areas being sited next to each other, such as a quiet area next to a ball-playing area. Making changes to existing outside areas will change the dynamics of the whole area, not just the parts involved in the new plan. Once any desirable changes to the outside area have been made, the next stage is to consider the planning and preparation for the activities that will be taking place.

Practical ideas to get you started in creating the outdoor environment

It is important to create an outside environment that is full of natural features that will both be a pleasant place to be for all the people who work, play or live in the setting and at the same time attract the maximum amount of wildlife possible for the size of the outside space to provide good stimulus for outside teaching and learning. An outdoor project that evolves over time will be more rewarding than calling in landscape gardeners to do it for you. However, that is not to say that successful results cannot be achieved quickly for those practitioners who cannot wait to get outside with the children. Growing seeds in the classroom before transplanting them to a garden patch gives children the opportunity to observe the initial growth stages and will help to build their interest in the various plants and how to tend them once they are transferred outdoors. They will be able to observe which seeds sprout first and whether they grow better in sun or shade. At a later stage these investigations can then extend into the planning and creation of the school garden itself. With obesity an increasing problem among children today and government healthy eating initiatives to encourage better eating, a good way to encourage children to eat well is by showing them how to grow nutritious, fresh and delicious foods themselves. Growing food in a school environment is not as difficult as you may think. Start with a sheltered sunny space near access to water and plan what you want to grow by browsing through gardening magazines and brochures with the children before you take them outside.

If space is limited, you can grow cress, lettuce, radish, tomatoes, strawberries, nasturtiums or even French beans in a container against a wall or in a hanging basket. Seeds are easy to grow and cheap to buy and can be started in suitable recycled food containers inside the classroom, then transplanted into their outdoor sites later. If you have a suitable outside space to include a garden patch, get the children involved in digging it and fertilising it with home-made compost.

The outdoor environment can offer rich learning experiences not found indoors and an outdoor classroom is ideal for an evolving curriculum, providing sensory experiences leading to greater levels of creativity and understanding. The outside area is full of wonderful things for children to experiment with, discover and explore. The HAO programme's approach to using the outside space has pioneered the use of the outdoor classroom, ensuring opportunities for quiet as well as active play whilst children are outside. Whether you choose to purchase a range of fitness- and agility-orientated play equipment or decide to make use of the natural features of the grounds for physical activities, the emphasis must be on open access and experimentation. The non-directive play in this programme will facilitate a wide spectrum of activities and exercises which are designed to expand and develop cognitive and motor skills whilst building strength and developing major muscle groups.

Social play teaches how to share and take turns, and observing each other and testing and discussing ideas can enhance individual development, creating an awareness of personal risk assessment and problem solving. Children's needs, views, abilities and interests are the starting point of the design and planning of any new play development and have provided many learning opportunities, which can be either informal or curriculum based. Collect the children's ideas and wish-lists for what they want outside in a manner that will help them be creative, have fun, explore, learn and communicate. Start with a mind-mapping session to get them thinking about the possibilities of an outdoor space which will match their needs and also provide a stimulating and challenging learning environment.

An insight into the school's ethos and how it works at all levels, over and above its ground development requirements, will help the outdoor design team to understand the values and ideals of the school which can be transferred across into the designs created for the outdoor environment. Encourage active involvement of all the school's stakeholders in the project, from pupils and staff to parents and governors. To make the project fully inclusive you may have to talk to experts across many disciplines throughout the design process. For example, the advice of occupational therapists may need to be sought concerning issues relating to mobility and wheelchair users. Taking advice from the experts means that the outdoor environment will be fully inclusive for everyone and will ensure that it works at all levels from activities to stimulate the senses to activities which provide children with physical challenges.

Activity panels and mazes

Activity panels are easy to create, especially if there is wire fencing around the site. Adults or children can create activity panels by attaching objects to the fence, either randomly or in connection with topics and themes. These panels are ideal for individual, paired or small group activity and encourage creativity and playful learning, for example in colour and shape recognition, eye and hand coordination, problem solving, and other developmental functions. Ensure they are safe, with no dangerous, removable parts, and make them bright and colourful using a wide range of textures, or make them subtle and natural. The opportunities for creativity and learning are endless and will transform the learning potential of those bleak outdoor sites that appear to offer little motivation for outside play. The activity panels offer a sensory adventure whilst developing sensorimotor skills and can be incorporated into play equipment, attached to posts or fixed directly to the wall at the appropriate heights for children to create an additional sensory experience.

Mazes are easy to create and make an exciting addition to any outside play space. They can be created from a variety of materials, and be either a fixed structure such as an interlocking system of walls; movable, using large construction materials or tyres; or living, by planting suitable shrubs.

Vertical space

Often the vertical space is overlooked when creating the outdoor environment. Interacting with walls (with permission) can be a major part of outdoor play for children and is full of exciting potential. Throwing or kicking a ball against a wall provides all kinds of opportunities for solitary or group play. Designate an area of wall away from windows and doors or purchase commercial ones which can be installed almost anywhere in the playground as long as they are tough and durable. Walls can be used as screens to separate areas, made into mazes, can be single- or double-sided, with targets, shapes, goals and stumps engraved into the timber. Kick-about areas can be set up to many specifications, according to size, system or security of the setting.

A range of fixed ropewalks, balance beams, ladders, trapeze rings, rock holds, climbing nets, platforms, fireman's poles, pull-up ramps, slides, rope tunnels and bridges adds a further dimension to the natural features of the outside space. The construction combinations for this range are endless and all are designed to challenge children physically. There are deliberately no start or finish points, allowing children to express themselves freely, expand their physical agilities, engage in exploratory play and develop a sense of accomplishment and independence. They can be enjoyed alone or in groups, thereby offering social development opportunities as well.

Pre-designed constructions to encourage imaginative role play such as boats and lighthouses, tractors and trains, pirate islands, bridges and theatres may become limiting as children sometimes tire of them unless they are included in session planning to foster creativity with a focus on empowering children to develop their imagination. The emphasis is on creating outdoor play environments which are non-prescriptive and which allow children to unleash the potential of their imaginations and bodies.

Play sculptures

Sculptures can be commercially produced or they can be artistic creations made by the children themselves. They can be designed as specific characters such as frogs and crocodiles, themes to address children's need for the mystical and magical and their sense of awe and wonder, or as living creations that will evolve over time. In addition, they can be used for play or seating if they are securely fixed to the ground. Adding sculptures to the outside space will create a magical, enchanting place for having fun messing around with friends or just to spend time.

Surfacing

Impact-absorbing surfaces are a crucial element to any play area, especially those surrounding fixed play equipment. From natural hardwood chips to recycled rubber wet pour they can be incorporated into an attractive design or become a feature in their own right. Surfacing can be made up of a variety of materials, for example:

- hardwood chips
- softwood bark
- sand
- impact-absorbing grass rubber matting
- wet pour.

All surfaces must be laid to comply with the appropriate health and safety legislation. If your outside area is just a barren playground then the very least you can do is to brighten it up by painting a variety of board games, puzzles, patterns, rainbows, mazes and other designs that will give children fun inventing their own games or simply following the pathways created by the painted lines.

Musical areas

Music is an art form that encompasses all areas of child development: physical, intellectual, social and emotional. Having musical areas will be magical for children and can include musical sculptures which will develop over a period of time and bring a new dimension to the outside play space. Creating a musical zone within the outdoor location with a variety of sound sources will encourage and motivate a child's playful exploration, interpretation and understanding of musical sound and will allow children to release energy and channel it in a creative, productive direction as they engage in the sense of sound (see activities p. 117, 161–2, 165).

Totem poles

Totem poles can be used in a variety of ways in the outdoor environment. They make unique assembly points and they help children develop orientation skills and an understanding of their bearing in relation to the environment. They can be designed as sensory posts, engraved with school emblems, logos, animals, characters from favourite stories and other current school projects, with a theme of your choice using designs created by the children. Sensory posts add interest to any outdoor play space and can be designed to be interactive rather than just ornamental; they can have spy holes, finger mazes and textured sections.

Fencing

It is essential that there is a robust fence around the outside area and that any pond or water feature is securely fenced off from children during free play activities. However, to create a sense of enclosure fences do not need to be solid because they can be a feature in their own right. The willow fence (see activities p.124) strikes a good balance between function and imagination and will become an attractive addition to any outside play environment. The fence will help to contain children within the relative safety of the play area and will give them a sense that it is their area and separate from the surroundings.

Shelters and shade

Children and young people are often outside during the middle of the day, so providing sufficient shade, or rain cover, for outdoor spaces in schools is very important. Every outdoor site needs some form of shelter, whether it is permanent, semi-permanent or taken down every day. Having a shelter is so much more than just having a roof overhead. Shelter has always been a basic human need and will create cool, peaceful, social spaces for quiet or passive play away from the more active play areas. Shelters can be used as story circles, theatres, stages and outdoor classrooms throughout the year and using them will be an opportunity to raise awareness about the elements children are sheltering from. Shelters will increase the amount of quality outdoor playtime throughout the year as they will provide welcome relief on a hot summer's day, and by providing sun protection they will help to promote sun-safe behaviour. In winter they will provide protection from the elements so that children can still enjoy going outside to play. Installing a pergola is a good starting point as pergolas are cheap and easy to put up, are not too ambitious for anyone new to outdoor practice and will evolve over time to provide a good natural shelter. Pergolas as natural canopies made from natural bamboo structures with climbing plants such as clematis and passion-flowers provide colour and aroma to alight the senses at the same time as protecting children from exposure to the sun.

Seating

Seating is an important consideration when creating the outdoor environment. Well-designed seating and improvised seating from logs provide a number of benefits and uses such as a place for gathering and social activity; a place to eat, read, work or play games; an area to wait; a space to divide the different uses of areas; and a place to stop, rest, relax, be and reflect. You might want to create seating areas for the entire class outside, or create peaceful smaller seating areas for small groups or individual children to go and complete a task or quietly look at books.

Figure 3.3 Children weaving fencing panels

Figure 3.4 Children using logs for seating

Trees and shrubs

There many reasons for planting trees, shrubs and other plants in your school grounds if you do not have any and some can even be grown in containers if you do not have a large enough outside space to grow them freely. Trees and shrubs will help to make the environment look attractive and pleasing to the eye at the same time as having many educational benefits. It is not expensive to buy young trees, especially bare-rooted varieties, from garden centres or local nurseries. It is important to remember not to plant a large tree too near buildings as you will lose natural light and the roots might damage the fabric of the building. Before you start planting trees ask yourself: what is your chosen site presently used for and how will the site be improved with the addition of trees and shrubs? In addition you will need to buy spades and a pH testing kit to determine if the soil in your outside area is acidic or alkaline.

A range of different trees and shrubs will provide a wealth of topics for study, according to their fruiting, flowering, leaf and pollination types. Children learn much through observing growth throughout the yearly cycle of changing seasons and through the maintenance and identification process of growing trees. There are also many creative opportunities from making observational drawings, paintings, natural mosaics to leaf printing and bark rubbing. In addition, trees and shrubs will attract a range of fascinating creatures to the outside space and will provide a natural resource for any study on wildlife habitats. Trees are also a useful addition to any outdoor space as they absorb dust and create barriers to wind, sound and any unsightly features around the grounds. Some good trees, shrubs and plants to grow in your outdoor environment are:

- oak – grows quite fast, produces acorns and pollinates through catkins. Of all native trees it can support the most (300) types of insect species;
- beech – grows well in the shade and with its autumn harvest of nuts attracts many birds, insects and small mammals;
- wild cherry – with its frothy pink or white spring blossoms it is ideal if your grounds are situated in an industrial area or near a busy road as it is very tolerant of pollution;
- buddleia – attracts many birds, bees and butterflies but needs regular pruning as it grows rampantly;
- willow – a fast-growing tree that will supply a harvest of willow withies to use for many of the activities described in this book.

Figure 3.5 Stretching up to reach the top of a tree

Living willow

Using living willow will engage children and raise their environmental awareness; structures such as arches, domes and tunnels can create shade and provide interesting, soothing learning environments. Including a willow structure in school grounds is a symbol for progressive environmental education, and because willow is fast-growing, it gains an established look in a short period and is thus ideal for quick, effective shelter. Growing willow shelters and sculptures is an adventure for children where there are no failures, just an exciting, meaningful opportunity to make positive links with the living world around us. A good place to start is by planting a willow tree well away from any buildings as willow's roots spread far and fast. Many fun activities can develop as a result of harvesting the withies every year. Harvested between November and January, they can be used to create many other willow structures and sculptures – for example the dream catcher on p.124.

Some trees are robust enough to be used as climbing trees, to make dens or even support tree houses which become places of adventure, imagination and make-believe. A tree house can be a special place to dream, a place to call your own to relax or have fun.

Planters and plants

Planters and raised beds are useful additions to any environment, with carefully selected planting to revitalise and transform any outside play space, provided you select the appropriate place to install them based on accessibility, amount of sunshine, availability of nearby water, and resolution of any security or inclusion issues that need to be addressed. Planters can be created to offer a heightened sensory experience. Whenever possible we encourage children to get involved in the planting and maintenance of their 'gardens'. Their interest and senses are stimulated by encouraging them to touch, smell and, if appropriate, taste a variety of carefully selected plants. Children take pride in their accomplishments as they watch their gardens grow and flourish. Planters and small patches of garden are a great way to catch children's imagination and get them interested in the garden. Rosemary, lavender and Choisya are easy to grow, are scented and have colourful flowers (see page 148 for growing activities).

Ponds

When planning a school pond it is essential that you find out about any regulations and requirements by talking to the experts from the LEA about their guidelines, as these are generally linked to insurance policies. In addition, it is important to consider the practical, ecological, educational and design issues. A pond should be as big as possible, 8 × 6m and at least 75cm deep so the water will not completely freeze during winter and kill any hibernating wildlife. If you do decide to include a pond in your outdoor setting, then late spring or early summer is a good time to start digging it for any pre-existing or new wildlife you hope to attract. A well-maintained pond will give real inspiration to any outdoor lessons about animal, bird, insect or plant life. Having a pond to look after will be a ready source of gentle exercise for the children, keeping it clear of litter, leaves and ice, topping it up with water and pruning any overhanging plants, at the same time as being a pleasant place to relax or go pond dipping on a warm, sunny day.

Pond plants

Ponds need plants and there are many pond plants to choose from; each one has a role to play in the life of the pond. For example, submerged plants oxygenate the water, emergent plants provide 'escape routes' for damselflies and dragonflies, and floating plants give the pond some shade and shelter. Bank-side plants, mainly long grasses and shrubs, can help to keep the pond safe by creating a 'safety zone' around the edges. This will also help to prevent too many unwary visitors disturbing any wildlife living in or around the pond. Depending on how many plants you choose, how quickly the plants become established and how natural you want your pond to look, there should be little maintenance to undertake throughout the year except during the autumn term. In order not to disturb the ecosystem you are developing it is important to do little and often and, with careful supervision, the children can take part in the regular maintenance tasks such as topping up the water and removing unwanted debris, leaf litter and rubbish.

Maintenance

Finally, it is important to reiterate that the inspection, maintenance and repair of any school grounds project must be given serious consideration when planning the creation or renewal of any outdoor play environment, and that practitioners taking on the project obtain advice from their stakeholders or local authority health and safety officers to ensure it is a safe, secure place for everyone.

4   Safety for healthy outdoor learning

Introduction

Safe outdoor education is an essential part of provision for all young children. And there are many arguments in favour of it. The HAO programme recognises the significant educational and social benefit of activities which take place outside in the fresh air. Outdoor education extends and enhances learning and personal development by exposing children to real issues and challenges. It is important, however, that anyone who leads young people in outdoor activities acknowledges to themselves and the young children in their charge the existence of a level of risk. Only in this way can an informed decision on participation be made by the leader, child and parent/guardian. It is not possible to remove all risk but through careful planning it can be reduced to an acceptable level. The national curriculum document *Aims for the School Curriculum* says that 'The school curriculum should...enable pupils to respond positively to opportunities, challenges and responsibilities, to manage risk and to cope with change and adversity' (DfES and QCA, 1999).

The information in this chapter provides a guideline regarding safety for outdoor learning but it cannot cover all aspects of safe outdoor education or every eventuality. Competence to lead groups outdoors safely will result from a combination of training, experience, assessment, professional judgement and informed use of the available guidance highlighted throughout this chapter.

The chapter includes practical advice on issues relating to health and safety, which include topics such as premises and security, statutory duties, frameworks and guidelines for outdoor provision, permission/medical questionnaire, complaints procedures, and organisation of adventure activities, supervision and risk assessments. It also includes a case study to demonstrate an example of a child taking the lead in an outdoor activity, emergency procedures, and some specific types of visit. The section on safe practice outdoors demonstrates the practical implications of the health and safety procedures as applied specifically to this programme.

This chapter also includes information about finding a suitable outdoor space to carry out the programme, what that space needs to include, and how to set it up and make the necessary risk assessments before the programme starts, for example making a reconnoitre visit, checking for possible hazards and what to do to make the area safe. It will include information about safe outdoor practice and the equipment needed to ensure safe practice. It discusses the importance of basic first aid training, and of gaining permission to do certain things such as having fires for barbecues or permission to take children off the site if a setting decides to venture further into the local community or woodlands. It will include information about basic personal safety, for example what to touch/not touch outdoors and what to do in case of an emergency.

In addition to the above, there are photographs of the children making the base to use as the meeting place at the start and finish of all activities and the 'hanging' tree which was chosen by the children as the constant recognisable feature to mark the meeting place to which the children returned after each activity.

The section on supervision discusses the issues of responsibility, the importance of making frequent head counts and using the 'buddy system' or a circular variation of it to keep children safe outdoors. It also explains the notion of 'remote supervision' and rearranging groups in relation to the programme. There is also an explanation of the important element of making risk assessments, paying attention to the local weather forecast and local knowledge alongside the

Figure 4.1 Touching base after a game

importance of making alternative plans, and considering any behaviour problems, illness or injury that might occur during the outdoor activities. Emergency procedures and adequate preparation for them are also considered.

This chapter will also include ways to encourage young children to play safely outdoors and look after each other. It will discuss the importance of risk taking and meeting challenges within a safe outdoor environment in order to gain the necessary experience to cope with the dangers of playing outdoors. In addition, this section will include examples of permission slips, health forms and video/photo consent forms to photocopy and send out to parents as safety precautions before the group starts.

Health and safety

Working outdoors with children has many implications for health and safety. The adult needs to be constantly aware of these. Whatever you are doing outdoors, be wary of the potential hazards for young children. It is important to consider all potential danger spots. Establish a set of basic outdoor ground rules which are always constant. Children need to know the outdoor boundaries, what they can or cannot do. They need to be constantly reminded of the dangers outdoors, as they tend to forget once they are engrossed in their play. As children will be running around outside, care must be taken to prevent them from bumping into each other or equipment. A code of safe outdoor practice needs to be established for everyone and understood by all involved. The amount and quality of supervision should be at least at the same level as for indoors.

Children will have accidents outdoors as even the best-planned outdoor activities can result in accidents. Minor accidents can be dealt with in the recommended way. Due to unforeseen circumstances, accidents of a more serious nature might occur. If so, proper medical advice must be sought as soon as possible. Concern for children's safety is paramount at all times. Minimising risk whilst maintaining the thrill of challenge is an important balance to strive for. Only by 'doing' will young children learn to assess risk and learn to be safe. However, it is also important to have an accident book or form to record all incidents.

Premises and security

School grounds are one of the few safe outdoor spaces that are available to children which allow them to experience the outdoors at the same time as providing them with a learning environment. Developments to school grounds that encourage the use of the outside spaces make a real difference to the children's lives. It is the responsibility of the programme facilitator to ensure that the outdoor space, furniture, equipment and toys are safe and suitable for their purpose. Fixed play equipment should comply with current recognised standards, such as British Standard 5696. All outdoor equipment needs regular cleaning and maintenance. Above all, the outdoors needs to be secure so that the children cannot get out and strangers cannot get in.

Equipment

The safety and suitability of outdoor equipment is primarily the responsibility of the employer. However, the employer will expect the employee to be vigilant, to address and report defects and to maintain a system of scheduled inspection. A logbook is an effective means by which to note the movement of a piece of equipment. Users can make comments in the log. The logbook can also show when an item was last checked, who checked it, and when it should be checked again.

Statutory duties, frameworks and guidelines

Settings should follow LEA guidance regarding safe outdoor practice although no guidance should be taken as an authoritative interpretation of the law, as only the law courts can provide that. Today there are many statutory duties, frameworks and guidelines that practitioners must adhere to regarding the education and care of young children and which apply to the setting up of outdoor provision. The Early Years Foundation Stage (EYFS) standards document *Setting the Standards for Learning, Development and Care for Children from Birth to Five* (DfES, 2007) spells out the statutory duties for early years providers regarding the use of outside premises for children and highlights that outside premises must be safe and secure. 'Providers must notify Ofsted of any change in the facilities to be used for care that may affect the space and level of care available to children. An early years provider who, without reasonable excuse, fails to comply with this requirement, commits an offence.'

The EYFS standards document (DfES, 2007) also states that:

CARDIFF
CAERDYDD

- providers must only release children into the care of individuals named by the parent;
- providers must ensure that children do not leave the premises unsupervised;
- providers must take steps to prevent intruders entering the premises.

The EYFS standards set out the statutory guidance which providers have to take into account where relevant when using the grounds. This includes ensuring outdoor security with regard to which doors are locked or unlocked, and the use of door alarms, security systems, intercoms and name badges. Early years practitioners should also be aware of the whereabouts of other people using the grounds. Posters and reminders should be displayed so that parents and visitors can easily access information about the need for security outdoors and the systems in place to maintain it. The outdoor programme facilitator needs to keep a visitor book or use a similar system to verify the identity of any visitors or volunteers to the programme so that names are recorded, along with the purpose of the visit, and details of arrival and departure times. The same procedure should be adopted for the arrival and departure of staff, children, parents and visitors, and written permission from parents where children are to be picked up by another adult.

> It is essential that children are provided with safe and secure environments in which to interact and explore rich and diverse learning and development opportunities. Providers need to ensure that, as well as conducting a formal risk assessment, they constantly reappraise both the environments and activities to which children are being exposed and make necessary adjustments to secure their safety at all times.
>
> (DfES, 2007: 19)

Health and safety needs to be monitored and evaluated so that activity outside the classroom is safe and poses reasonable challenges and risks for the children and adults taking part. It is vital that young children learn how to manage challenge and take risks for themselves in everyday life situations so that they can develop to become confident, capable adults. Staff should be able to manage the outdoor programme so that it is safe for all taking part. The educational benefits for young children getting outside for learning experiences should be the main driving forces for outside learning.

Responsibility for the safety of taking children outside the classroom into the grounds or local community to take part in the programme rests entirely with the setting. Staff should have the necessary training to enable them to tackle the programme with the confidence that all safety policies and guidance documents are fully understood and followed in order to sensibly manage any risk. Keeping young children safe is of paramount importance and all programme leaders/facilitators should work together to meet health and safety standards and share expertise and best practice. It is good practice to help children understand how to behave outdoors by talking about personal safety, risks and the safety of others.

If children are going to be taken outside the premises of their setting, which was the case for the HAO programme, there are statutory requirements that must be met to keep them safe. For each specific outing, providers must carry out a full risk assessment, which includes an assessment of required adult:child ratios. This assessment must take account of the nature of the outing, and consider whether it is appropriate to exceed the normal ratio requirements set out in the early years statutory document, in accordance with providers' procedures for supervision of children on outings.

The EYFS document (DFES, 2007), the statutory guidance relevant to the HAO programme, which, depending on how it is adapted for use in each individual setting, may include an outing such as a visit to the local woods if they are within walking distance or visits to carry out surveys in the local community, sets out the following requirements:

- Providers should obtain written parental permission for children to take part in outings.
- Providers should take essential records and equipment on outings, for example, contact telephone numbers for the parents of children on the outing, first aid kit, a mobile phone.
- Providers should ensure that they have sufficient information about the medical condition of any child with long-term medical needs.
- Providers must notify Ofsted and local child protection agencies of any serious accident or injury to, or serious illness of, or the death of, any child whilst in their care, and act on any advice given. An early years provider who, without reasonable excuse, fails to comply with this requirement, commits an offence.
- At least one person who has a current paediatric first aid certificate must be on the premises at all times when children are present. There must be at least one person on outings who has a current paediatric first aid certificate.
- Providers must have a first aid box with appropriate content to meet the needs of children.
- Providers must keep a record of accidents and first aid treatment. Providers must inform parents of any accidents or injuries sustained by the child whilst in the care of the providers and of any first aid treatment that was given.
- Providers should discuss with parents the procedure for children who are ill or infectious. This should include the possibility of exclusion as well as the protocol for contacting parents or another adult designated by the parent if a child becomes ill or receives minor injuries whilst in the provider's care.

(DfES, 2007: 24)

Safety management needs to be practical and proportionate to what is going on regarding the use of the outside area or field trips to the local community. Any safety-related paperwork needs to be manageable and kept to a minimum, otherwise staff will be deterred from taking advantage of using the endless natural teaching resources found outside. Again the EYFS standards document clearly spells out the statutory guidance to which providers should have regard. It is as follows:

- All practitioners should have an up-to-date understanding of safeguarding children issues and be able to implement the safeguarding children policy and procedure appropriately.
- Policies should be in line with LSCB local guidance and procedures.
- Staff should be able to respond appropriately to significant changes in children's behaviour; deterioration in their general well-being; unexplained bruising, marks or signs of possible abuse; neglect and the comments children make which give cause for concern.

(DfES, 2007: 22)

There is also a section in the EYFS standards document (DfES, 2007) which gives practitioners statutory information on how to deal with giving parents and carers information about the programme and dealing with any complaints they might receive about it. It states that providers must engage with parents and provide information about:

- the type of activities the children will take part in;
- the daily routines of the provision;
- the staffing of the provision;
- food and drinks provided for the children;
- the provider's policies and procedures, for example the policies for taking children outdoors, equality of opportunity policy, safeguarding children, the complaints procedure, details for contacting Ofsted and an explanation that parents can make a complaint to Ofsted should they wish;
- the procedure to be followed in the event of a parent failing to collect a child at the appointed time and the procedure to be followed in the event of a child going missing.

(DfES, 2007)

Information needed in advance of a child taking part in the Healthy, Active and Outside programme

According to the EYFS standards document (DfES, 2007), providers must obtain certain necessary information from parents in advance of a child being admitted to the provision. The necessary information is listed below:

- emergency contact numbers
- the child's special dietary requirements
- food allergies the child may have
- the child's special health requirements
- information about who has legal contact with the child and who has parental responsibility for the child
- written parental permission must be requested, at the time of the child's admission to the provision, to the seeking of any necessary emergency medical advice or treatment.

The setting in which the programme takes place may already have all the above information but it would be precautionary to complete the parental consent form (Figure 4.2, p. 38) with parents or carers of children before they start the programme.

Complaints about the programme

Usually the setting in which you run the programme will be responsible for following the statutory complaints procedures but it may be necessary to follow up procedures for yourself or at least be aware of their existence so that they can be followed if the situation arises. The EYFS standards document (DfES, 2007) states that providers must put in place a written procedure for dealing with concerns and complaints from parents and keep a written record of these complaints and their outcome. If you are running an outdoor programme you must follow the setting's complaints procedures to investigate all written complaints relating to the requirements and notify complainants of the outcome of the investigation within 28 days of having received the complaint.

THE HEALTHY, ACTIVE AND OUTSIDE PROGRAMME
Parental consent form

Child's name...

Parent/guardian/next of kin, full name...

Home address ....

....

Contact telephone number in case of emergency: Home...........................

Work.................................Mobile...

Name and address of family doctor ....

....

Telephone number ....

Has your son/daughter had any of the following:

Asthma	YES	NO
Sight or hearing disabilities	YES	NO
Heart condition	YES	NO
Fits, blackouts	YES	NO
Severe headaches	YES	NO
Diabetes	YES	NO
Allergies to any known drugs	YES	NO
Any other known allergies, e.g. material, food, pollen	YES	NO
Other illnesses or disability	YES	NO

If the answer to any of the questions above is YES, please give details in the space below including details of medication.

Has your son/daughter received vaccination against tetanus in the last year? YES/NO

As a parent/guardian of the child named above I have read, fully understood and am satisfied with the details of the Healthy, Active and Outside programme and agree for my child to take part. I know of no medical reasons why my child should not take part.

Signed................................….... Date......................................

Name......................................…… Relation to child ....

Figure 4.2 Permission/medical form

Providers must supply Ofsted, on request, with a written record of all complaints made during any specified period, and the action which was taken as a result of each complaint. The very least you should do is to make dated records of all incidents of complaint and the outcomes.

Policy of Safety and Guidance for Outdoor Education

All settings which include an element of outdoor education should have a policy of Safety and Guidance for Outdoor Education. There are many health and safety policies which can be adapted to suit individual settings. The best place to begin is to contact the Local Education Authority in which the programme takes place and read the following, adapted from one by the Dorset County Council which was found on the Safegard website.

The following government documents should be read before embarking on any form of outdoor education:

- 'Standards for Adventure', aimed at the practitioner teacher who leads young people on adventure activities.
- 'A Handbook for Group Leaders', aimed at anyone who leads groups of young people on any kind of educational visit. It sets out good practice in supervision, ongoing risk assessment and emergency procedures.
- 'Group Safety at Water Margins' is aimed at anyone who organises learning activities that take place near or in water, such as a walk along a river bank or seashore, collecting samples from ponds or streams, or paddling or walking in gentle, shallow water.
- 'Health and Safety: Responsibilities and Powers', which was sent out to schools and LAs in December 2001.

(Adapted from the Safegard website, Dorset County Council)

Practitioners should seek to resolve internally any disagreement about health and safety management affecting children in their care. On the rare occasion when a practitioner believes a safety risk has not been adequately dealt with, it may be necessary to raise concern about risk management. The law protects a practitioner from getting into trouble with their senior management when they make a disclosure if it tends to show, for example, a danger to the health and safety of an individual. Employees can disclose their concern to a manager, their employer, the Health and Safety Executive, even other outsiders in certain circumstances.

The Health and Safety Executive highlights the immense benefit of outdoor education when based on proper risk management. The guidance published by the DfES is available and highlights ten vital questions that should be answered before an educational visit takes place.

Standards for Adventure

The 'Standards for Adventure' document is Part 2 of a three-part supplement – *Health and Safety of Pupils on Educational Visits: A Good Practice Guide* (*HASPEV*, 2002). For policy information see also 'Health and Safety: Responsibilities and Powers' and the other parts of this supplement: 'Standards for LEAs in Overseeing Educational Visits' and 'A Handbook for Group Leaders' (*HASPEV*, 2002). This document does not replace local or other professional guidance or regulations and all settings must follow LEA guidance as a first recourse but it does contain useful advice about school-led adventure activities and information about the responsibilities and tasks of the supervisor, the educational visits coordinator and the technical adviser (*HASPEV*, 2002, Chapter 8, paragraphs 172–174). Adventure activities are the core activities as defined in the 1996 Regulations such as climbing, caving and water activities. Second, they include the range of other activities that present hazards over and above those in everyday life. Some of the guidance will be useful for *all* kinds of outdoor activities and off-site visits, whether overtly adventurous or not. Tragedies can happen on ordinary visits where the risks are not obvious. Routine educational visits may seem safe but they still require good risk assessment and management.

Organisation of adventure activities

The facilitator of the outdoor programme should seek advice from the LEA's outdoor education adviser or an appropriately qualified technical adviser as necessary. Under current legislation the HAO adventure programme is not subject to national inspection or licensing as it is organised and led as part of the core activities of the setting, and schools are not required to hold a licence when making provision to their own pupils.

However, adventure activities taking place in any setting are subject to the management and approval of the education employer under health and safety law. This is because the employer must, in law, ensure the health and safety of both pupils and staff. The local authority (LA) has this responsibility for community and voluntary controlled schools. The governing body is the employer in foundation and voluntary aided schools. The proprietor is the employer in independent schools. 'Health and Safety: Responsibilities and Powers' explains the legal framework for each type of school. 'Standards for LEAs in Overseeing Educational Visits' gives guidance on the role of the LEA, with read-across for other types of education employer.

Competence

It is important to ensure that activities are supervised by people of suitable competence. LEA guidance may prescribe the levels of competence required. In leading adventure activities, teachers or other school staff will have the great advantage of knowing their pupils well. But they may not regularly instruct an activity nor be familiar with the activity site. This could affect their awareness of specific risks. Facilitators may need to hold a national governing body leader or instructor qualification for some outdoor activities. These qualifications will need to be supplemented by the verification of other qualities such as maturity, general supervision skills, ability to supervise different types of group and relevant experience. For other activities, teachers may have their competence ratified in-house by a suitably competent person, if their employer considers that appropriate.

Some adventure activities need the following evidence of competence:

- National Governing Body (NGB) awards/qualifications;
- National Vocational Qualifications (NVQs); NVQs are work-related, competence-based qualifications that reflect the skills and knowledge required to do a job effectively. NVQs represent national standards that are recognised by employers throughout England. They are based on the National Occupational Standards (NOS) and will be most relevant to outdoor learning where they incorporate the relevant NGB qualification;
- OCR Off-Site Safety Management Certificate;
- local or in-house validation;
- site-specific assessment which refers to a situation in which an individual is trained to cope.

For visits or activities such as a walk in the park, a site-specific induction, rather than a formal assessment, might be sufficient as long as supervisory competence in general had been satisfactorily assessed, perhaps by a senior member of school staff. This assessment might include the ability to hold the attention of a group during the visit and to brief pupils in a range of circumstances.

Experience

Competence in outdoor adventure activities derives from a balance of personal experience of trial and error and learning from the errors made, and related training. Technical competence can be attained through formal training. But safety judgements are most soundly based on enlightened experience, which takes time to accumulate. Proof must therefore exist of suitable and sufficient experience in the activity. An employer who is unsure about assessing the competence of an individual to lead a particular activity should seek the guidance of a technical adviser.

Programme facilitators may find it useful to consider categories of activities, when determining an appropriate course of action in respect of activities presenting different levels of potential risk. However, accidents can happen in any activity regardless of whether it is classified as high, medium or low risk. It is important to be aware that low risk does not mean no risk. Low-risk activities that present no significant risks should be supervised by a teacher who has been assessed as competent to lead this category of educational activity or visit. The activities should be conducted following the LEA's or school's standard visits procedures. Some LEAs classify these as activities needing level 1 supervisory skills; examples might include:

- walking in parks or on non-remote country paths;
- field studies in environments presenting no technical hazards.

Activities next to open water, such as pond dipping, might rate as category B, which is a medium risk. Winter camping might rate as category C, which is a high risk, as might other outdoor activities in bleak winter weather or over steep terrain.

In assessing the appropriate category in which to place an activity, the outdoor education leader should take account of the environment in which the activity will take place. An activity might be rated in a higher category if it takes place:

- in or near water
- in winter conditions
- in an area subject to extremes of weather or environmental change.

There are many handbooks to provide practical information that might be helpful to group leaders of outdoor activities, particularly regarding health and safety. These handbooks are no substitutes for good outdoor training but nevertheless provide a good grounding in the theory of safe outdoor education. It is recommended that all group leaders have access to training before taking children outside for educational purposes.

Risk assessments

This section aims to enhance practitioners' understanding of, and confidence to address, the issue of risk in outdoor play. To do this, first the factors that affect practitioners' judgement must be looked at, including their concerns about the potential for parental complaint or being thought negligent. A risk assessment is undertaken by the leaders of the programme as a regular part of their practice and should involve discussion which explores the link between risk assessment and creating the best possible outside play environment for the children.

The risk assessment process itself is mandatory for providers but practitioners should also consider:

- what exactly outdoor play means to them;
- just how you get the balance right in risk assessments between taking positive risks and safety;
- how you can show that you make reasonable judgements about risk levels;
- the difference between negligence and an accident;
- what constitutes a serious injury;
- how 'health and safety' and our present culture of anxiety affects judgement.

Criteria by which judgements should be made concerning making risk assessments

Children and young people need opportunities to engage in beneficial risk taking within acceptable levels of risk. But what does this mean in practice? This section of the book explores how attitudes and anxieties about risk affect so many aspects of decision making in respect of outdoor play; for example:

- the physical design of play places;
- whether play is supervised or unsupervised;

- creation of self-induced 'artificial scarcity' in play budgets;
- modes of supervision;
- balance of adult-initiated structured activities and child-initiated free play.

Leaders should recognise that there are many hazards in school grounds and take the appropriate action to manage risk by making thorough risk assessments before each session begins. As with all outdoor learning, you will need to write risk assessments, but these need only be written when an activity is done for the first time, and then kept on record. You should find that many outdoor lessons are similar enough that a fairly generic risk assessment can be quickly adapted. Useful information can be obtained from the following websites: http://www.hse.gov.uk ('A Guide to Risk Assessment Requirements') and http://www.hse.gov.uk ('Five Steps to Risk Assessment').

Although risk assessment is an ongoing process, it is good practice for the group leader to first draw up a plan and timetable for the programme by considering the questions why, who, what, when, where and how? The group leader should then consider what could go wrong during the outdoor programme and how to avoid the risks or, for overtly adventurous activities, how to manage them. The plan of action will need modifying until the control measures are satisfactory. Any new information arising out of an activity should be fed back into the process. There should be regular, ongoing reassessment of any risks that might occur during the programme. Risk assessment in relation to the outdoor programme can be usefully considered as having three levels:

1 Generic activity risk assessments, which are likely to apply to the activity wherever and whenever it takes place.
2 Site-specific risk assessments, which will differ from place to place and group to group.
3 Ongoing risk assessments that take account of, for example, illness of staff or pupils, changes of weather, availability of preferred activity or use of specific tools.

Written risk assessments

Good practice in assessing the risks of outdoor education allows for a wide range of written evidence to be used as part of the risk assessment procedure. This includes:

- The initial activity approval form, which is generally completed by the programme/group leader and is designed to lead him or her through a suitable and sufficient assessment of the risks involved. See, for example, *HASPEV* (2002, pp. 45–47, Form One). This can be modified as necessary.
- Minimum evidence of risk assessment; this could comprise: a reference to the generic risks associated with that activity; the corresponding qualifications and experience of the leader; a list of site-specific hazards (e.g. accident black spots); and a corresponding list of control measures to be applied which takes account of the age and abilities of the pupil group. See 'Standards for LEAs in Overseeing Educational Visits'.
- For higher-risk activities, a comprehensive induction for all adult supervisors; this would establish the significant hazards and how these will be met. An appropriately completed induction checklist is part of the risk assessment.

Acknowledgement of risk

When considering the subject of acknowledging risk in connecting with the outdoor programme it is essential to recognise that a condition or set of circumstances may be hazardous to one group, or to one group member, more than to another. No assumptions should ever be made, especially where the children's individual levels of knowledge are uncertain. It is good practice for a setting or school to share aspects of the risk assessment with parents and pupils. Both should be made aware of the likely risks and their management so that consent can be given or refused on an informed basis. Some organisers of outdoor activities ask parents to formally acknowledge the risks. Neither this nor parental consent absolves the LEA or school staff of their responsibilities under health and safety law.

Ongoing risk assessments

Making risk assessments for outdoor activities also includes an ongoing element of reassessment. This continual reassessment might be necessitated by objective observation, such as changing the activity because of adverse changes in the weather or by reason of subjective feelings if, for example, someone in the group becomes frightened, ill or overtired during the activity. Risk assessment does not end when the outdoor activity begins. Changes to the plans, changes to the weather, incidents (whether minor or major), staff illness – all or any of these may cause children to face unexpected hazards or difficulties and give rise to the need to reassess risk.

The group leader (and other adults with supervisory responsibility) prepares ongoing risk assessments the whole while the outdoor programme is taking place. These normally consist of judgements and decisions made as the need arises. They are not usually recorded until after the activity when there is planned time for debriefing, recording and planning for the next outdoor session. These ongoing risk assessments should be informed by the generic risk assessment for the programme as a whole and the site-specific risk assessments made prior to the start of the outdoor programme. It is good practice to have briefings after each session to take stock and assess the circumstances for the next session. It is also good practice to spend time explaining arrangements for the session's programme of activities to the children at the start of each new session.

Check the local weather forecast

Before going outside, always check the local weather forecast to inform decisions on appropriate clothing as it is important that the children taking part in the outdoor activities are safe from any potential harm caused through inappropriate clothing. Children need outdoor clothing that is appropriate for the weather conditions and which allows freedom of movement. They need shoes with sturdy grip which can be securely fastened and clothes with no loose parts to get caught on equipment; they also need sunhats and/or protective clothing. At times it might be too hot, too cold, too wet or too slippery for children to play outdoors.

Seek knowledge of potential hazards

Before the children arrive for each outdoor session, check the outside area you are using to run the programme for any hazards that might have cropped up between sessions such as fox faeces, broken glass thrown onto the premises, broken perimeter fences or latches on security gates. If taking children outside the setting into the local community, check for any hazards such as rivers or streams that might be prone to sudden increases in flow, newly fallen trees and branches in the woodland area, difficult terrain or crossing points for the road.

Alternative plans

It is always useful to have alternative plans for outdoor activities. Good forward planning will always include alternative plans in case the activities need to be changed due to unforeseen circumstances. A flexible plan allows activities from later in the programme to be substituted for earlier activities if those are prevented by unexpected circumstances. Group leaders faced with potential difficulties will feel more confident to change the plan if an alternative is available. Even if an alternative plan has been pre-assessed, always reassess risks if the planned activities change. On arrival at an alternative site or activity that has not previously been risk-assessed, the group leader should risk-assess the situation before allowing the pupils to take part. An unknown location might involve hazards not covered in the original risk assessment; for example, if the original intention to visit a land-only site has to be changed at short notice, there may be an unexpected hazardous water feature such as a pond or a stream.

Supervision

Every outdoor programme needs a named group leader who manages the whole programme. However, for individual activities within each session, it is better for some groups to be small, each with a supervisor, who will normally be an experienced early years practitioner teacher or another member of the staff.

Supervision of outdoor activities is most effective when:

- the aims and objectives of the activity are clearly understood by all the group leaders;
- the activities have been carefully risk-assessed and will be managed safely;
- practitioners and children have contributed to the overall plan, including the risk assessment and risk management;
- the group leader has laid down clear guidelines for standards of behaviour and everyone has agreed them;
- group leaders have a reasonable knowledge of the pupils, including any special educational needs, medical needs or disabilities;
- each activity has an alternative plan for bad weather;
- volunteers have provided evidence of Criminal Records Bureau clearance, where required, depending on circumstances and individual settings.

Close and remote supervision

Supervision of groups playing outside can be close or remote. Close supervision occurs when the group remain within sight and contact of the group leader. Remote supervision occurs when, as part of the planned activities or during free play, children move away from the supervisor but are subject to stated controls. The leader is present though not necessarily near or in sight, but his or her whereabouts are known by the children and other adults outside. Free play may involve close or remote supervision, but should not be unsupervised, and at all times the leaders continue to be in charge.

In close supervision all supervisors usually:

- have prior knowledge of the children in the group;
- carry a list/register of all the children;
- regularly check that all the children are present;
- have appropriate access to first aid.

Remote supervision will normally be the final stage of a phased development programme. When supervision is remote:

- Group leaders must be sufficiently trained and competent for the level of activity undertaken by the group of children, including in first aid and emergency procedures.
- Children will be familiar with the environment.
- Children will have details of the meeting points.
- Children fully understand the length of times they can be away from the supervisor.
- Clear and understandable boundaries will be set for the group.
- There must be clear lines of communication between the group and the leader.
- The leader should monitor the group's progress at appropriate intervals.
- The supervisor will be in the activity area and able to reach the group reasonably promptly in an emergency.
- There should be a recognisable point at which the activity is completed.
- There should be clear arrangements to abandon the activity when it cannot be safely completed.

It is essential that everyone involved in the activity understands the supervision arrangements and expectations. At certain times during the programme there is a higher risk that things might go wrong – for example, when a large group is split into smaller groups for specific activities, when groups transfer from one activity to another and change supervisor, during transition periods between activities or when small groups re-form back into the large group.

It is therefore important that the facilitator supervising each group takes responsibility for the group when their part of the programme begins, making sure that all children in the group are aware of the changeover. It is equally important that supervisors pass on responsibility for the group when their part of the programme is finished, together with any relevant information ensuring that the children know who their next supervisor is. To ensure absolute clarity at all times regarding these points there may be some benefit in differentiating between a group leader/supervisor of the programme and an activity leader.

Supervision ratios

Normally there should be individual supervision by an adult for every child younger than 12 months, a ratio of one adult for two children for children between ages one and two, and gradually increasing ratios up to one adult for eight children for children between the ages five and eight. Ratios may vary in the course of the activity and will often become obvious when making the defined educational objectives and the risk assessment. The factors that must be taken into consideration include:

- the specific activity
- the experience of the group involved
- the needs of individuals within the group, including those with special educational needs
- the environment
- the conditions in which the activity takes place
- the experience of the staff (e.g. newly qualified teachers/volunteers)
- the nature of the venue.

Supervisors must be competent to undertake the role and may include other school staff or parent volunteers. Any person acting as a supervisor who is not employed by the LEA or setting cannot hold the same responsibility as regular staff. They should not normally be given sole charge of any pupils, unless, perhaps, for a short time in clearly defined circumstances where the teacher is readily to hand.

At times a pupil may be sufficiently competent to supervise other children in certain teacher-controlled circumstances or even for a technically competent pupil to instruct (but not to supervise) a teacher who will remain as the pupil's supervisor. At times the outdoor programme included older children in the school in which it was run. They provided role models for younger children or were given the opportunity to take part in the outdoor programme because they were having difficulties coping with their behaviour indoors or because older brothers and sisters had been invited to take part as a specific activity. This worked well and gave a family structure to the group, especially when parents were also taking part.

Case study

During the outdoor programme that was running throughout the academic year of 2005/6 an older boy in Year 5 who was experiencing difficulties staying in class due to behaviour problems was on the verge of exclusion. He was particularly good with younger children and also liked outdoor physical activities. To keep him out of trouble and to build on his strengths he was invited to join the programme for a term as a 'helper'. Knowing that it was a privilege, not a punishment, to join the group, he rose to the occasion and provided an excellent male role model for the Foundation Stage children and took great care to work within the boundaries and limits set by the group leader. He took the lead in many activities and spent a great deal of his own time preparing a 'keep fit for toddlers' course which he set up around the woodland space used for the activities at that time. He made 12 activity cards depicting different exercises that he hung on branches around a predetermined course prior to the children attending the session. He led the group and demonstrated each exercise and counted out the number of repetitions to help the younger children with their counting before helping them (and the group leaders!) to carry out the instructions on the cards. He was able to take on the leadership role throughout the activity and although still supervised by the teacher he was able to instruct her on some of the finer technicalities of the exercises he had set up for the keep fit course. His behaviour during that summer term was better than it had been for the rest of the whole year, and since. The young children responded to him without their usual fear and he in turn showed respect for both the programme leaders and the young children taking part. In addition he also ensured that the base used by the Foundation Stage children stayed intact when older children used the area during play times.

Practical advice on supervision 'in the field'

This section aims to give practical advice on supervision 'in the field'. During the outdoor programme it was made quite clear that everyone involved had a certain amount of responsibility for themselves and for others, whatever their age or position in the group. These main categories of responsibility are:

1   responsibility of the programme leader/facilitator
2   responsibility of the supervisor/activity leader
3   responsibility of the child.

Responsibility of the programme leader/facilitator

The programme leader has overall responsibility for the group at all times. In delegating supervisory roles to other adults in the group, it is good practice for the group leader to:

- allocate responsibility to each adult for named children;
- ensure that each adult knows which children they are responsible for;
- ensure that each child knows which adult is responsible for them;
- ensure that all adults understand that they are responsible to the group leader for the supervision of the pupils assigned to them;
- ensure that all adults and children are aware of the expected standards of behaviour.

Responsibility of the activity leader

Each activity leader should:

- have a reasonable prior knowledge of the pupils, including any special educational needs, medical needs or disabilities;
- carry a list of all group members;
- directly supervise the pupils (except during remote supervision) and regularly check that the entire group is present;
- have a clear plan of the activity and its educational objectives;
- be able to contact the group leader or other supervisors in the case of an emergency or when needing help;
- have prior knowledge of the outside space being used for the programme – the group leader should normally have made an exploratory visit;
- anticipate a potential risk by recognising a hazard, by arriving, where necessary, at the point of hazard before the pupils do, and acting promptly where necessary;
- continuously monitor the appropriateness of the activity, the physical and mental condition and abilities of the children and the suitability of the prevailing conditions;
- be competent to exercise appropriate control of the group, and to ensure that children abide by the agreed standards of behaviour;
- clearly understand the emergency procedures and be able to carry them out;
- have appropriate access to first aid.

Responsibility of the child

Each child attending the programme should:

- know who their activity leader is and how to contact him/her when necessary;
- have been given clear, understandable and appropriate instructions;
- rarely if ever be entirely on their own;
- alert the activity leader if they know someone is missing or in difficulty;
- have a meeting place to return to, or an instruction to remain where they are, if separated from the main group;
- understand and accept the expected standards of behaviour.

Head counts

Whatever the length and nature of the activity, regular head-counting of pupils should take place when learning outside. It is good practice to have a head count checklist to tick off, of all pupils and adults who are involved in the programme. When taking children outside it is also good practice to ensure that they are readily identifiable, especially if the outside area is shared by others or the outdoor programme is taking place outside the grounds of the setting. Brightly coloured caps or T-shirts can be seen more easily amongst other children or in dense woodland. It is a good idea to give the children badges displaying the name of the setting, group leader and an emergency contact number as useful safety measures, but avoid name badges as they could put children at risk. It is important to ensure that all children are aware of the meeting point and that they know what to do if they become separated from the group.

Using 'buddy' systems

Encourage children from a very young age to take responsibility for themselves and their friends. One way to do this is to use the 'buddy' system where each child is paired with a buddy who regularly checks that the other is present and is OK, or use a variation of the buddy system, the 'circle buddy', where children form a circle at the start of the outdoor session so that each child has a left-side 'buddy' and a right-side 'buddy'. He or she will check on these when asked during random points in the session in readiness to use the system in case of an emergency. Two pupils cannot disappear together without being missed by the third, which might happen when using the paired 'buddy' system of checking in.

Behaviour problems, illness or injury

Agree a set of behaviour standards at the start of the programme and reiterate them before every session and at specific points throughout the activities to help reduce the likelihood of behaviour problems. Although the outdoor programme is a good opportunity for staff to get to know children away from the confines of the school, they should resist any temptation to accept lower standards of behaviour. The different hazards that children may be exposed to outdoors will require them to observe standards of behaviour that are at least as high as, or higher than, those expected for indoors in the classroom.

If a situation arises where one adult has to give prolonged attention to one child in the group, the leader should reassess the supervisory roles of the other adults and reallocate children to different groups, ensuring that they know who is responsible for them. In this specific case or similar situations, activities may need to be amended until the adult is able to return full attention to the group in his or her charge. Group leaders need to listen to their instincts and trust their own knowledge of the young people at the same time as relying on their own professional judgement. At times a situation might arise where it is necessary to challenge an activity leader if another adult in charge of supervising groups of children outdoors has superior knowledge of the children. In some cases the challenge might also involve intervening to prompt a change of plan.

Emergency procedures

By their very nature, emergencies usually catch us out unexpectedly, but careful emergency planning can help everyone cope with the trauma faced in the difficult circumstances of being caught up in an emergency. It is good practice for the group leader to establish an agreed emergency action plan prior to the outdoor activities, stating clear roles for the group leader, school/LEA contact and head teacher. The plan should also include ways to manage specific emergency situations, for example when a child has been injured, which include ways to support parents of the injured child.

It is also the leader's responsibility to ensure that all members of the group are made aware of what action to take if there is an emergency. A practical way of doing this is to hold regular debriefing meetings at the end of each outdoor session with all the adults involved in running the programme to discuss issues for the next session and to spend time at the start of each session explaining arrangements to the children to ensure that they all understand and follow the code of conduct. Also, spend time practising emergency drills, for example fire drills or evacuation from the outside area where the programme is taking place.

In addition, to help keep children safe when taking part in outside activities there should be a named first-aider on the premises or all the adults should be encouraged to hold up-to-date competence in first aid or other competencies necessary for the activities that the children are taking part in. It is the group leader's responsibility to ensure that the first aid kit is properly stocked and accessible (see Guidance on First Aid for Schools, paragraph 60, http://www.teachernet.gov.uk/firstaid). It is also the leader's responsibility to ensure that all children's medical conditions such as asthma, diabetes, epilepsy and anaphylaxis are known and that staff are competent to handle them if the occasion arises (see Supporting Pupils with Medical Needs: A Good Practice Guide, http://www.teachernet.gov.uk/medical).

At times it might be necessary to advise children attending the programme about the dangers of over-exertion in the heat and of dehydration, which can cause headache, dizziness and nausea, and encourage them to stop for drinks of water. When the climate is warm and children are engrossed in outdoor play activities they need to be encouraged to keep fluid levels high by being told to stop for drinks of water. At times it may also be necessary to encourage children to play in shady areas and to advise the parents to dress their children appropriately in loose, lightweight

Figure 4.3 Stopping for a drink in a shady area

clothing, preferably made of cotton or other natural fibres, sun hats and glasses and to apply high-factored sun protection creams before they arrive for the start of each outdoor session.

If an emergency occurs during the outside programme, the group leader should maintain or resume control of the group. The main factors to consider include:

- establishing the nature and extent of the emergency as quickly as possible;
- ensuring that all the group are safe and looked after;
- establishing the names of any casualties and getting immediate medical attention;
- ensuring that a teacher accompanies casualties to hospital with any relevant medical information, and that the rest of the group are adequately supervised at all times and kept together;
- notifying the police if necessary;
- ensuring that all group members who need to know are aware of the incident;
- ensuring that all group members are following the emergency procedures and the roles allocated to them – revising procedures and re-allocating roles as necessary;
- informing the school contact. The school contact number should be accessible at all times during the outdoor activity;
- passing on details of the incident to the school; these should include nature, date and time of incident; location of incident; names of casualties and details of their injuries; names of others involved so that parents can be reassured; action taken so far; action yet to be taken (and by whom);
- contacting parents, providing as full a factual account of the incident as possible;
- writing down accurately and as soon as possible all relevant facts and witness details and preserving any vital evidence;
- keeping a written account of all events, times and contacts after the incident and completing an accident report form as soon as possible.

Advice on specific activities

When taking part in specific outdoor activities such as a walk in a wood or a visit to a farm it is important to look out for hazards such as glass or barbed wire. It is also important to adopt and explain the signals of distress and carry out regular head counts. Supervisors should ensure that there are adequate clean and well-maintained washing facilities and that all children wash their hands thoroughly before eating or drinking. They should prevent children from touching animal droppings, and if they do, then they must wash and dry their hands.

Figure 4.4 Listening carefully to explanations of safety regarding berries found on trees

Case study: Safe practice in the HAO programme

This section of the chapter demonstrates the practical application of health and safety procedures relating specifically to the HAO programme itself. Safe practice was a major consideration when leading the outdoor programme. The Local Education Authority Guidelines for outdoor adventure were followed (Bristol LEA, 1998) and risk assessments were made regarding the woodland environment itself and any tools that the group might be using during each particular session. Before the programme got under way the children were taught:

- to respond readily to instructions;
- to recognise and follow certain rules, etiquette and safety procedures for different kinds of activities or events;
- about the safety risks of wearing inappropriate clothing, footwear and jewellery and why certain clothes are worn for different activities;
- to negotiate safe pathways through rough terrain, to use alternative routes or to ask and give each other help, especially when negotiating steep, slippery slopes in wet weather conditions;
- to handle tools safely;
- how to lift, carry, place and use equipment safely;
- how to warm up and recover from exercise.

Figure 4.5 Children negotiating safe pathways through rough terrain

Figure 4.6 Children lifting and placing equipment safely

A safety ethos was established through a progressive approach to the activities which encouraged children to take responsibility for themselves and each other at every stage. For some children it was necessary to adapt the activities that had been planned to enhance their learning opportunities and to ensure that safe practice took place. Looking out for each other was encouraged throughout every aspect of the programme.

The outdoor space used during the programme was checked for hazards by a member of staff before each weekly session. The boundaries were set and any particular hazards were pointed out to the children at the start of every session. These included the pond area, which although already drained and abandoned by the school sometimes filled up with water when it rained heavily. They were taught to stay within the perimeters of the woodland area, which although part of the school field was not fenced in. Incidentally, there were no problems at all regarding children staying within the physical boundaries even though there were no fences and several of them were known 'runners'.

The safety tree

The safety tree was marked out as the base to group together for any recall such as the end of an activity, a need to call the group together in an emergency, to prevent unsafe practices or to explain what was going to happen next. A game called '1, 2, 3 Where Are You?' is a hide-and-seek safety game adapted from one learned during the researcher's training at the Forest School in Bridgwater College and was developed to encourage safe practice and used during every outdoor school session. When hearing the call of '1, 2, 3 Where are you?' from one or other of the group leaders the children knew it was time to quickly and safely return to the tree marking the base. The children were also taught a safety game to use if they got into trouble when out of sight and needed to call for help.

The game encourages children to make choices and take turns; it requires communication, listening, negotiation, problem solving, observation, physical and decision-making skills. The game also fosters children's willingness to explore and take risks, their independence, high levels of involvement, care and concern for others, themselves and the environment as children develop a sense of trust and make meaningful relationships. The game allows children to move in a variety of ways as they negotiate appropriate pathways back to base. The children playing can express their thoughts and ideas with confidence and reflect about them during the review at the end when they are all counted in for a safety check.

Figure 4.7 The safety tree

5 Moving outdoors

Introduction

This chapter will discuss the importance of creating the right atmosphere and ethos for the group work process to be effective. It will include information about setting up groups and will focus on the importance of building genuine relationships with all concerned parties in order to make the intervention an enjoyable process which is effective for all concerned. It will include the children's stories which unfolded during the intervention and comments from the children themselves, their parents/carers and school staff.

This section of the book will also set out the basic structure of the outdoor activities for each week, linked into the three seasons and six school terms. It will also show how the full-length programme can be adapted into a short six- to ten-week intervention to be used as part of the curriculum for all children. It will provide practitioners with an easy-to-follow structure for the process of running an outdoor physical activities programme. This section will include photocopiable sheets to use for planning and recording individual and group evaluation and a blank timetable of activities.

Moving outdoors will complement any work already going on in the classroom or indoor setting as there is nothing that cannot be covered outside in an open-air classroom. Each session is different and constantly stimulating as children learn to be creative by building their dens or practise numeracy skills as they collect and compare objects found in the woodland space, negotiating their way up slopes and collecting dead wood for the campfire. Gradually, over the weeks of the programme children become increasingly more confident in the outside woodland environment until they are ready to take on the more difficult skills involved in using real tools such as saws and mallets and helping to light the fire.

Figure 5.1 Bringing a long stick back to base

Moving outdoors for learning gives children a unique educational experience as the primary purpose is to adapt an educational curriculum to a participant's preferred learning style. There are a broad range of benefits for the children who attend the outdoor programme regardless of their age, gender or social backgrounds and these benefits will be explored in the final analysis of the research later in this study.

The philosophy is to encourage children to develop through the mastery of small, achievable tasks in an outdoor environment. The programme studied had access to a small piece of woodland in school grounds and access to a public wood next to it. However, a wood is not a requirement as the activities can be adapted to any outdoor setting, including a park, the school field or a beach. Children can work towards curriculum goals as even the simplest of outdoor games are learning experiences and the activities are an integral part of the delivery of the early years curriculum, not just an add-on. Learning in the HAO programme takes place wholly outdoors in a classroom without walls. The children experience the changing weather and seasons, use real tools for real reasons, build shelters to protect them from the weather and light fires to keep warm and cook. The children learn to respect themselves, each other and the environment, working within agreed safety boundaries as they grow together as a team.

There are no permanent features in the woodland used for the programme studied and as such each group can take complete ownership of and responsibility for the location during their time within it. The outdoor life presents a way of learning that is fully inclusive, as it is accessible to everyone. Experimentation and play are acknowledged as being a vital part of every child's learning experience and what better way to achieve it than by moving outside? Transforming your outdoor space is not just about formal, tick-box assessment. Start with a 'walkabout' that will create the context for a mutual exploration of ideas, discussing specific sites and opportunities, testing and stretching thinking.

It is important to have an outdoor play policy to establish the values, understandings, principles, objectives and criteria that will underpin and inform action; and an outdoor play strategy that establishes the priorities and actions required to fulfil the play policy in specific situations. A play strategy without a play policy is like a house without foundations. Creating an outdoor play policy is the foundational work of any new venture that aims to take children outside for playing and learning. Formulating that policy together creates the context for developing a widely shared,

Figure 5.2 Climbing up steep slopes

informed consensus on often contentious issues and is a good process for staff to tackle all those knotty little problems that affect outdoor play provision. A good policy development process engages and challenges everyone and much is learned, through thrashing and ironing out the difficulties and differences that will inevitably be part of the process. Both the outdoor play policy and strategy take account of other strategies and plans that are in place in the setting. Of equal importance, other strategies and plans must take account of the outdoor play policy and strategy. Achieving this is as much about the 'politics' of a situation as it is a technical act.

There are many issues to tackle when formulating the policy and you may need to take legal advice on risk and outdoor play. It is important to decide what actually makes a good place to play outside and what gets in the way of creating good outdoor places for children to play, including the all-important connection between outdoor play and beneficial risk taking. Remember to consider the potential positive impact it has on children's development, and in every setting regardless of its place on the outdoor provision ladder there is scope for designing more interesting, stimulating, imaginative outdoor places for play.

During the policy- and strategy-forming process it is important to consider the attitudinal and cultural changes required to secure better outdoor play for children, whether it is supervised or unsupervised, as much practice is still driven by a deeply ingrained, hardly acknowledged defensive practice. It is important to understand how to support a less defensive practice. All too often, attitudes are backward-looking and uncritically mimicking the defective outdoor practices of the past. Alongside this defensive practice, often in many of the same settings there is an equal amount of frustration and a desire for change.

To make change a possibility, the rationale for a different approach needs to be clearly and publicly articulated. This is not an easy matter but is nevertheless an urgent one, and before embarking on moving outside in ways suggested in this programme, many questions of how to go about that change need to be addressed.

The aim is to create with the children and their families places for outdoor play in and around the grounds of the setting in which the programme takes place. The aim is to cast a light on key issues affecting play in both unsupervised and supervised designated outdoor play spaces. Outdoor play environments should be beautiful, individually designed, should please and stimulate the senses, and be sources of delight and surprise. Quality play environments are those that offer children and young people opportunities to engage with their natural surroundings, be sociable and solitary, create imaginary worlds, test boundaries, construct and alter their surroundings, experience change and continuity, and take acceptable levels of risk.

The sessions are intended to educate children to:

- communicate effectively
- listen attentively
- work and play cooperatively
- express feelings without acting up or withdrawing
- manage anger and stress productively
- solve problems and negotiate
- develop self-discipline
- develop high levels of self-awareness and self-esteem
- understand the feelings that drive behaviour
- have realistic expectations of others and themselves
- develop empathy for and understanding of others.

The HAO programme

The outdoor programme setting

The Healthy, Active and Outside programme is based in a small woodland area in the grounds of a primary school in north Bristol. Due to the size and layout of the existing outdoor environment there is the scope for diversity of work patterns within the project base to enable the leader to set up an 'outdoor classroom' in the school grounds.

Figure 5.3 The woodland site on the edge of the school grounds

Figure 5.4 Finding a way down a slippery slope

Figure 5.5 Stopping for a rest on the edge of the woods

The children taking part in the programme are given access to a natural outdoor play environment with a high level of diversity throughout the changing seasons and weather. The features of this area include slopes of varying gradients, natural and manufactured pathways, hard tarmac and grassy surfaces, trees and bushes, a natural pond, log piles and large stones.

Programme components

The components of the programme are relatively simple and can be easily duplicated or adapted to other settings. Many of the outdoor physical activities used in the programme are based on ideas from the 'Top Outdoor Programme', as, at the time, the teacher involved in the project held the post of Outdoor Curriculum Focus teacher for Early Years on behalf of the Local Education Authority, who were trialling the TOPS programmes (Youth Sport Trust, 2000). The activities include the generic skills of team work and cooperation, trust communication, planning decision making, as well as skills specific to the individual activities. The programme includes physical challenges, trails and hashing (basic orienteering but without using maps). Activities are designed to ensure progression for children, who are encouraged to move from dependence to greater independence in learning by:

- performing given tasks to be able to devise their own challenges;
- using given criteria to judge performance of others so as to develop their own criteria by which to evaluate their own performance and that of others;
- progressing from simple tasks to more difficult, complex ones;
- working individually, through pairs activity, to group problem-solving activities (see Figure 5.8, p.58).

Figure 5.6 Child's drawing of working together to problem-solve

Curriculum planning

Each activity in the programme is designed to comply with the Early Years Foundation Curriculum (DfES, 2007) and the Key Stage 1 Curriculum (DfES, 2000). There are easier and harder stages planned into the activities to suit the different abilities of younger, inexperienced children or older, more experienced children to assist differentiation and progression. The programme is designed to be an effective resource which can be integrated into the whole school planning for Physical Education and Development, and Personal, Social and Health Education. Although it does not provide settings or schools with a complete unit of work for outdoor education, it will provide them with resources to support outdoor adventure activities which can take place in the school grounds even if there is no access to woodland areas. The programme is an effective way to integrate outdoor activities into the usual school curriculum so that wider teaching and learning opportunities are opened up to include all children. As in any other programme, children will progress at different rates in response to the activities planned for them.

Equipment

There is little cost outlay to set up the programme as it relies on the use of very little equipment except some gardening tools and the natural resources that are freely available in the outdoor environment. During the pilot programme any equipment used during physical challenges was improvised from what was available in the woodland setting in which it took place. In addition to the generic risk assessment which formulated before the programme took place, weekly assessments were carried out for specific activities including the ones which required the use of real tools.

   The pilot programme was led by the teacher carrying out the action research, and a learning support assistant, with the back-up of a social worker on the team who covered staff absences. The groups of children attending the programme were between the ages of three/four and five/six years, from the nursery and reception classes of local schools. As part of the programme, children are encouraged to both explore the woodland area freely and take part in structured adult-initiated physical activities based on the child's interest at the time, or

Figure 5.7 Deeply engrossed in learning outdoors

need, particularly in respect of their personal, social, physical and/or emotional development. Respect for the environment alongside respect for themselves and each other is an integral part of their early childhood education during the programme. During the trial of the programme, when it was decided that the children were ready in terms of safety and confidence, they were taken outside the school grounds to explore and use the natural facilities of the huge expanse of public woodland that is situated next to the school grounds. Permission to use this woodland, in particular to be able to light fires there, was gained from the Forestry Commission responsible for its upkeep. However, it is for each individual setting to decide if they are going to move beyond the grounds, in which case they need to consider the extra implications explained in Chapter 4, pp. 36–50.

There is a wealth of research regarding the effectiveness of working in an experiential way, using outdoor physical activity for children with social, emotional, behavioural and/or mental health difficulties. Using the outdoor environment, children are encouraged and inspired to grow in confidence, independence and self-esteem. As the child grows in self-esteem, the tasks become more challenging. The whole programme is based upon the theory that success encourages more success, and on a progressive development of skills. Consequently, a child always experiences a level of success no matter how small the step is, and it is standard practice in the programme never to set up a child to fail by setting tasks that are beyond their capability. Children are encouraged to develop personal, social and physical skills through the mastery of small achievable tasks and adventure activities. Each task is designed to be achievable at the same time as being challenging.

During the programme children learn social, emotional, physical and practical skills in an experiential way through looking after themselves, others and the environment. Using a holistic approach to learning, children experience outdoor adventure activities. Children work individually, in pairs or collaboratively as part of a team and within structured boundaries to encourage a feeling of success and self-worth. The skills children learn are transferable to other areas of their lives such as home and school. Working wholly outdoors throughout the seasons, children can take part in fun activities such as creating objects of art from natural resources, den and shelter building, making pathways, building bonfires, tracking, planting trees, sharing food, role play, storytelling and singing.

Figure 5.8 Working together to problem-solve

Figure 5.9 Carrying heavy logs together

Why teach in the grounds instead of going off-site?

Inevitably it is quicker, easier and cheaper to teach on-site. This makes it easier for practitioners new to outdoor learning to ease themselves in gradually. It also means that outdoor education can take place more frequently – this increases not only the number of opportunities for children, but also their quality. When children are able to go back outdoors when necessary, it is easier to construct child-led, discovery learning opportunities. They are able to gather initial information, develop and test hypotheses, and then refine their ideas, in a way that would not be possible in a one-day trip out. They are also able to explore the effects of time, making observations at different times of the day or across the year. Teaching outdoors in the school grounds will also benefit the setting or school in other ways. Hawkins' integrated model for outdoor education (Hawkins, 1987) proposes that awareness and acclimatisation activities based on personal experience of the environment lay the foundations for later investigation and enquiry, which in turn lead to feelings of personal responsibility and a desire to participate in actions and decisions to protect and improve the environment. Using the grounds as a focus for learning allows plenty of time to progress through these stages, and the resulting sense of ownership of the grounds reduces levels of vandalism, improves behaviour at break times, and supports a greater sense of belonging. Taking children outdoors into the grounds enhances the learning that takes place on more extended activities by equipping them with the skills to make the most of the opportunities they are offered.

Practical ideas for using the school grounds for structured learning

The traditional adventure-style outdoor learning activities are an obvious starting point for making more use of your school grounds for teaching and will be a valuable element of the Early Years Foundation Stage (DfES, 2007) or PSHE or PE Key Stage 1 curriculum (DfES, 2002). Many activities can make use of existing equipment, but you might want to consider investing in oil drums, parachutes etc. to extend the range of team-building games you can run. Setting up orienteering trails around the grounds is a good way to introduce children to more structured outdoor activities. On a more ambitious scale, many schools have built adventure play trails in their grounds for use at free play times, as well as during structured group work. It is even possible to create a traversing wall by using rock-climbing holds across a strong, high wall already existing in the school grounds.

Taking the curriculum outdoors

Knowledge and understanding of the world and the science curriculum are obvious starting points for outdoor learning, as are geography lessons, as much of the curriculum in these areas cannot be taught effectively without using the outside environment. Outdoors there are plenty of opportunities to develop pupils' planning and investigation skills. Most fieldwork activities can be adapted to take place in the school grounds, and often they benefit from the close proximity of the environment being studied. Topics normally taught indoors can also be more easily understood by pupils through exploiting the space outdoors. For example, in science, pupils can investigate the effects of light, water and food on growing plants. A dramatic experiment is to use large sheets of carpet or black polythene cut into shapes to prevent sunlight reaching the grass. After a couple of weeks, the covers can be removed to reveal a pattern of yellowed grass. Air resistance is another topic which benefits from going outside – children can run against or with the breeze, pulling different types of material. Children can make detailed observation of the climate and its effects on the environment – for example, investigating where frost builds up in the playground or the effects of heavy rain on the soil or play area. The grounds can provide a real context for exploring concepts and developing children's skills. They can explore shapes, measurements, positions and movement. Data-handling activities can be based on collecting a whole range of different objects from around the outdoor space, and 'archaeology' digs can be set up within the grounds by burying artefacts or 'treasures' for pupils to discover which can then be buried again to be rediscovered by future outdoor groups or in the years to come after the completion of the outdoor programme.

Many creative activities can take place outside in the grounds. Children can be encouraged to draw features within the grounds. They can also research, plan and produce new features to enhance the grounds. For example, they can create murals, mosaics, sculptures or seating. When children make any kind of artwork to enhance the grounds, it is invariably well cared for by other children, even long after the original designers have left or in schools where vandalism of adult-chosen features is commonplace. Outdoor performances have a special nature of their own and benefit from the greater space outdoors, and the change in atmosphere often offers fresh sources of inspiration. Music performed in the grounds and other outdoor environments can be inspirational.

Children can explore the grounds and collect objects that will make a good sound either on their own or when used with something else such as when they are placed inside a container: different sizes of stones knocked together, plastic scratching against itself, sticks being banged against one another, bits of gravel shaken in a yoghurt pot. The children can practise each of the

Figure 5.10 Using sticks to explore sound

sounds, choose their favourite 'instrument' to play in an open-air concert or 'conduct' other children playing instruments made from things found outdoors in the environment. The performance could be a structured adult-led activity by the whole class, smaller groups playing their own individual compositions or individual children giving a live performance to their friends during free play.

When you make more use of your grounds for teaching and learning, you may subsequently be inspired to make changes to the grounds to make them even more useful. These changes could include subject-specific features such as habitats, gardens, outdoor classrooms or outdoor musical instruments. Children should always be involved in the planning, design and implementation of such changes as they will gain an immense amount of learning from it. Schools that improved their grounds have found that a structured process of change yields more success. Follow the steps below to ensure maximum success:

- Tell everyone, including staff, children, parents and people in the local community, why you want to improve the grounds.
- Set up a management team to share the workload and capitalise on people's different strengths.
- Survey your site to see what you already have and how people feel about it.
- Decide what you want to do in the grounds.
- Inspire everyone by developing a long-term, whole-site vision.
- Design the changes that are needed.
- Make the changes.
- Celebrate success.
- Maintain the improvements.

Schools wanting to improve the use, design or management of their grounds can join Learning Through Landscapes (LTL), which is a national school grounds charity. Members receive twice-termly mailings of teaching ideas and materials, and are given access to specialised advice and support. Training is organised nationally to cover all aspects of teaching in school grounds as well as improving them.

Improving the outdoor area is a good way to get the school and community working together on a project that will reap rewards for years to come. It is important to carry out research before any changes are made by thinking carefully about what you've already got, how you use it and how people feel about it. A thorough survey of the grounds and their use will enable you to recognise any problems or issues and will prevent you from making mistakes or destroying useful resources. When you have a clear idea of the needs of the school the next step is to create a vision plan to summarise everything you have learned and explaining what you hope to achieve in the future. You don't need lots of time or money to make better use of your school grounds. There are plenty of positive steps you can take that require no physical changes at all.

Get involved

Successful developments of school grounds are achieved by active participation of people who use them. Nobody knows your school grounds better than the children, who will be enthusiastic and full of practical ideas. Involving the children will help them develop a sense of ownership and responsibility for the finished project and will also be a valuable learning activity in its own right. There will be many opportunities for children to learn about sustainable development and to develop skills in many subjects above and beyond those targeted in the programme, as it is based on the principles of cross-curricular learning. Involving children in decision making and gaining the support of both teaching and non-teaching staff is vital to the success of the project. Alongside contributing to the planning process of developing the school grounds and implementing the outdoor programme, staff can help raise the profile and status of the outdoor environment by making more use of the grounds for everyday learning and play.

Try things out

Expensive mistakes can be avoided by taking time to experiment with the space you have. For example, if seating has been identified as a priority, put classroom chairs out in the playgrounds during lunchtimes for a couple of weeks. Allow children to put the chairs where they want, and map out the various arrangements to give you an accurate picture of where seating is needed. Experiment with logs or blankets – you may find that standard-issue benches are not what pupils need.

Make a start

Once you have a shared vision for the school grounds, it is time to start developing and implementing your ideas. If you want to make large or complex changes, you may decide to bring in a professional to help you, but do not overlook sources of expertise closer to home. Undertake a skills audit of your school community, including staff and parents – enthusiastic amateurs can be as valuable as professionals. However, you must be aware of health and safety and insurance issues if you are managing your own project, as you are responsible for ensuring work is of appropriate quality and that helpers are working safely.

Some practical ideas for involving children in the initial stages of planning and developing the outdoor environment

Creating plans

The learning objective is to generate and explore ideas about improving the school grounds before the programme is implemented. Take the children outside and give them a variety of objects to represent the different features they may want to include in their plan for the outside space and ask them to try out different arrangements. Good experimentation tools include hula-hoops, chalk, skipping ropes, pallets, lengths of fabric and pieces of wood. Discuss with the children how well the plan might work and take photographs for further discussion and consultation.

Contributing to decision making

The learning objective of this activity is to take part in making a decision on a school issue. There are many ways children can be involved in giving their opinions about the outside play space. Try out the following ideas.

Ask the children to draw a map of the school grounds, encouraging them to pay particular attention to the areas of the grounds that are under-represented on children's maps. Why might this be? How can these areas be put to better use? Use disposable or digital cameras to do a photographic survey of the grounds and make a display showing children's favourite and least favourite areas. Put up a plan of the site and give children sticky dots to use to show which parts they like and dislike. You could use different-coloured stickers for boys and girls, or for different year groups. Older children can collaborate with others in a group to solve a problem or make a decision and they can be involved in drawing together the different opinions about the grounds and helping to create the final plans. Give groups of children a summary of previous presentations, a large copy of the site plan and laminated illustrations of the different features that people would like to include. Encourage the children to move the cards around on the map to experiment with different layouts. They may need prompting to think about any conflicts of interest and issues that might arise such as supervision and security. When groups have reached a decision, they should stick the pictures onto the map to create rough plans to present to the rest of the group. Children can then vote on which plan they think will work best.

Once the plans have been finalised the next stage is to move outdoors to make them happen and to begin to think about the more practical aspects of running an outdoor programme such as planning the general activities that will take place in the school grounds, the planning of the session routine and the more specific learning activities found in the next chapters.

Lastly, but most important of all, when thinking of moving outdoors in the ways suggested in this book, it is important to consider the quality of leadership and management because the calibre of the leader is crucial to its success. Practitioners who lead the outdoor programme need the skills to implement it as part of a holistic curriculum rather than compartmentalising it into separate isolated areas. In addition, they should be practitioners who demonstrate the ability to deliver a fully inclusive practice which fosters creativity and consideration of the individual needs of all children to allow for their personal growth and development. Teaching and learning, health and safety, and equality of opportunity all need to be monitored to ensure that high-quality experiences with built-in continuity and progression are offered to all children taking part in the programme. When you are moving learning outdoors, the focus for the practitioner should always be on what children can do, rather than on what they fail to achieve. Ability should not be a fixed and predetermined property, as belief about ability can have a profound effect on ability itself (Bandura, 1977).

6 Theory into practice

Introduction

This chapter will look at the relevant areas of the early years curriculum and link the theory into the practical activities. It will show how the outdoor activity programme can be an inclusive practice for all children. Information will be included about ways to handle difficult situations outdoors through the use of problem-solving skills. The use of the welcome and complementary circle will be discussed to show how to make the most of any new learning that has occurred during the session, including the use of songs to accompany outdoor activities. This chapter will also include case studies to demonstrate the use of positive reinforcement. It will discuss the importance of non-verbal behaviour and role modelling, showing respect and using clear communication to encourage children to do well. In addition there is information about the importance of setting time aside at the end of the programme for reflection.

Philosophy of the programme

The philosophy underpinning the programme is based upon a desire to provide young children with an education which encourages a healthy active outdoor lifestyle alongside an appreciation of the wide natural world which will encourage them to have an environmental awareness in later life. This philosophy fits with the current Early Years Foundation Stage Framework (DfES, 2007), and references are made to the standards, guidelines, strategies, principles and policies throughout the book. The idea behind this outdoor programme is to bring learning to life through a fully inclusive, holistic practice that concentrates on getting children fit and healthy within a safe outdoor context. Making prudent use of natural resources and having some good old-fashioned outdoor fun, young children begin to learn about the need to take an interest in the issues of healthy lifestyles, conservation and sustainable development in order to ensure a better quality of life for everyone now and for generations to come (*A Better Quality of Life*, Defra, 1999).

The outdoor programme is based on the humanist approach to teaching and learning (Rogers, 1967). One of the most important factors in determining the success of the programme is the attitude of the facilitator. According to Rogers (1967), the qualities that facilitate learning are:

- realness or genuineness in the facilitator of learning
- prizing, acceptance, trust
- empathic understanding.

Realness or genuineness in the facilitator of learning

When the facilitator is a real person, being what she is, entering into a relationship with the learner without presenting a front or a façade, being herself, not denying herself, she is much more likely to be effective. The feelings that she is experiencing are available to her, available to her awareness; she is able to live these feelings, be them, and communicate them if appropriate. It also means having a direct personal encounter with the learner and meeting them on a person-to-person basis.

Prizing, acceptance, trust

The other attitude that stands out in successful facilitating of learning is 'prizing' the learner, the learner's feelings, opinions and person, and having a non-possessive caring for the learner, whilst at the same time accepting the other individual as a separate person, having worth in their own right. This attitude is having a basic trust, a belief that the other person is fundamentally trustworthy. This is what Rogers (1967) describes as 'a prizing of the learner as an imperfect human being with many feelings, many potentialities'.

Empathic understanding

A further element that establishes a climate for self-initiated experiential learning is the empathic understanding of the leader. With the ability to understand the child's reactions from the inside, a sensitive awareness of the way the process of education and learning seems to the child, the likelihood of significant learning is increased. Children feel deeply appreciative when they are simply understood – not evaluated, not judged – from their *own* point of view, not the teacher's (Rogers, 1967). Linked to this is the importance of building genuine relationships with the children's families to build trust, have high expectations and give them the security they need to cope with the demands of the programme and to secure its success.

Social learning theory

Social learning theorists (Bruner, 1985; Vygotsky, 1978) believe that socialisation emerges from awareness of self and then awareness of others within the immediate surroundings. The acquisition of social skills depends on the ability to observe, interpret and imitate the behaviours of competent others. According to the 'Social Learning Theory' (Bandura, 1986), positive reinforcement consolidates appropriate behaviours and attitudes, and sanctions and rewards play an important role in dealing with children's behaviour (Bandura, 1986). Bandura suggests that behaviour is the result of personal, behavioural and environmental factors and that these three factors influence each other. Bandura argues that personality is an integrated self-system involving beliefs, systems and structures. He emphasises the importance of cognitive factors in developing our sense of self and argues that the three key components that make up this integrated system are:

- observational learning
- self-efficacy
- self-regulation.

Much of our behaviour is the result of observational learning and it is more likely to occur when the person observed is attractive, trustworthy, and similar to the observer. Vicarious reinforcement, whereby we witness the person observed being reinforced or punished, can motivate the observer, inform them about the consequences of their actions, and generate arousal and fear (Bandura and Rosenthal, 1966; Bandura *et al.*, 1963). According to Bandura, people learn to do what they do because of the direct reinforcement of their responses to stimuli and they learn by 'observing the consequences of other people's actions'. It is hoped that the children attending the programmes will imitate the behaviours that bring rewards and avoid those that are punished. To achieve this, the adults constantly need to point out the behaviour that they want to see more of so that the children become aware of the desired behaviour through observing others who are modelling it.

However, children do not learn by observational learning alone; other factors such as self-efficacy and self-regulation are important too (Bandura, 1986). Self-efficacy describes the beliefs we have concerning our ability to cope with a particular task or situation and whether we think we will achieve the desired outcome. According to Bandura (1986), our self-efficacy is determined by:

- our previous experiences of success and failure;
- relevant vicarious experiences (e.g. seeing someone else cope successfully);
- verbal/social persuasion (e.g. being told you have the relevant skills);
- emotional arousal.

Self-regulation is linked to both observational learning and self-efficacy. Self-regulation involves using our cognitive processes to regulate and control our behaviour. It involves self-observation, judgemental processes and self-reaction. Thus actions that give us self-satisfaction and a sense of self-worth are more likely to be pursued than actions that lead to self-censure (Bandura, 1986). In Bandura's view, reinforcement is both external and self-evaluative. A specific behaviour, besides merely producing an external outcome, also leads to a self-evaluative reaction. Reinforcement is not as straightforward as the behaviourists believe (Bandura *et al.*, 1963) but external reinforcement certainly works, although it is most effective when it is consistent with self-reinforcement and least effective when it directly contradicts the self-evaluative response. It is not clear how observational learning, self-efficacy and self-regulation relate to each other, but research has suggested that all three aspects of Bandura's theory (observational learning, self-efficacy and self-regulation) do play a part in determining our behaviour.

In addition, parallel theories need to be considered too, particularly the humanist approach to learning and its impact on relationships, and the biological, maturational and emotional factors which all influence children's behaviour (Rogers, 1967). Depending on the situation, a variety of behaviour management tools are used throughout the programme, including modelling, role play, consistent boundaries, guidelines, ground rules, policies and the security of a warm, consistent ethos which is conducive to learning through experiential methods and being able to make mistakes. In addition, it is important to have clearly communicated expectations, use genuine labelled praise, with consistent positive support and reinforcement, and above all the ability to establish positive relationships built on trust and high expectations (Canter and Canter, 1993). These tools should be used to help guide children towards choosing the appropriate behaviour needed to enable them to experience and build upon success throughout their time in the programme – although at times, providing corrective actions for the children may not always be enough on its own, and at some point the children must be held accountable for their own actions (Canter and Canter, 1993).

Current theoretical guidelines

The programme follows the guidance set out in the Early Years Foundation Stage (DfES, 2007), a comprehensive framework which sets the standards for learning, development and care of children from birth to five. This new government document builds on and will replace the existing statutory *Curriculum Guidance for the Foundation Stage*, the non-statutory *Birth to Three Matters* framework, and the regulatory frameworks in the *National Standards for Under 8s Day Care and Childminding*, and should be in place from September 2008.

Educational benefits

Helping children to apply their knowledge across a range of challenges, learning in an experiential way outside the classroom, bridges the gap between theory and reality. Good-quality learning experiences in 'real' situations have the capacity to raise achievement across a range of subjects and to develop personal and social skills which are all transferable to other situations. The indoor and outdoor environments should work as one, and be planned for as one. All outdoor experiences need to be well planned and organised. They need to be safely managed and personalised to meet the needs of every individual child taking part in them. The benefits that a child will experience as a result of attending the outdoor programme may include any or all of the following:

- improved attitude to learning
- improved academic achievement
- independence
- opportunities for informal learning through play

- an awareness of the environment
- opportunity to be creative
- reduction of emotional and behavioural difficulties
- improved motivation
- stimulation
- inspiration
- engagement to learning
- ability to deal with uncertainty
- challenge
- opportunity to take acceptable levels of risk.

(DfES, 2007)

The programme sits well with key education priorities which focus on personalised learning and will support the current strategy for children as it provides a clear route into the *Every Child Matters* (DfES, 2003a) framework, which identifies the key outcomes for children and young people's service provision as:

- being healthy
- staying safe
- enjoying and achieving
- making a positive contribution
- economic well-being.

This outdoor programme focuses on how the provision of good-quality outdoor play opportunities for young children can contribute to the achievement of these outcomes for all children, especially those who may be systematically excluded from these benefits. Children will learn from their own successes and failures and take responsibility for achieving the above outcomes, as learning outside in the fresh air will provide them with the direct and relevant experiences that will naturally deepen and enrich learning.

Aims

The aims of the programme are linked to the 'Every Child Matters' framework (DfES, 2007).

Be healthy

- Enjoy good physical and mental health by living a healthy lifestyle.

Enjoy and achieve

- Give children the opportunity to enjoy themselves and have fun through free exploration and free-flow play within the safety of a controlled woodland environment.
- Teach positive interaction skills, communication skills, problem-solving strategies, anger management and appropriate behaviour. Children exhibiting challenging behaviour are given the opportunity to develop control over their behaviour, improve in their concentration, independence, and social and physical skills.
- Learn in an active, 'hands-on' way.
- Enhance children's progress in school and lifelong learning through all of the above.

Make a positive contribution

- By being involved with the community and society and not engaging in anti-social or offending behaviour. Children learn to respect their environment, to abide by rules and standards of behaviour, to work in teams and to respect one another.

Stay safe

- Be protected from harm and neglect – safety outdoors is given priority at first as children learn about the boundaries within which they must work. Children have the opportunity to access the freedom of the outdoors in a safe environment where they can learn to take reasonable risks, meet challenges and learn how to deal with danger.

Vulnerable children and those likely to be excluded from school may benefit from the programme as they will be able to work away from the usual classroom environment, giving them a fresh approach in a more manageable small group. With support, the skills acquired can be transferred back into the classroom, the school and the child's family. The topics of personal safety outdoors, giving children opportunities to be active and let off steam, looking after and using the local outdoor environment, the importance of exercise and getting active outdoors are covered as a means to improve mental health and well-being for both parents and children. At the same time, children and parents are encouraged to take ownership of the outdoor community in order to gain a sense of responsibility for their environment.

National Framework for Sustainable Schools

Based on the notion that all children need a range of indoor and outdoor play opportunities, this book aims to identify ways in which the use of the outside spaces can become a more sustainable part of provision for all children in any early years setting. The programme demonstrates a way to change the way we work and think in early years settings to encourage children to look after our most precious resource – the planet. It will teach children to care for the environment and encourage them to become part of the solution for bringing about changes in the way we treat our environment by learning love and respect for it, by developing skills such as cooperation, listening, tackling real problems, participating in decision making and making informed choices. In doing so, children will learn to protect the natural environment.

The Healthy, Active and Outside programme encompasses the recommendations of the *National Framework for Sustainable Schools* (DfES, 2006a), as it is an inclusive practice which enables all children to participate fully and encourages a respect for human rights, freedom, cultures and expression. In keeping with the sustainable schools recommendations the HAO programme enables children to learn about the natural world around them through food growing and biodiversity conservation.

A well-thought-out outside space provides a rich resource for learning, not only about the outside environment but also through benefiting the children's sense of well-being and behaviour.

Figure 6.1 Children taking responsibility for the outside space by spreading wood chips to make a base

Some of the activities that take place in the programme help to improve the environment and quality of life for the children and the local community and give them the opportunity to learn together in order to strengthen relationships.

Methods used in the programme

Many different methods and styles of teaching are used in the delivery of the programme, depending on the situation at the time. Some of these methods include:

- experiential adventure activities such as tracking;
- environmental awareness;
- positive role modelling;
- structured activities to give children the opportunity to practise specific target play to develop physical, social, emotional and behavioural skills;
- constant feedback and positive reinforcement;
- social rewarding of appropriate behaviour by labelling the specific behaviour when praising a child;
- giving social rewards such as smiles, hugs and hand signs;
- giving children roles of responsibility and leadership;
- free exploration of the woodland;
- opportunity for sustained free-flow play;
- child-initiated activities;
- adult-led, structured activities from observation of need and interest;
- personal and group reflection.

Content of the programme

The content of the programme covers a wide range of life skills that will build on children's personal development and social and emotional skills such as:

- development of self-esteem, confidence and well-being;
- self-awareness, independence and safety;
- relationship building;
- team building;
- using initiative;
- taking the lead and following;
- detecting, understanding, accepting and verbalising feelings in themselves and others;
- interpersonal cognitive problem-solving skills;
- anger management and self-control;
- how to be friendly (help, share, teamwork);
- effective communication skills;
- effective school behaviour;
- group skills.

In addition, the underlying philosophy of the outdoor programme is based on the following guidelines for play:

- Keep the motivation intrinsic.
- Orient learners towards the process, not the goal.
- Use non-literal frames of reference.
- Keep rules simple.

Keep the motivation intrinsic

- Avoid using rewards as part of the play process.
- Encourage children to become so engaged in the activity that they do not think about external gain. Greater learning is associated with activities that avoid rewards (Pintrich and Schunk, 1996).
- Orienting learners towards the process, not the goal, will encourage children to take charge of their own learning and shift their goals if or when necessary. This is valuable as it will lead to greater creativity, self-efficacy and extension of existing learning (Jenson, 2000).
- Use non-literal frames of reference.
- Allow children to take on new roles, try out new behaviours and experience things they might never experience.

Keep rules simple

Ensure the children understand the ground rules before even attempting an activity, particularly the safety rules and what to do in an emergency. Be prepared to alter the rules as necessary for each particular group of children. Encourage children to be part of the rule-making process so that they take some responsibility for their own behaviour.

Include everyone

Use games that everyone can play and adapt them if necessary. The games played in outdoor school are not just for the most intelligent, best-versed or fittest children. Everyone should be able to get involved and everyone can learn.

Kinaesthetic learning

The programme concentrates on kinaesthetic learning, for example by encouraging children to stand up and demonstrate concepts, by using clapping and the stomping out of rhythms. The start and end of every session include the repetition of a favourite 'theme song', for example 'If you're happy and you know it clap your hands' based upon the physical actions of the activities that take place during that particular session. Examples might include 'If you're happy and you know it walk to the woods', 'stamp the ground', 'jump up and down' or 'turn around'. The actions accompanying the song should always be linked to both the new learning taking place and activities from previous sessions to reinforce learning at the end of each session. By the end of the programme children will know many variations of the song and will have practised many new actions and learned much new vocabulary without even realising it.

Using role play to give quick reviews of the learning that takes place during the session is another good way to encourage children to learn through practical physical activity. Before the start of every outdoor session always warm up with energisers to engage the brain to use both left and right hemispheres by including lots of cross-lateral fun activities. For example, encourage children to rub their tummies with one hand whilst patting their head with the other (cross-overs), with the left hand pat the right shoulder, elbow, knee etc. (cross-laterals) (Dennison and Dennison, 1989; Hannaford, 1995). During the warm-up encourage lots of stretching to get more oxygen into the brain and throughout the session encourage lots of laughter and joke telling as there is much evidence to suggest that even a few moments' laughter is good for both the body and the mind (Dhyan, 1995).

Incorporate energisers (pp.117–19) into the programme into every session to keep children moving, especially when the weather is particularly inclement during the colder months. These energising activities can include games such as 'Simon says...' with content of the session built into the actions carried out – for example, 'Simon says – go off and find five sticks as long as your arms or as small as your little fingers.'

Methods

The research was organised into eight phases (see Figure 7.1 on p.79) and the programme was implemented through a cyclical process based upon a balance of adult-led and child-initiated activities. The structure of each session mirrored this cyclical action research process of:

- plan
- perform (do)
- evaluate (review and reflect)
- transfer learning (to meet the next task or other learning opportunity).

The methods of whole group, small group, paired and individual work regarding discussion, decision making and action should always be followed by review and reflection, and a time to plan for the coming week should be included in each session.

The activities which take place in the outdoor programme can make a significant contribution to the development of cross-curricular skills through the use of problem-solving methods and approaches. Verbal and communication skills can be reinforced when the children or the group leader describe or evaluate the activities during the review at the end of each session. The programme will enhance many areas of the early years curriculum as there is the opportunity to develop a whole range of cross-curricular activities alongside encouraging the children to become more self-confident and self-reliant and to work cooperatively to solve problems.

Policy and theory into practice

The underlying policy, theory and philosophy of the programme are explained in the section above. Now it is time to think about moving outdoors to look at the practicalities of setting up the outside play space ready for the programme to begin. A good way to begin is to set up zones for different activities to take place.

Zones

It is sensible to zone off the outdoor space into themed areas; for example:

- imaginative play with a variety of props depending on current level of interests;
- performance area for drama, impromptu concerts etc.;
- creative area for musical activities or artistic representation with a changing variety of resources (such as chalk, large painting materials, water painting);
- building and construction on a large scale, dens etc;
- sandpit;
- water with gutters, pipes etc.;
- discovery area for observing minibeasts, weather watching, pulleys, finding out box;
- growing area for digging and planting;
- quiet area with an element of privacy and some comfortable seating, to rest, read and think, or just be;
- large apparatus for physical activity such as balancing and climbing;
- small apparatus with a variety of resources including beanbags and balls to promote hand–eye coordination;
- tracks and pathways for pushing and pulling toys, bikes, prams, trailers etc.

It is not always necessary to set up all of the above every session but they are all desirable some of the time. It is a good idea to plan the permanent areas or structures you want for the outdoor area with flexibility in mind and to buy or acquire resources that are flexible and can serve many purposes. If vandalism is a potential problem, you will need a lockable shed or similar to store portable equipment or make sure it goes back inside at the end of every session.

Ideas of general practical activities to set up outside

This section presents some general ideas which are linked to the Early Learning Goals (ELG) to inspire the practitioner to move learning outside followed by more specific practical activities in the next chapter that can be used or adapted when planning adult-initiated activities for outside learning. They are not intended to be followed in any particular order but are presented as ideas to dip into to set up the outdoor area with resources which will inspire children's learning.

Physical development

ELG 106a – Move with control and coordination

RESOURCES

Water, buckets and a variety of containers of different shapes and sizes, sponges, syringes, washing-up liquid bottles, spray bottles, soap dispensers, hosepipes and chalk.

ACTIVITY

Help children to improve their hand–eye coordination by inviting them to use the resources during free play, for example by throwing a ball into a bowl of water or a sponge into a bucket. Invite children to fill up water pistols, plastic washing-up liquid bottles etc. with water to aim at targets such as a chalk wall target, plastic ducks in a water tray, skittles in a row.

ADULT'S ROLE

The adult's role is to ensure children remain on task and to show them how to aim, encourage accuracy and increasing difficulty as they improve by adding smaller targets for the children to aim at or by increasing the distance they aim from. Adults should also encourage children to evaluate their own performance and plan how to get better.

Communication, language and literacy

ELG 58a – Use language to imagine and recreate roles and experiences

RESOURCES

Tents or clothes drier/table, drapes or blankets, torches, backpacks, sleeping bags, picnic rug, stove or BBQ (real or pretend), camping table and chairs, cooking equipment, crockery, cutlery, washing-up bowl, bats and balls, water carrier, sun hats, Wellington boots, map etc.

ACTIVITY

Set the scene by telling the children a story. Discuss what is needed for a camping trip. Gather together everything that is needed with the children's help and take everything outside. Negotiate a good place to set up camp and pretend to go camping.

ADULT'S ROLE

The adult's role is to set the scene for the play by leading the discussion and encouraging the children to imagine that they are going camping. Encourage them to talk about the activity in an imaginary way, joining in if appropriate.

Other ideas

There are many other ideas of imaginary play that take can place outdoors to encourage communication, language and literacy. It is important to seize the moment to fully utilise any outdoor experience that might crop up when taking children outside to play, such as seeing an aeroplane or birds flying overhead, hearing different sounds and frosty or snowy weather.

Below are just a few ideas for setting up imaginary role play outside to encourage learning in communication, language and literacy:

- fire fighting/stations – climbing frame with a pole, helmet and hose;
- petrol station/garage to wash wheelie toys with water, hoses, and soap suds etc. as props;
- road safety – police, traffic warden, lollipop person using props such as cones and mark-making materials;
- washing/laundries;
- outdoor market (see p.136 for more details);
- table-top sale;
- going on a bear hunt after reading the book (details on p.132).

Problem solving, reasoning and numeracy

ELG 80c – Use language such as 'circle' or 'bigger' to describe the shape and size of solids and flat shapes

RESOURCES

Giant cardboard boxes, small and large tubs and tubes, springs, metal bits and bobs, rubber gloves, large foil containers, cogs, art straws, 2D shapes, paper plates, PVA glue, string and child-safe fastenings.

ACTIVITY

Children and adults work together to make a funny monster with moving parts that a child can fit inside, and decorate it with shapes.

ADULT'S ROLE

To use and develop children's understanding of the language of shape and size, and ensure that children experience being inside a 3D shape.

Other ideas

- Blowing bubbles – use water tray and hoops for large-scale bubbles.
- Streamers for making shapes.
- Finding out what large shaped boxes roll down a slide.
- Use different-shaped food to make a picnic.
- Mark out a hopscotch grid on the ground with squares and circles.

Knowledge and understanding of the world

ELG 90a – Build and construct with a wide range of objects, selecting appropriate resources, and adapting their work where necessary.

IDEAS FOR RESOURCES

Large wooden bricks, tunnels, cones, drapes, chairs, crates, chalk, planks, tyres, buckets, steps, trestles, ladders, boxes, ropes and nets.

ACTIVITY

Invite the children to build themselves an assault course. Talk about exciting activities that might be included, such as crawling under, over, through, balancing, jumping over. Provide children with a range of resources and encourage them to select and build imaginatively and safely.

Figure 6.2 Building with natural materials

ADULT'S ROLE

The adult's role is to ensure that resources provided are safe and the construction is safe (e.g. no holes to jam feet, keep low); to support children and supervise the children (avoid direction); to encourage the children to adapt their work where necessary (e.g. make something higher to crawl under successfully).

Other ideas

- Make dens (clothes horse, drapes, elastic bands, pegs and string etc.).
- Large-scale junk modelling (e.g. a train, fire engine).
- Build an imaginary play area (e.g. shark-infested sea, an island, pirate ship).
- Build a stone pile, or rockery for minibeasts to hide.
- Build a log pile to watch it decomposing over time and the creatures that use it as a habitat.
- Set up a plumber's yard using offcuts of plastic guttering, pipes, joints etc.
- Set up a series of pulleys and ropes.

Creative development

ELG 126a – Respond in a variety of ways to what they see, hear, smell, touch and feel

ACTIVITY

Children and adults walk through the different environment such as a street, park, wood, beach, fish market, the docks, a flower garden or churchyard.

ADULT'S ROLE

The adult's role is to explore alongside the child, encouraging conversation and valuing their reactions, and above all to ensure safety; to draw attention to sensory experiences (e.g. feel the textures of building materials, smell flowers, herbs etc.) and to encourage children to use all their senses. It is also their role to encourage responses to both pleasant and unpleasant stimuli using facial expressions, body language as well as verbal responses.

Figure 6.3 Looking at objects found outside

Other ideas

- Chasing shadows.
- Minibeast hunt.
- Observe signs of spring, summer, autumn and winter.
- Find a collection of pleasing sensory objects.
- Blindfold games.
- Splash in puddles.
- Scavenger hunt to find materials for a project or object for a collage, display or sculpture.

Once the practitioner has a good working knowledge of general ways to set up the outside, it is time to get down to the planning of each session. Below is one version of the session routine on which to base ideas for individual settings. This structure is continually evolving and changing because no two settings, groups, practitioners are the same.

A typical outdoor session

The programme set out below is an example of a typical session routine for a morning outdoors with young children. With a little imagination it can be adapted to fit into the structure of the routines already in place in individual settings, to take place for part of a session or to take place throughout a whole day. The venue will determine the length of the session. Many settings will have a suitable outside space on-site and will not necessitate a walk to a woodland area as described below. The programme has been extended to take in the local wood and therefore more time was allocated to cover all aspects of the programme. It has also been adapted to take in a day trip each week to an outdoor play site or area of natural beauty. If this is the intention when using the template for outdoor education then the usual precautions for school trips need to be strictly adhered to. It is also important to gain permission from the site warden if using an area of outstanding natural beauty as there may be restrictions concerning what can take place. The country code should also always be followed when taking children outdoors to public places.

8.30 – 9.00a.m. – Preparation

Time for staff to organise the session, go over plans, visit the woodland area to check for hazards and make the risk assessment (see pp.41–3 for information on risk assessment).

9.00 – 9.15a.m. – Staggered arrival

The arrival time for children attending the programme is staggered. One member of staff greets the children and their parents whilst others continue the preparations for the group, including lighting the fire.

9.15 – 9.30a.m. – Welcome, handover and introduction

At the start of the session children dress for the weather conditions that day – normally wet-weather clothes and Wellington boots! During this time parents talk to group leaders and each other in order to develop relationships and find out about their children's activities that day.

9.30 – 9.45a.m. – Walk to the woodland area and shelter/den building

Children take turns to lead the way to the woods. Children attending the school on the same site as the woodland area are picked up en route. The shelter is built as protection from the elements. This is particularly necessary during wet or very hot and sunny days when everyone sits down for refreshments or during the plenary at the end of each session.

---

*9.45 – 9.55a.m. – Safety games (see p.51) and review of previous
session*

Each week, boundaries are re-established through the repetition of two important safety games. The first is to establish the signal for calling children safely back to the base in case of emergency or when the group need to get together to start a new activity. The second game is to give the children a means of having a safety procedure if they get into difficulty or need an adult's help. This is followed by a review of previous sessions and the children's choice of activity.

9.55 – 11.00a.m. – Free exploration of woods

Children are given the freedom, within well-established and consistent boundaries, for free exploration of the woodland area where they can practise what they have learned previously or merely enjoy exploring the space. It is also an opportunity to have some healthy fresh air, and to exercise and let off steam.

11.00 – 11.20a.m. – Structured, adult-led/initiated activity

This activity is based upon observation of need, children's interests or the social skills training theme for the session. The planned activity reinforces the concepts taught throughout the session. Children take part in structured, individual, paired or group activities, planned to reinforce the new behaviours learned during the session.

*11.20 – 11.30a.m. – Snack, drink (also available throughout the session
if children choose/need them), song and complement circle*

The song is chosen to complement the content of the session and to reinforce any new learning, giving the children another chance to take on board the new concepts through constant repetition. During the complement circle, the children are encouraged to reflect on the activities they have taken part in during that session to reinforce all new learning through modelling and sensitive, open-ended questioning by the leader. They are also encouraged to say something positive about the session or each other and are thanked for their cooperation.

11.30 – 11.45a.m. – Reflection, clear up and walk back

Children are encouraged to reflect on the session, to help each other take down the shelter, clear up tools and equipment and carry them back to the base from which the outside programme takes place.

11.45 – 12 00a.m. – Hand-back and discussion with parents

A short time at the end of each session is set aside for discussion about the day's activities or to share any concerns about the children with their parents.

12.00 – 12.15p.m. – Clear-up time

Staff finish clearing up such as returning washed/clean equipment to cupboards.

*12.15 – 1.15p.m. – Debrief for reviewing, reflecting, recording and
future planning*

Figure 6.4 Time for reflection and a well-earned break after the programme

Time for reflection

An hour is planned at the end of every session for the debriefing of staff and the opportunity to discuss any events that take place during the morning. It is also a time to discuss and write up group and individual observations and to plan for the next session. Reflection time should always be planned for the end of each outdoor session to enable practitioners to recover, reflect on practice, look at how well examples of outdoor learning are reflected in their observations and assessments of children, consider whether the outdoor provision meets the needs of all the children, as both a place to feel 'at home' and a place to learn, and ensure that the deployment of staff is flexible enough to respond to the flow and movement of children between indoors and outdoors (DfES, 2002).

When the programme takes place over a whole day the adult-initiated tasks and activities such as shelter building and safety games take place in the morning, the snack time becomes an outdoor picnic lunch, and the free exploration period then takes place after lunch. All activities are extended accordingly to maintain a balance between the child-initiated play and the adult-led tasks that take place. Obviously this structure can be adapted to suit the needs of the group taking part in the outside programme at the time. More detailed practical activities to use during the programme can be found in Chapter 9, page 120.

7 Assessing children outdoors

Introduction

There are many different ways to make assessments of children, including the decisions made using daily observations about a child's development and/or learning and their interests or abilities, which are often referred to as 'assessment for learning' or 'formative assessment'. Another form of assessment gives a summary of a child's achievements and progress and is known as a 'summative assessment', such as the EYFS Profile documenting each child's achievement at the end of the EYFS.

This chapter will include the value of note taking. It will look at the use of questioning, observation, and information needed about the parents and children, and at the importance of making baseline assessments, recording, and reporting back relevant information to parents and class teachers and any other relevant people, bearing in mind the Data Protection Act. It will include the importance of taking a baseline assessment and using the process of action research as a tool to provide evidence-based practice. Case studies will be included to show the positive changes in some children as a result of attending the intervention.

Observation and assessment

All good practitioners regularly assess children's progress by making observations of them to inform the Foundation Stage Profile, which provides a framework for summarising children's progress and learning needs at the end of the Foundation Stage. The observations made during the outdoor programme can be used by practitioners when completing these profiles. Further information can be found in the QCA Foundation Stage and Key Stage 1 Assessment and Reporting Arrangements sent to schools in October each year. This chapter will give an insight into the record keeping that was made during the outdoor programme but it is for individual practitioners to use their professional judgement as to how much record keeping they want to do and how they keep the records.

Assessment

Assessments and observations were made throughout the eight phases of the programme (see Figure 7.1). Before the start of the programme, several meetings with parents were arranged. An initial meeting was set up to explain the programme and the required level of commitment from both parent/s and child. Meetings took place either at home, at the project rooms or at the child's school, wherever the parent felt most comfortable. The majority of parents decided to have their initial meetings and interviews at the project base although one parent was visited at home and another parent decided upon a meeting in her son's nursery school.

A second parent meeting was set up to collect historical information. A third, sometimes fourth, meeting took place for parents to complete assessment questionnaires.

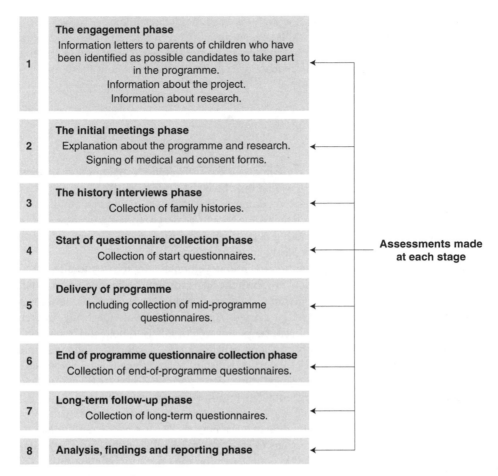

Figure 7.1 Schematic diagram of the eight phases of the programme

Assessment tools

Many assessment tools were used during the pilot programme because it was important to ascertain whether the programme actually worked before putting it into place for children and recommending its use in other settings. Children, parents, carers/guardians and staff were given the opportunity to take part in the research and asked to complete questionnaires before the programme started and midway through it. The assessment tools used at this stage were:

- History Interview and Questionnaire
- Conners' Rating Scale – Revised
- The Eyberg Child Behaviour Inventory
- The Achenbach (Parent)
- The Achenbach (Teacher)
- Webster-Stratton Parent Defined Problems
- Beck's CDBI-11 (Depression Questionnaire – for parents)
- Beck's BAI (Anxiety Questionnaire – for parents)
- Children's Activity Rating Scale.

These questionnaires, with the addition of a Participant Satisfaction Questionnaire, were repeated at the end of the programme. They were also administered several months (between 12 and 18 months) after the completion of the programme in order to determine whether there had been any long-term benefits for the children and parents involved in the project. After the difficulties experienced by the team before the start of the project through setting up interview meetings with parents and school staff to administer so many questionnaires, it was decided to use fewer questionnaires for final evaluation purposes. Children referred to the programme were observed in school or at home before being accepted as participants, in order to assess the suitability of the referral. Verbal feedback was given at the time about these observations to the class teachers and parents involved.

Observation, assessment and planning

Starting with the child

The main method of record keeping recommended for the outdoor programme is observation. Children should be regularly observed to find out about their needs, what they are interested in and what they can do. The practitioner should make observations of individual children's development and learning. It is good practice to involve parents as part of the ongoing observation and assessment process. During the debriefing session after the programme it is important to talk about the observations and how to document children's learning.

Observation skills and an understanding of child development are the key to effective learning in outdoor play. Careful observation will form the basis for future planning and will help the adult to give effective guidance to individual children. To make the most of observation in the outdoor setting it is essential to be well organised. When working outdoors with children it is advisable to carrying a small notebook, sticker pad or role of labels to note children's responses in different situations so that the observations can be analysed later to highlight children's achievements or their need for further support. It is useful to jot things down as you see them. Include in your notes such things as context, time, date, group size, type of activity, language used by the children, evaluation and recommended follow-up activities (Figure 7.3).

Outdoor movements can be fleeting, so it is difficult to observe and record them. Focus on specific areas such as a child's coordination or balancing skills, or whether a child can use the equipment effectively. Restrict observations to short bursts of between two and five minutes so that you can still give the children the time and attention they need to maintain interest and to extend their learning. Outdoor observations should be used to inform future planning. As children progress at different rates, you may need to make more frequent observations for some children, being particularly sensitive when making observations of children with special needs.

Video recordings

A camcorder was used to make recordings every session for observational, research and training purposes. In the first instance the video material was used by programme staff as an observational tool for evaluation purposes to inform practice and for in-house training. Later a compilation tape and a DVD were made from snapshots of the weekly sessions to share with parents in the final consultation with them after their children had completed the programme so that they could see exactly what their children had been doing during the programme. Later, this demonstration tape was used to inform other agencies and engage new families for subsequent groups. The training tape and DVD of the outdoor programme were particularly useful to the multidisciplinary staff team during the research aspect of the programme in order to arrive at a common understanding of terminology and to enable them to have a common understanding of the different activity levels and areas of assessment. The compilation tape of the outdoor programme was also used to disseminate findings at training sessions for other nursery settings and during the conference held at the end of the project. Video consent in writing was sought prior to the group starting. If your setting decides to follow the idea of using video recordings as a means of assessment then it is necessary to have a parental consent note held on file for every child and to make the purpose of the recording quite clear due to issues surrounding confidentiality and safety of the child.

Using video recordings or DVDs naturally takes time and extra resources in terms of both equipment and personnel. As this method of observation proves costly, serious consideration needs to be taken by individual settings regarding its viability and purpose. There is no point in

...unioning and Establishing
a Base.

In order to work in the area in all weathers we
needed to establish a base and some shelter.

Chanelle and Dyson are securing the ground
sheet we have tied in the trees to make
a shelter. Working together is a strong feature
of the Outdoor School.

The Den/shelter is used as protection from
the wind and rain in the winter and
the Sun in the summer. Here Sophie,
Chanelle and Dyson are sheltering from the
rain during a much earned break from 'work.'

Figure 7.2 Example of a programme recording log using photographs

taking endless recordings of children if you have not given careful consideration concerning what you are going to do with them. The programme on which this book was based had a budget for research and time for reflection in a debriefing session after each weekly group. Not all settings can afford to work in this way. It is important to set aside time in the debriefing session to view the video recording to inform future practice and for assessment. There is not much point in using this technique for observational purposes unless you have sufficient finances to provide the time for staff to look at the recording together as a team to discuss what has been recorded and to use it to inform practice and contribute towards children's individual assessments.

The recordings of the outdoor programme were frequently shared with the children during their times for reflection at the end of each session and the demonstration tape was particularly useful to show other children in settings what their friends were doing when they went to the woodland to take part in the outdoor programme. Ideally, all children in any setting should have the opportunity to take part in the programme but as the original programme was a service for children, their families and schools in a particular geographical area, the children taking part were drawn from a variety of different settings across that area.

The voice of the child

If the children are able, it is important to include them in any form of assessment. In the outdoor programme children were asked to complete a child's version of the visual analogue (PDP)/Likert (Olier and Hobday *et al.*, 1999) scale both before and after the programme to set targets and assess their own outcomes. As not all children involved in the research project were able to do this, the outcomes of the child's visual analogue scale were not included in the final analysis of the programme but were recorded in their individual profiles.

Children's comments

Some of the children were asked about their experiences of the outdoor programme. The majority of children expressed their enjoyment of the programme. One child said, 'I love playing in the woods with you, when can I come again?' when he spotted us many months later in his nursery setting. After the programme another child said, 'I can find lots of good things outside to play with, like snails and woodlice now; before I didn't even know they were there.' One boy who was loath to come outside at first reported, 'This is great. I love it. I like building dens most of all.' And one little girl who was almost too frightened to step outside the classroom door at first was caught on video saying to her friend, 'I want to go outside all the time 'cause it's fun.'

As the children were central to all the research that took place during the programme they were also shown some of the video material and given the opportunity to comment on what they had seen or to comment on their feelings about their experience in the programme. Some of their comments can be seen below. They were also able to reflect on their participation in the programme through drawing activities which took place alongside the parent interviews and during the weekly end-of-session group review (see Figures 7.3–7.7).

Case studies

Tara

Tara was very shy and withdrawn when she first attended the outdoor programme. She was always immaculately dressed in clothes which were inappropriate for play. She worried about spoiling her clothes and getting her hands dirty, which prevented her from accessing the curriculum at nursery. She did not mix or talk to other children much and rarely spoke out in groups.

At first Tara did not like attending the programme because she did not like going outside to play. Gradually she grew in confidence and began to take lead roles in the group and talk freely in group discussions. After she had attended the outdoor programme for ten weeks her nursery teacher said that she could not believe the change in Tara. Tara always had lots to talk about after coming back from the outdoor programme and could not wait to tell the other children all about it. She became much happier at nursery and began to play outdoors with the other children. Her mother now dressed Tara more appropriately for outdoor play at nursery and she no longer worried about spoiling her clothes or getting herself dirty.

Dan

Dan is now in reception; he is nearly five years old. When he attended the outdoor programme he hardly talked. Developmentally he was approximately two years behind his peers. Dan cried for his mum constantly. He had no friends at nursery as other children were wary of him. Dan's mother also attended the programme alongside him as she was keen to do all she could to support him. Dan has one sister and his mum is separated from the children's father and admits that she cannot cope with her children. She also suffers from depression and has been taking anti-depressants for many years. She enjoyed the support she found in the outdoor programme and felt that being outdoors had helped to lift all their moods.

Dan is prone to violent temper tantrums, which his mum deals with by shouting, smacking and grounding him for days on end in his bedroom, which he then 'trashes'. We were able to offer support to change the pattern of negative parenting and to encourage the mother to play with Dan. At first Dan's mother said she found it impossible to meet her children's needs as she always felt tired and depressed herself at home. During the programme she enjoyed the parent–child activities and started playing with her children more at home. Dan's mum gained much from the self-esteem and confidence-building part of the programme but continues to need the ongoing support which she is receiving from the linked parenting programme.

Dan enjoyed the programme and had the opportunity to take part in many new first-hand experiences. Dan's mum recognised he had a good time and continued to attend the support

Figure 7.3 Children's record of the safety game

Figure 7.4 Children's record of a pick up sticks activity

Figure 7.5 Children's record of favourite outdoor activities

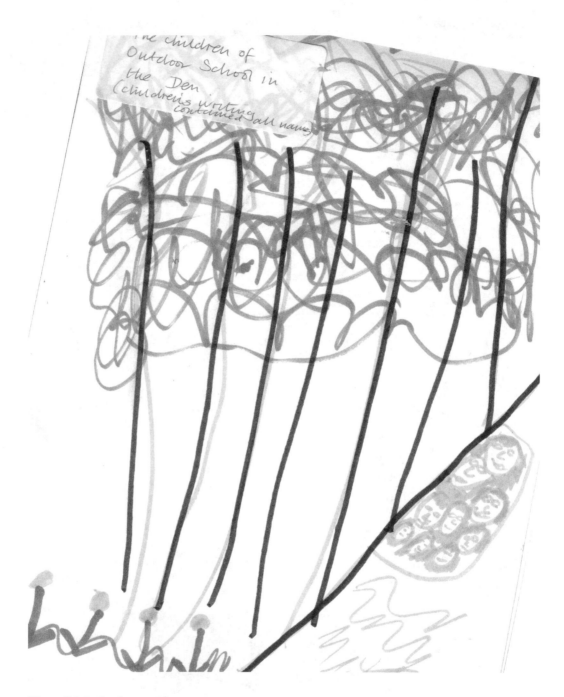

Figure 7.6 In the den

Figure 7.7 Finding spiders

group as she wanted things to improve for her family at home. At home he did not have so many temper tantrums and no longer trashed his room. He stopped hitting out at his mum, and his mother no longer smacked him as she found other strategies to deal with his difficult behaviour from coming to the group. She no longer shouted at him and time shut in his room was reduced to 5 minutes instead of every night for the whole week. He gets on better with his sister and the whole atmosphere has changed for the better at home except on bad days. Dan's mum says that:

> Although we still have our ups and downs and bad days I realise that smacking and shouting does not work...I feel more confident in myself now, not so stressed all the time. I know that playing with him helps as I can get on with my own things later on...every day used to be a bad day and don't get me wrong, I love my kids, but I could not stand them most of the time. I loved them but did not like them. I could not be in the same room as them as they made me feel so bad. Now I can sit down and play with them and know how to handle them because I've got more idea about what to do. I know that if we all go outside to play we all feel better, so most days we spend some time outdoors even when it's cold or raining.

She attributes this change to what they have all gained from coming to the programme. Dan's class teacher said that the experience had changed Dan and that although he continued to have special needs he was no longer quite so difficult in class.

Comments from school staff

> We have already noticed the difference in children coming to Outdoor School after only five weeks. They are more confident and talking more now. Some are playing with each other now rather than alone. We know how well it works, it's a shame more children don't get the chance to come.

8 Links with home

Introduction

The programme bridges the gap between school and home and enables parents to make more positive home–school relationships. This chapter draws on evidence from research to highlight the importance of parental involvement in their children's education and the challenges to parents becoming involved. Alongside this, ideas from the original outdoor programme are highlighted to show practitioners how to involve parents effectively. In addition it considers the issues of making genuine partnerships with parents and of making links with home by having high expectations of families to commit to the programme from the outset. It shows how parents of the children attending the programme are encouraged to make as much or as little commitment as their individual circumstances permit. Ways to entice parents to join in and increase their participation are explained alongside ways to encourage parents and staff to share information about children and to make genuine, positive relationships to enhance healthy, active lifestyles that will promote lifelong learning.

An information sheet about the Healthy, Active and Outside programme was given to parents in advance to familiarise them with the aims and purpose of the project (Figures 8.1 and 8.2). A welcome letter was given to the children who had been chosen to participate in the programme (Figure 8.3).

The impact of parental involvement on children's learning

The benefits of outdoor experiential programmes on physical and mental health are well documented in research. Parents and children working together may find a healthier way of living through exercise and appreciation of their natural surroundings. Parents' self-esteem and confidence rises alongside that of their child as they work together using the free, natural resources of outside areas. Many of the parents have negative feelings about school from their own childhood experiences but are happier to get involved with outdoor programmes as they feel more confident away from the classroom setting.

In the early years, parental involvement has a significant impact on children's development and achievement. It is well documented that educational failure is increased by lack of parental interest in schooling although most parents still believe that the responsibility for their child's education is shared between parents and the school. Many parents want to be involved in their children's education. In a recent study in England, almost three-quarters of parents said that they wanted more involvement (Williams *et al.*, 2002). There is conclusive evidence that parental involvement does make a difference to children's engagement and their achievement and it indicates that parental involvement benefits children, parents, teachers and schools.

The initial Healthy, Active and Outside programme aims to help parents learn about Education for Sustainable Development (ESD) issues via the design, use and management of their children's school grounds. Parents who originally signed up to be part of the programme received regular feedback about their children's progress and behaviour, and the evaluation report (Filer, 2002) clearly demonstrated that when parents are motivated to get involved they make a significant difference. Many of the parents who were involved with the programme felt motivated to do more for the environment and also believed it would be of direct educational benefit to their children. In addition, as a direct result of being involved in the programme more parents were more likely to be involved in other school-based projects.

The Healthy, Active and Outside programme

What is the programme all about?

The Healthy, Active and Outside programme is based upon the philosophy of the Forest Schools developed in Denmark in the early 1980s, where children are allowed the free exploration of the outdoor environment as an integral part of their early education. The programme was developed by Dr Janice Filer during her teaching years as environment and outdoor play coordinator in a Bristol nursery school from 1989 to 1999, where she created an outdoor environment to enable children to learn and develop through outdoor experiential activities.

In the HAO programme the content of the early years curriculum is taught wholly outdoors. Working outside in the fresh air, children are encouraged to develop personal and social skills through the mastery of small, achievable tasks. Through the exploration of the outdoor environment, children are encouraged to grow in confidence and self-esteem. Children learn to respect their environment, to abide by rules and standards of behaviour, work in teams and learn to respect one another in an active, experiential way. The benefits to the children are on many levels as they grow in confidence and learn to appreciate the natural world around them.

The programme particularly supports the emotional, behavioural and social development of children. Children exhibiting challenging behaviour are given the opportunity to develop control over their behaviour and improve their concentration, independence, and social, personal and physical skills. Safety outdoors is given priority as children learn about the boundaries within which they must work. The sense of freedom from being outdoors is well suited to children who need to learn in an active, 'hands-on' way. The programme takes place entirely outdoors, with the children going out in all weathers. By the end of the programme children will have experienced the changing seasons whilst working towards developing self-esteem, concentration and social interaction skills that will enhance their lifelong learning and start the process into an active, healthy adulthood. Children have the opportunity to access the freedom of the outdoor environment within safe boundaries, to learn in an experiential way.

Figure 8.1 The Healthy, Active and Outside programme information sheet

Healthy, Active and Outside
Information for parents about programme evaluation

The Healthy, Active and Outside (HAO) programme is a new project for children and families in: (NAME OF SETTING).

As it is a new project, it is important to find out if it works. We are going to set up an outdoor programme that will be evaluated. As well as talking regularly to staff and teachers of all the children attending the programme, we will also be talking to children and their parents to find out what they think about the programme.

Involvement in the research evaluation of the HAO programme is optional. If you do not want to take part, it will not affect your child's right to attend. For the parents who choose to take part in the evaluation, there will be TWO interviews, which will last no longer than one hour each.

INTERVIEW 1: before the programme, to find out how you think it might help you and your child.
INTERVIEW 2: after the programme to find out what you thought about it.

Any information that you give will be anonymous and confidential. Anything you say will be recorded on tape (with your permission) or written down. The information may be used in reports about the programme but only in anonymous form, i.e. it will not have your name on it or any other characteristic that could identify you or your child.

If you are interested in taking part in research of the HAO programme, please let me know and I will arrange a time to meet, either in your home or at the setting in which the programme takes place, whichever you prefer.

Many thanks for your help.

Yours sincerely,

Programme facilitator/leader

Figure 8.2 Information for parents about programme evaluation

Dear

Welcome to the Healthy, Active and Outside (HAO) programme. We hope you enjoy the time you spend taking part in the programme, meeting new friends and exploring the natural woodland area.

While attending the HAO programme, you will learn all about playing safely outdoors with other children. You will learn how to make new friends, play within safe boundaries, listen to commands and meet exciting challenges alongside activities such as making shelters, having picnics, playing hide and seek. You will be able to explore the natural resources that are readily available in the outdoor areas. You will be encouraged to work in small groups and experience being part of a team as well as building independence skills.

You will be working outdoors in all weathers and we hope you look forward to taking part in all the activities we have planned for you.

Best wishes from

-- the HAO team

(PS – Don't forget your outdoor clothes)

Figure 8.3 Welcome letter for participants

What is parental involvement?

There are two main educators in children's lives:

- parents
- teachers.

Parents are the prime educators until the child attends nursery or starts school and continue to remain a major influence on their children's learning throughout school and beyond. There is no clear demarcation to show where the parents' input stops and the teachers' begins. Although both play a crucial role in children's educational development, the impact is greater if parents work in partnership with the setting. There is still no universal agreement on exactly what parental involvement actually is, but there are two broad strands:

- parents' involvement in the life of the setting
- parents' involvement in supporting their child both at home and at school.

The impact of parental involvement in early years education

Parental involvement in early intervention programmes has been found to equate with better outcomes for the child. The Effective Provision of Pre-School Education (EPPE), a large-scale longitudinal study which monitors 2,800 children, has found that the most effective early interventions involve parents in pre-school children's development. According to this research, in common with the outdoor programme, play, fun and scope for physical activity seem to produce the most effective outcomes. In addition, parents' self-esteem is very important in determining long-term outcomes for both themselves and their children (EPPE, 2005). Research evidence also clearly shows that children's progress can be hindered by lack of parental involvement. It appears that children are disadvantaged not by social class, but rather by lack of parents' interest (Williams *et al.*, 2002). The study found that children whose parents showed a high level of interest, regardless of social class, had higher test scores at age eight and 11, whereas the scores of those children whose parents showed little interest deteriorated. The children with interested parents pulled ahead of the rest whatever their initial starting point (Douglas, 1964). In another study, the childhood experience and parental factors tested were linked to a wide range of outcomes in adulthood (Hobcraft, 1998).

Challenges to parents becoming involved

We know that many parents are already routinely involved in their children's education. However, some parents face challenges which prevent them from being involved. The Department for Education and Skills (DfES) commissioned research with parents in 2001 in order to identify whether parents were involved, to what level, and to discover the perceived barriers to involvement (Williams *et al.*, 2002). When they were asked about barriers to becoming involved, parents cited the competing demands in their lives such as work commitments, other children, childcare difficulties and lack of time. Parents' difficulties with basic skills are also a barrier to being involved in their children's education. In addition, it is well documented that parents who themselves did not enjoy school or had a bad experience at school may have difficulties communicating with teachers, which may affect their level of involvement.

It is surprising just how many parents want their children to have daily access to the outdoor environment with its special nature and broad benefits. They want their children to have the opportunity to play outside in the mud and rain getting messy, in all weathers in a safe, supported environment, but are often not able to provide it at home for a variety of reasons – perhaps they live in flats with no garden space, have too many responsibilities with family, work and chores, worry about safety outdoors or just do not know how to start or what to do.

It is well recognised that in today's climate children need to be discouraged from sedentary lifestyles and encouraged to be more physically active. From the hands-on practical experiences they share with their children during the programme, parents realise the role physical activity plays in keeping their children active and healthy. Most important of all, parents who attend the outdoor programme alongside their children can join them in the fun of good outdoor physical exercise that will help set them up for healthy, active lifestyles well into adulthood.

Links with home

Play is central to children's learning as it provides them with opportunities to explore, develop their imagination, communicate with others and extend their language and thinking. The outdoor play that takes place in the programme links well with the kind of play children often take part in at home. If the child has access to an outdoor play space at home, many of the activities can be repeated or adapted without the need for any specialist equipment. Children who have no access to outdoor play space can be taken outdoors even if it is only for a walk to the shops. Getting outdoors with children enables them to meet the challenges of their own environment. Children are innately inquisitive about their natural surroundings and any outdoor area is an unequalled wealth of resources just waiting to be explored. Taking part in the programme alongside their children will help parents to understand the importance of getting outdoors on a daily basis.

Learning together

What happens at home is important because learning is for life, starts from birth and continues throughout our lives. From the moment they are born children start to learn and begin to acquire important life skills such as communicating with others, making relationships with them and developing certain attitudes and habits. The outdoors is the one environment that naturally lends itself to the idea of families and settings to experience the enjoyment of learning together. Although there are many ways that families can learn together, it can be easier to accommodate their inclusion in programmes of this type as they take place outdoors in a space that is much larger than the one indoors. This addresses the problem of the way some settings avoid including parents in daily sessions because some staff believe that high numbers of adults are overpowering to young children in a small, confined space. With the will and confidence alongside good organisation and planning to include parents, it is possible to overcome this problem. Following or adapting this programme and by moving learning outdoors into the open spaces that surround the premises, both on-site and into the wider community, will greatly reduce this tension.

Taking the family-based approach to learning encouraged in this outdoor programme builds on the notion that learning takes place anywhere and everywhere and helps to finally eradicate the idea that when children are enjoying themselves outside in the fresh air, they are just playing about and wasting time. Inviting parents to attend the programme alongside their children will soon convince them that learning does not just take place in schools or when sitting down with children to do 'work'. They will see for themselves that it can take place anywhere at any time: in the home, the street, outdoors in the school grounds or in the local community. By attending the outdoor programme parents can find out how to introduce their children to a wide range of outdoor learning activities that can be replicated at home for little or no cost. It is surprising how little convincing parents need as they see first-hand how to take advantage of everyday opportunities to help their children develop the essential skills for lifelong learning. During the outdoor programme parents are encouraged to work alongside staff to enable their children to develop the skills of communication, asking questions and listening, increasing their vocabulary, working independently or as part of a team or taking the lead or following the direction of others. They are also helped to understand the problem-solving process and to gain more confidence and increased self-worth and well-being. In addition, family times are encouraged so that parents and their children can enjoy each other's company and have good times together playing outside in the open air, talking, listening or having good fun together.

Parents as partners

Parents make a real difference as they play a crucial role in the education of young children. As the child's first and key educator, they know the child better than anyone else. There is a wealth of research evidence which shows that children do well when:

- parents show a keen interest in their child's education and make learning a part of everyday life at home;
- there is a close working partnership between the home and the setting;
- there is information sharing about children's learning, development and background by everyone involved in the child's successful development;
- children are actively involved in making decisions about their own learning.

Children enter the education system at three and sometimes even earlier, and they continue to need their parents' interest and support as they move through the phases of formal education if they are to make the most of opportunities offered to them. Partnership with parents is an essential component of the outdoor programme, and genuine mutual relationships need to be forged through weekly information-sharing opportunities and regular low-key social events. Before the outdoor programme starts, invite the parents to attend a pre-group coffee morning to learn all about it and discuss their child's individual needs. Repeat this process at specific times during the programme, at ends of term if it is being run throughout the academic year, and at the end of the programme, to give parents as many opportunities as possible to attend.

There are many ways to entice parents to join in and increase their participation in the outdoor programme. Rather than just hoping to catch parents on the hop, allocate a designated time at the start and the end of each weekly session when they come to drop off or collect their children to share information and give feedback about the outdoor session that day. Adults can cover this time on a rota basis which can be displayed for parents to see so that they have the opportunity to choose which day or member of staff they want to talk to about their child. Regularly remind parents that they are invited to attend all or any of the weekly sessions with their child and especially encourage them to attend the end-of-term celebrations and barbecues. Have high expectations of parents to be involved without haranguing them and they will rise to the occasion and soon learn to enjoy being outdoors with their children. If the programme is to have a research element then it is particularly important to encourage parents to attend consultation meetings to collect data from them about their children. It is always important to encourage parents to contribute to the regular assessments of their children that settings have to make regarding children's development and learning achievements. The staff should always be happy to discuss children's strengths, interests and needs with parents and it is beneficial to all concerned if parents do likewise. As part of the process of partnerships with parents regarding the outdoor programme parents should be expected to be committed to getting their children to the outdoor programme every week dressed appropriately for spending the session outdoors.

The parents of the children attending the outdoor programme are actively encouraged to share knowledge about their children in many different ways depending on need, time and ability. One way this can be achieved is by encouraging parents to attend parent and family workshops to find out what their children are learning in the programme and how they might best support them. Other ways to encourage sharing of knowledge about the child with parents could include any or all of the following:

- initial information-sharing meetings about the programme;
- low-key social coffee mornings;
- completion of assessment questionnaires together;
- giving them the opportunity to take part in the research element of the programme;
- setting aside a designated time for parents at the start and end of every session for formal discussions and informal conversations;
- inviting them to attend sessions alongside their child;

- encouraging them to join specific outdoor activities such as gardening days, barbecues and celebrations;
- getting them to volunteer to help on a regular basis;
- enlisting their help for off-site visits;
- inviting them to contribute to children's profiles and observations;
- giving them a report at the end of the programme.

The ratio of adults to children is much higher when taking children outdoors, particularly if they are of a very young age or activities take place off the school site, in which case parents, carers and volunteers may be needed to give essential support to ensure that the outdoor activities take place safely. The contribution parents are able to offer in terms of working outside with children can greatly enrich the effectiveness of the learning experiences of the children and the planned activities. Engaging parents helps develop a sense of community and foster a widespread understanding of the value of outdoor learning. It is down to the leader to encourage parents to participate in the outside learning with their children to foster a deeper understanding of its value and importance.

Parents can make a real difference to the success of the programme as they play a crucial role in their child's education and know their child better than anyone else. As seen above, research shows that children do better when there is a close partnership between home and school. Involving parents in the outdoor programme will help parents to know what their children are doing at school so that they can help them to develop their interests. Parents sharing information about their child will help the programme leaders to provide appropriate personalised learning. They can help build upon all the learning that has already taken place before the child started school. Likewise, the adults leading the programme can help parents build on their knowledge to support their children's learning at home. Sharing of knowledge about the child with practitioners will ensure that learning is as effective and enjoyable as possible.

Increasing awareness of outdoor education

To increase parents' awareness of the importance of outdoor education it is important to engage in regular formal and informal conversation with them and send home regular newsletters, photographs or examples of activities. This will help them understand what learning experiences the children are having during the outdoor programme and give them ideas of how to extend the activities at home. Explain that children need the freedom to explore, meet challenges and take reasonable risks outdoors and that even the smallest outdoor space can provide a wealth of opportunities for children to play. Build upon children's own outdoor experiences to maintain a link with home. Making use of the local outdoor area for visits and walks will help children to recognise features and make their own links with home. If parents do not wish to attend the outdoor programme or the setting cannot readily accommodate them on a regular basis, invite them in for picnics, to take part in outdoor activities, to play games, to help with outdoor maintenance or to watch outdoor performances so that they can see for themselves the value of using the outdoors. Above all, help parents to understand that the weather should not prevent them from taking their children outdoors, by holding outdoor events all year round, not just during the summer months.

Initial meeting with parents

A few weeks before the programme starts it is important to set up an initial meeting with parents to give them an overview of the programme that their children will hopefully be taking part in. It is essential to gain parental approval and permission for children to take part in the programme before it begins. During this initial meeting take the opportunity to inform them of the high level of commitment they will be expected to make. Aim to make every aspect of the involvement process as easy as possible for parents who are prepared to make time to take part in the programme by organising a crèche for important meetings and by planning activities to include siblings.

Case study

On one occasion an older sister of one of the children joined the programme to learn how to play with her so-called difficult brother. They had had difficulties around sibling rivalry and prior to her joining the outdoor programme she had always been the one to get things right and her brother was always in trouble. She soon learned that some of the outdoor activities enabled him to shine and gain a feeling of self-worth that he did not get from indoor education. She could see that he could work well in a practical way although he could not read or write things down. This helped improve family relationships at home because both children could begin to recognise that they had different abilities which were equally valid. The boy's confidence improved as he showed his sister how to carry out some of the outdoor tasks that were new to her but that he could do well because he had had hands-on experience and practice. She in turn grew to respect his practical ability as throughout the programme he was the one to help her rather than as previously, when she was always the one to take the lead or get things right.

Encouraging parental support

Family circumstances should be taken into consideration and respect shown for home situations without being judgemental of parents if they find it difficult to make a commitment to attending any of the outdoor sessions. It should be made as easy as possible for busy parents with family responsibilities, mental health problems, low confidence, no time, aversion to school or younger children etc. to become involved with their children's education outside the home.

Some parents may have literacy problems that the setting may not be aware of. A great deal of embarrassment often accompanies this situation and parents may not be confident enough in themselves or the setting to reveal this difficulty. Sensitive observation and handling of the situation by programme leaders or staff will help alleviate any potential difficulties. Care must be taken not to put parents in an embarrassing situation at the start of the programme by expecting them to complete questionnaires or forms that they may not be able to read or understand. It is important that programme leaders are sensitive and discreet in how they first tackle the issue of written assessments to avoid excluding illiterate parents from the process. Sometimes it may be necessary to set up individual interview situations for all parents so they can answer questions which the leader records.

Parents should be consulted on a regular basis and given the opportunity to express their thoughts and feelings about the programme, and invited to contribute to it under the guidance and supervision of the group leader, if they so wish. It should always be understood by everyone that levels of commitment will naturally differ from family to family. Although expectations of parental involvement in the programme are high, no parent or child is judged or penalised if parents can only commit to the minimum expected involvement set out in the agreement at the start of the programme.

Parents attending the original pilot programme were expected to attend a linked parent support group and end-of-term celebrations, and to sign up for at least one session to join in the outdoor activities with their child. A video viewing session was also arranged for the parents to view a video of their child taking part in the programme. Expectation for parental involvement in the pilot programme was extremely high and at the time was regarded by some professionals as too ambitious because the general trend in the area was of little or no parental involvement at all. The actual level of involvement of parents recorded in the research was significantly higher than expected. A higher than average percentage for parental attendance was recorded during the research programme for meetings, interviews to provide the data for the research project and the weekly programme sessions. The findings show that only one parent made no extra commitment to the programme except for the expected times set out during the initial meeting and, sadly, that was due to severe mental illness that erupted midway through the programme. It was acknowledged that the high level of involvement was due to high expectations and the sensitive handling of the whole process by the leaders of the programme. If you expect parents to work with you and you make it possible for them to do so, it is surprising just how much they will rally to make the effort, whatever their circumstances at home. In addition, ensure that parents have regular opportunities to add to records and make sure that records are clear and accessible to everybody who needs to see them.

Research evidence supports the fact that collaboration between teachers and parents is effective. Parents express great satisfaction in being involved and their teachers report that the children of the parents involved in the programme show an increased keenness for learning and are better behaved at school. Parents bring specific skills to outdoor activities as well as the valuable resources of time and energy. Within the parent body there may be painters and decorators who can help with murals, fences or painting playground markings to zone off areas or create games to play. There may be joiners who can help make seating, decking or pergolas to create shady areas, builders with the skills and machinery to build raised flower beds or walls, or even a landscape architect or garden designer who can help transform your outside space. There may be groups or individuals in the local community who may be able to offer help and expertise such as allotment societies, wildlife organisations, older children, sports celebrities or artists.

Settings that maintain and develop strong links with parents and the wider community share responsibility for children's behaviour and their social and emotional well-being both in and outside the setting. Adopting the programme in the spirit it which it was intended will help those settings to build and maintain effective relationships.

Comments from parents

At the end of the pilot programme parents were asked about their children's experiences in the outdoor programme. Below you will find one parent's comments about their child, who was not settling well into his nursery class at the start of the programme:

> My child really loves going to the outdoor programme. I know he has a good time at nursery on Mondays because he always comes back muddy and looking like he's had a good time. It's good that the children can get out because they always stay in at home playing on their PlayStations and watching TV. It's not safe to play out these days 'cause you don't know who is about any more. I don't have time to get outdoors to play with them so it's nice that they can do it at nursery. They need to play outside because they can't do it at home. My child just loves it now. He always asks if it is Monday because he looks forward to going to nursery on that day, which is a benefit to me because at least I can go home on a Monday without worrying about him all morning now. We're all much happier now and he is getting the idea of how to cope back in the nursery too. I wish he could play outside every day and I expect he does too.

At the end of the programme children and their families are invited to a celebration open day where they receive a certificate of attendance.

There are many ways to encourage links with home and forge genuine two-way relationships with parents as partners. It is up to each individual setting to decide how they can include parents in outdoor activities but it is important to stress that if it is the first time that the setting has ventured outdoors to implement the programme, they need to plan a staged development of inclusion which is manageable, agreed and owned by all staff.

9   The planned activities

Introduction

When you are planning, remember that children learn from everything, even things you have not planned for. Plan to observe as part of the daily routine and analyse observations to help you plan 'what next' for individuals and groups of children. Ensure that there is flexibility in planning for the group, while keeping a focus on children's individual and present learning needs, or interests and achievements.

The outside space is the perfect place for children to be as active as possible to get their bodies working to burn off energy and lift the spirits, at the same time as having some good old-fashioned fun! By using the activities in this chapter to encourage children to apply their knowledge across a range of challenges, learning outside the classroom will build bridges between theory and reality. Quality learning experiences in 'real' situations have the capacity to raise achievement across a range of subjects and enable children to develop better personal and social skills. According to the government manifesto, when these experiences are well planned, safely managed and personalised to meet the needs of every child they can:

- improve academic achievement
- provide a bridge to higher-order learning
- develop skills and independence in a widening range of environments
- make learning more engaging and relevant to young people
- develop active citizens and stewards of the environment
- nurture creativity
- provide opportunities for informal learning through play
- reduce behaviour problems and improve attendance
- stimulate, inspire and improve motivation
- develop the ability to deal with uncertainty
- provide challenge and the opportunity to take acceptable levels of risk
- improve young people's attitudes to learning
- give young people responsibility for achieving these outcomes, thereby helping them to learn from their successes and failures.

(DfES, 2006b)

Planning and preparation

Outdoor activities must be carefully planned and well taught, and should extend learning before and after the event as quality should be the defining factor influencing participation in outside learning. Planning learning outside the classroom is as important as individual learning and there should be a balance of the two. Outdoor activities need to be planned well in advance but there needs to be some flexibility because you can never depend on the weather. All the resources need to be prepared and collected together beforehand. You need to know how you are going to introduce the activities to the children, what you will say to them, what questions they might ask and what the children will do if they finish the activity more quickly than was anticipated. The programme provides support for planning activities in many different curriculum areas, and being linked to the Early Years Foundation Stage curriculum, the activities in this chapter provide direct and relevant experiences that will deepen and enrich learning. The activities are primarily designed for the early years age group from approximately three to five but with a little imagination, they can be adapted for any age!

The programme is all about getting outside and exploring the outdoor space. Following the ideas about developing the outside environment discussed in previous chapters, alongside the more specific activities in this chapter, will facilitate the creation of non-prescriptive play environments which enable children to unleash the potential of their imaginations and the feelings associated with having fun. The planned activities are designed mainly to focus on helping children develop their imagination and encourage playful learning and other non-academic development skills such as social interaction. The activities have been developed to entice children to use their imaginations and help promote original thinking, flexibility, adaptability, empathy and the ability to generate multiple solutions to a problem. They should be used in the context of the ethos of the setting and what is generally accepted as effective pedagogy in the early years: 'In the excellent and good settings the balance of who initiated the activities, staff or child, was very equal, revealing that the pedagogy of these effective settings encourages children to initiate activities as often as the staff' (Siraj-Blatchford *et al.*, 2003). The author has acquired knowledge of the activities in this chapter from many various sources over a prolonged period of experience in the field of physical education in the early years and as such the sources are no longer identifiable. Many of them have been passed down from activities demonstrated during training or from organisations such as Learning Through Landscapes.

This chapter includes a programme of work (Table 9.1), how to adapt the programme to fit into a shorter period of time, examples of blank session and activity planning sheets (Tables 9.2 and 9.3) and HAO session pro formas (Table 9.4), and many ideas of practical activities to help the practitioner build on their knowledge to extend children's interest in particular areas. It also includes information about the components that are part of every session such as adopting a theme song, warm-ups, energisers and reflection activities to capture the views and feelings of the children themselves.

Any planned activity should be adapted to suit the situation and to ensure a balance of structured adult-initiated activities and free exploratory play. Any heavy emphasis upon direct teaching and programmed instruction should be avoided in the early years as young children should be engaged in free outdoor play as much as possible. The planned activities in this section of the book are particularly effective when young children have freely chosen to take part in them. Before you start, always remind the children of any safety issues, boundaries or guidelines concerning what they can or cannot do in the outdoor play space and check out the area you are using to ensure safety, make sure there are no dangerous objects lying around and that the children cannot get out and strangers or animals such as dogs cannot get in.

Programme of work

Over the next pages you will find a programme of work for running 30-week outdoor sessions throughout the academic year to take into account the changing seasons with planning sheets and pro formas (Tables 9.1, 9.2, 9.3, 9.4).

Adapting the programme

The scheme of work should be used as a guide to inspire you or get you started if you are new to working outside. The programme is designed to be used in a flexible way and to be adapted to fit into any situation in any setting. The programme can be followed as it stands or you can select a 'pick and mix' of activities depending on children's interests at the time, what themes or schemas are most prevalent or what events are happening in the setting. Add practical activities from the ideas in the planned activity section later in this chapter. The programme can be run as a ten-week intervention using parts 1–10 if it takes place during the autumn/winter, parts 11–20 for the January to Easter term and parts 21–30 if the programme is going to take place during the warmer summer months as five sessions of the programme are designed to fit into each new academic term.

Table 9.1 The Healthy, Active and Outside programme

THE HEALTHY, ACTIVE AND OUTSIDE PROGRAMME – part 1

AIMS:
To encourage children to develop awareness of themselves, others and the outdoor environment
To provide opportunities for children to learn outside in the open air
To provide children with practical skills and ideas for use in the development of their physical and personal, social and emotional skills
To enhance children's self-confidence and esteem as individuals and their progression to further learning opportunities
To support parents in developing their role as partners in the educational process

Every session

1 At the start, review previous week and sing theme song 'If You're Happy and You Know It' (p.117) with actions and words to match activities of the previous session
2 Choose a different child each session to be the leader, to choose a favourite activity as the repeat activity/lead games etc.
3 Play safety game '123 Where Are You'
4 Make the shelter/base
5 New activity
4 Repeat previous week's main activity to review and consolidate new learning
5 Have an active warm-up/energiser game: Simon Says (use leader's name), Traffic Lights (p.127), Collecting Tails (p.157), Magic Shoes (p.165), Clear the Decks (p.155), Sandy Girl/Boy (p.161), Captain's Calling (p.143) or Fruit Shop (p.154). Always link actions and vocabulary to weekly activity
6 Balance of free exploratory/discovery play
7 Snack
8 Reflection time at end of every session with discussion and repeat song 'If You're Happy and You Know It' (p.117) with actions and words to match activities that session. Sing more songs if appropriate
9 Take down shelter if not permanent and clear up

Terms 1 and 2:	Group			Facilitator/s:		
Session	New Activity	The Child Will:	Methods of Assessment/ Teaching Methods	Evidence of Learning	Warm-up Energiser/ Song/Extra Resources	Page
1	Ground rules Safety game '123 Where Are You?' Making the base and pathways	Learn how to be safe outdoors, decide on the whereabouts of the base and leave the area as they found it	Leader talk and facilitation Demonstration/modelling Guided discovery Individual Pairs Whole group Joint activity	Site-located observation Return to base Observation of loud/clear calling of leader's names Base set up	Simon Says Walk to the Woods Make the Base Make Some Pathways	71 121

Table 9.1 The Healthy, Active and Outside programme continued

Terms 1 and 2:		Group		Facilitator/s:		
Session	New Activity	The Child Will:	Methods of Assessment/ Teaching Methods	Evidence of Learning	Warm-up Energiser/ Song/Extra Resources	Page
2	Stop, Look, Listen Dens, Bases and Secret Places	To learn to stop, look, listen To play cooperatively to create dens for role play	Leader talk and facilitation Demonstration/modelling Pairs	Observation Can listen, respond and ask appropriate questions	Traffic lights	127
	Shelters	To work cooperatively to make a shelter	Small group	Can feed back verbally after request to 'Stop, look and listen' Pairs dens made	String, penknife/scissors Branches Groundsheets, plastic sheets	157 126 128
	Seats	To organise logs into a seating circle	Joint activity Whole group	Group shelter made Seating circle in place	Seat-sized logs	71
3	Pass the stick Find small sticks	Learn to take turns Find twigs the same size as their fingers	Individual Whole group	Observation Collection of dead wood ready for bonfire		
4	Find big sticks	Find sticks as long as their legs	Leader talk and facilitation Demonstration of frame	Observation Can listen, respond and ask appropriate questions	Metal pole to make holes for frame	137
	Scavengers letter links Word Map	Recognise the initial of their first name	Demonstration of in and out 'like a snake' Guided discovery of using/ properties of willow/natural materials	Knows initial letter sound for name Can make weaving actions with hands	6 strong, straight sticks/branches approx 1 m for frame Willow branches to weave in/out of sticks	125 136
	Willow weaving – fences	Make a willow fence	Individual practical activity Small groups Joint sustained activity	Can weave willow into frame of sticks Over several weeks can complete the fence to be used as a wind guard Can feed back verbally	Natural materials collected by children from area to decorate fence: ivy, fir cones, leaves and twigs etc.	

Table 9.1 The Healthy, Active and Outside programme continued

Terms 1 and 2:

Session	New Activity	Group The Child Will:	Methods of Assessment/ Teaching Methods	Facilitator/s: Evidence of Learning	Warm-up Energiser/ Song/Extra Resources	Page
5	Dress Up Warm Lost and found	Understand why they need to look after themselves when playing outdoors	Demonstration/modelling Individual Small group Joint activity	Observation Can listen, respond and ask appropriate questions Can feed back verbally	Hide and Seek Voting Pots Play people	129 138 120
	Planting bulbs	Bulbs planted	Leader talk and facilitation Demonstration/modelling		Various spring bulbs	
	Scooping Conkers	Conkers collected and used during free play	Individual Whole group			
6	Windy, Windy Weather Weather Watch	Develop communication skills by discussing weather and playing weather games	Leader talk and facilitation Demonstration/modelling Guided discovery	Observation Can listen, respond and ask appropriate questions	Pick a Place	130 134
	Catch a Fallen Leaf	Develop hand–eye coordination	Individual Small groups with leader Joint weather watch activity sustained over a few weeks Whole group	Observation Can describe weather Can join in cooperative game	Containers for leaf collection	121
7	Follow me Stop, Look, Listen. Think! Puddle Play Crossing the swamp	Can follow instructions Experiment with water Play a cooperative game with others	Leader talk and facilitation Demonstration Small group Whole group Joint activity	Observation Can listen, respond and ask appropriate questions	Simon Says	157 146
8	Hashing (following trails) Photo trails Blindfold rope trail Stop, Look, Listen, Think and Check! Checking twice Concentrating	Follow instructions Play a cooperative game	Leader talk and facilitation Demonstration Guided discovery Individual Pairs Whole group	Observation Can listen, respond and ask appropriate questions	Hide and Seek Ball of string Various objects to hide	157 120

Table 9.1 The Healthy, Active and Outside programme continued

| Terms 1 and 2: | | Group | | Facilitator/s: | Warm-up Energiser | |
Session	New Activity	The Child Will:	Methods of Assessment/ Teaching Methods	Evidence of Learning	Extra Resources	Page
9	Laying trails Footprints All Around	Lead an activity Follow instructions and a trail	Leader talk and facilitation Demonstration of natural decoration by leader	Observation Can listen, respond and ask appropriate questions	Simon says	154 135–6
	Nature's art – twig decorations Decorating trees	Make a decoration from natural materials found outside Hang decoration tree	Individual practical activity Whole group Joint activity		String, penknife or scissors Collection of natural objects found in area to join together: twigs, feathers, fir cones	
10	Children's choice	Tell/show favourite activity	Leader talk and facilitation Individual	Observation Can listen, respond and ask appropriate questions	Pick a Place Barbecue materials/fire basket etc.	163 121
	Outdoor Bands	Perform	Whole group Joint activity		Sausages, rolls Flasks of soup/ hot chocolate etc.	
	Winter celebration – safety re: lighting fires and cooking food outdoors					
	Hidden surprise	Game played/hidden surprise found				

THE HEALTHY, ACTIVE AND OUTSIDE PROGRAMME – part 2

| Terms 3 and 4 | | Group | | Facilitator/s: | Warm-up Energiser | |
Session	New Activity	The Child Will:	Methods of Assessment/	Evidence of Learning		Page
11	Re-establish base and set ground rules	Play within boundaries	Leader talk and facilitation Demonstration/modelling	Observation Can listen, respond and ask appropriate questions	Simon says Hide and seek Animal Transfer	131 120
	Review of previous sessions	Tell others about previous activities enjoyed/played	Guided discovery Whole group	Can feed back verbally Base set up and shelter made		
	Children's choice	Make choices	Individual Pairs			
	Bird Watch 1	Spot and mark birds on a chart	Joint activity			

Table 9.1 The Healthy, Active and Outside programme continued

| Terms 3 and 4: | | | | Group | Facilitator/s: | | |
Session	New Activity	The Child Will:	Methods of Assessment/ Teaching Methods		Evidence of Learning	Warm-up Energiser Extra Resources	Page
12	Ice art	Make an ice picture	Modelling/demonstration Individual		Observation Can listen, respond and ask appropriate questions	Animal Transfer Collecting Tails	164 120
	Woodland animals game	Follow instructions to play a cooperative game	Whole group Small group Joint activity				
13	Bird Watch 2	Spot/identify birds and record them on a chart	Whole group		Observation Can listen, respond and ask appropriate questions	Simon says Actions linked to session activity	131 154
	Footprints All Around		Small group			Animal Transfer	136
	Puddle Play	Explore the properties of puddles	Joint activity		Explore the woodland		
14	Bird Watch 3	Spot/identify birds and record them on a chart	Demonstration/modelling Individual		Observation Can listen, respond and ask appropriate questions	Fitness Circuit Animal Transfer (Using different species of birds)	131 133
	We're Going on a Bear Hunt	Play a cooperative game	Small group Joint activity				
15	Dream catchers	Make a dream catcher from willow	Individual		Observation Can listen, respond and ask appropriate questions	Fitness Circuits Pick a Place	125 142
	Finding Families	Follow instructions to play a game	Small group Joint activity				119
16	Fill It Up	Follow instructions to play a game	Individual Pairs		Observation Can listen, respond and ask appropriate questions	Dodge Ball Ball Swap – hoops 20 metres apart	137 120
	Market Stalls	Take part in imaginary role play	Whole group Small group Joint activity		Can find and identify minibeasts found in woodland		
17	Patchwork Plot	Make a garden patch and plant seeds	Individual Whole group Small group Joint activity		Observation Can listen, respond and ask appropriate questions	Fruit Shop – pick vegetables to match planting activity Hop, Skip, Jump	149 155

Table 9.1 The Healthy, Active and Outside programme continued

Terms 3 and 4:		Group		Facilitator/s:		
Session	New Activity	The Child Will:	Methods of Assessment/ Teaching Methods	Evidence of Learning	Warm-up Energiser Extra Resources	Page
18	Treasure hunts: Pick up a Rainbow, natural or manufactured	Play a game Sort objects found in the outside area	Individual Whole group Small group Joint activity	Observation Can listen, respond and ask appropriate questions	Hide and Seek Skip On	143 145 120
19	Nature Search Find surprise Vegetable People	Find natural objects Find surprise Make a character from a vegetable	Individual Small group Joint activity	Observation Can listen, respond and ask appropriate questions	What's the time, Mr Wolf? Number Bundles Voting Pots	139 120
20	Children's choice Spring celebration picnic Egg hunts	Identify at least one previous activity Explore the area looking for eggs Bring found eggs back to base to share	Leader talk Presentation Group discussion/ verbal feedback Individual and pairs activity Whole group	Observation Can listen, respond and ask appropriate questions Can make choice of activity	Energy Stations Pick a place Small wrapped chocolate eggs/boiled eggs Container/basket to count eggs back Picnic blankets and food	119

THE HEALTHY, ACTIVE AND OUTSIDE PROGRAMME – part 3

Terms 5 and 6		Group		Facilitator/s:		
Session	New Activity	The Child Will:	Methods of Assessment/ Teaching Methods	Evidence of Learning	Warm-up Energiser	Page
21	Re-establish base and set ground rules Review of previous sessions Lift Some Litter	Explore and identify guidelines/ground rules Identify previous activities Collect litter from outdoor area and produce artwork from it	Demonstration/modelling Leader talk Whole group Pairs Joint activity	Observation Can listen, respond and ask appropriate questions Return to base Can identify at least one previous activity Can give verbal feedback to group Made resource	Animal Transfer – use names of the litter spotted in the area Containers for litter Plastic/garden gloves Example of artwork made from litter	135–6

Table 9.1 The Healthy, Active and Outside programme continued

Terms 5 and 6:	Group		Facilitator/s:		
Session	New Activity	The Child Will:	Methods of Assessment/ Teaching Methods	Evidence of Learning	Warm-up Energiser Extra Resources	Page
22	Hide and Seek	Explore outside area and find hiding places Play the game within rules Count up to 20	Whole group Small group Joint activity	Observation Can listen, respond and ask appropriate questions Observation of clear and concise instructions	Captain's Coming – extend the game to include features found in the outside space and call it 'Leader's Coming'	144 120
	Signs of new life	Find evidence of new life and report back to group		Can hide and accept being found/return to base Can wait whilst others hide and then find them Observed following instructions when looking for signs of new life		
23	Minibeasts 1 – Making homes Wildlife Treasure Hunts	Use tools to make the resource of animal home for next week's activity Find minibeasts Report back to group.	Leader talk/modelling Whole group Small group Joint activity	Observation Can listen, respond and ask appropriate questions Explore the woodland	Simon says Hide and Seek Animal Transfer	146 145 151 120
	What Lives in a Place Like This?	Show evidence.				
24	Minibeasts 2 – habitats	Handle minibeasts/homes	Demonstration/modelling	Observation	Animal Transfer – minibeasts Follow Me Number Bundles Pick a Place Windy day! Warm clothes	146 157 120–1
	Classifying flowers, trees etc.	Show a basic understanding of biodiversity Identify some wild flowers by name	Individual Small group Joint activity	Can listen, respond and ask appropriate questions Can work with others collaboratively		

Table 9.1 The Healthy, Active and Outside programme continued

Terms 5 and 6:		Group		Facilitator/s:		
Session	New Activity	The Child Will:	Methods of Assessment/ Teaching Methods	Evidence of Learning	Warm-up Energiser Extra Resources	Page
25	Dream Catchers	Make dream catcher Use materials to join objects together	Individual Small group Joint activity	Observation Can listen, respond and ask appropriate questions Dream catcher completed Verbal feedback to group	Bull's-Eye String, penknife/scissors Length of willow per child Range of natural objects to decorate	125 121
26	Lost and found A Bowlful of Bubbles	Awareness of feelings when lost and found Able to describe feelings Take the lead to hide the 'lost' play people/items	Leader talk Whole group Small group Joint activity	Observation Can listen, respond and ask appropriate questions	Ball swap Hide and Seek Simon Says	148
27	Playful Shadows Scribbling in Sand A Waxy Rub (bark rubbing)	Understand the concept of a shadow Follow own shadow, not step on other shadows Follow process Find materials to make rubbing and produce artwork	Whole group Small group Joint activity	Observation Can listen, respond and ask appropriate questions Can distinguish between shade and light patches	Skip on Pick a Place	148 161
28	Where's my hat? Treasure hunt	To learn to look after personal property by playing searching games Able to find hat	Whole group Small group Individual Joint activity	Observation Can listen, respond and ask appropriate questions Child can hide treasure Treasure found brought back to base Can count treasure back	Hoop La Fruit Shop – include losing hat on the way Treasure to hide Make progressive, i.e. plastic toys, children's sweatshirts/peaked caps Large bright objects/smaller natural objects, etc.	129 145

Table 9.1 The Healthy, Active and Outside programme continued

Terms 5 and 6:		Group		Facilitator/s:		
Session	New Activity	The Child Will:	Methods of Assessment/ Teaching Methods	Evidence of Learning	Warm-up Energiser Extra Resources	Page
29	Natural designs Marks in Mud Where's teddy?	Make a piece of artwork To learn positional language and find teddy	Individual Small group Joint activity	Observation Can listen, respond and ask appropriate questions	Balance Beams Voting Pots Story	136 132 159–60
30	Targets of Ten Children's choice End of programme celebration/teddy bears' picnic Performance, art display Lost teddies – Found teddies	Be confident to take part in a performance Complete a piece of artwork Understand and name feelings, begin to show empathy	Presentation Whole group Verbal evaluation by children Written evaluation by parents and staff	Observation Can listen, respond and ask appropriate questions Can choose and demonstrate favourite activity Can take part in group discussions Can evaluate the programme	Energy Stations Voting Pots – re whole programme Certificates Artwork from course displayed Sandwiches from food grown, i.e. egg and cress, salad Drinks Picnic blankets Wooden sticks/homemade instruments	141 163 119–20

Table 9.2 The Healthy, Active and Outside programme session planning sheet

The Healthy, Active and Outside Programme Planning Sheet

Date:	Group/Children:		Session no:	Venue:	Leader/s:
Activity:					
Area of Experience	What do you want the children to learn?		How will you enable the learning to take place?	How will we know what learning has taken place?	What next?
	Learning intentions based on the stepping stones/early learning goals	Vocabulary	Activities/routines	Assessment	Notes on how assessments will inform new plans
PSED					
CLL					
KUW					
PD					
CD					
PSRN					

Abbreviations: PSED = Personal, Social and Emotional Development; CLL = Communication, Language and Literacy; KUW = Knowledge and Understanding of the World; PD = Physical Development; CD = Creative Development.

Table 9.3 The Healthy, Active and Outside programme activity planning sheet

THE HEALTHY, ACTIVE AND OUTSIDE PROGRAMME **Activity Planning Sheet**			
ACTIVITY			
DATE	GROUP	CONTEXT	LEADER/S
MAIN LEARNING INTENTION/POSSIBLE LEARNING OUTCOME			
RESOURCES		KEY VOCABULARY/QUESTIONS	
INTRODUCTION			
STEP-BY-STEP CONTENT			
ADAPTING THE ACTIVITY FOR INDIVIDUAL CHILDREN			
Younger/less able children	Older/more able children	Children for whom this activity is particularly appropriate	
FOLLOW-UP ACTIVITIES/PROGRESSION/EXTENSION IDEAS			

Table 9.4 Healthy, Active and Outside programme session pro formas

THE HEALTHY, ACTIVE AND OUTSIDE PROGRAMME Session planning				
Date:	Leader/Facilitator:		Co-leader/s	
Session:	Theme		Focus child:	
Greeting Safety activity before start of session	Time Initial	**Review last week's session**		Time Initial
START PROGRAMME:		Introduce new learning		
New learning activity 1 2 3 4		**New strategies** 1 2 3 4		
Team/game activity		**BREAK: Snack and free play**		
Story/song		**Reflection/review**		

Table 9.4 Healthy, Active and Outside session pro formas continued

| THE HEALTHY, ACTIVE AND OUTSIDE PROGRAMME |
| Observation notes |

Focus child: Date of birth   Observer:

No of adults: No of children: Date: Time:

Individual (I)   Pairs (P)   Small group (SG)   Whole group (WG)

Solitary (S)   Parallel (PP)   Cooperative (CP)   Joint activity (JA)

Context/setting:

| PSED | CLL | PSRN | KUW | PD | CD |

Additional key: eg FC: focus child, A: adult

Activity	**Language**

Levels of engagement

Fully engaged   1   2   3   4   5   Not engaged

Notes for future planning

Themes/schemas

Table 9.4 Healthy, Active and Outside session pro formas continued

THE HEALTHY, ACTIVE AND OUTSIDE PROGRAMME		
Session recording		
Date:	Leader/Facilitator:	Co-leader/s:
Session	Focus child:	Setting:

Main group issues

Strategies used

Working together

New learning

Activities and games

Free play/children's main interests

Review/reflection

Ideas to take to supervision

Table 9.4 Healthy, Active and Outside session pro formas continued

THE HEALTHY, ACTIVE AND OUTSIDE PROGRAMME **Individual Records**
Focus child: D.O.B: Setting:
Date: Session
Date: Session
Date: Session
Date: Session
Date: Session
End notes

Table 9.4 Healthy, Active and Outside session pro formas continued

---

THE HEALTHY, ACTIVE AND OUTSIDE PROGRAMME
Individual Session Report

Name: **Date:**

At Outdoor School today I:

Learning Goals I worked towards are:
Personal, Social and Emotional Development

Communication, Language and Literacy

Problem Solving, Reasoning and Numeracy

Knowledge and Understanding of the World

Physical Development

Creative Development

Member of staff's comment

Staff signature:
Parent's comments

Parent's signature:
Please return this form to a member of staff, as it is put into the child's profile. It will be returned to you when your child leaves the project.

Components of every session

Some parts of the programme are designed to give it a containing cyclical structure which will provide the children with the security of a regular routine with some activities. Some of the features which take part during every session include the theme song, a warm-up, an energiser and activities to use for reflection and evaluation during the review to capture and record children's own ideas and views about the programme. Here are some ideas:

The theme song

Choose and sing your own theme song at the start and end of every session; for example:

'IF YOU'RE HAPPY'

If you're happy and you know it
Walk to the woods × 2
If you're happy and you know it and you really want to show it
If you're happy and you know it
Walk to the woods.

Use the song above as the programme's theme song by singing it at the start of each session as a review of the previous week/s and again at the end to reflect on the activities that day. Change the action or the feeling to link to the activities that have taken place that session, or if the song is being sung at the end celebration, use it to reflect on favourite activities etc. The variations are endless. Give the children the opportunity to choose what action or feeling they sing about by including a 'children's choice' in the activity which can be linked to the leader for the day if there is not enough time for all children to choose.

Think of some ideas for actions to replace the words 'walk to the woods' and emotive words to replace 'happy'. The list is endless but here are a few ideas to get you started:

Dreamy – make a dream catcher, catch some dreams
Lost – look high, look low/look all around/call out loud
Sad – find the play people/get some exercise
Caring – take care of a friend
Hurt – hop on one leg/walk on all fours
Tired – sit down and rest
Bored – splash in puddles/play outside
Cold – build a shelter/wrap up warm/jump up and down/weave a fence
Hungry – sizzle some sausages/grow some food
Friendly – show your friends
Angry – stamp the ground, punch the air
Safe – run back to base
Healthy – get fit outside
Dirty – wipe off the mud/wash your hands

Warm-ups and energisers

Try any of these activities to get the children warmed up and their hearts beating to increase cardiovascular fitness and as energisers for mental alertness.

Energy Stations

Resources: skipping ropes, hoops, chalk, balance beams and balls

Set out a course of five activity stations around the grounds. Use chalk to create the stations and any markings required.

1   Skip On – do 20 skips on the spot with a rope.
2   Ball Swap – transfer five balls, one at a time, from one hoop to another.
3   Hoopla – run up and down the course, collecting an object from the first hoop and returning to the start before running on to hoop 2 and so on. The next person could then run up and back replacing the objects.
4   Hop, Skip & Jump – follow the instructions to go up and down the course, first hopping, followed by skipping and then jumping.
5   Balance Beams – walk along three balance beams with a beanbag on your head.

Split into small teams to move around the activity stations. Give each team a clipboard and ask them to record how many times the whole team is able to complete each activity. Move the groups on after a set period of time.

Fitness Circuits

Resources: laminated exercise cards, question cards and coloured signs/markers

Place the laminated cards with exercises and numbers of repetitions shown on them to warm up all parts of the body, including small parts such as hands, neck and feet, around the outside area. Tell the children to go off and repeat the exercises on each card around the course.

YOUNGER CHILDREN/OLDER CHILDREN

Younger children can be led around the course missing alternate exercises, missing out different exercises each session or doing fewer repetitions of them. Take them to try out the first few exercises, depending on fitness levels. Older children could demonstrate exercises, make up their own exercises and laminated cards, or do the course as a timed/competitive activity. They could lead the activity. Older children could a follow a course where there are question cards at ten different places in the grounds for them to answer. For example, the cards could include mental arithmetic for the day, questions about a current project or relating to each place – e.g. What type of tree is this? How many pieces of rubbish can you see?

The course could be set up as a mapping activity where children are asked to mark the same points on a map of the grounds with small coloured dots. Give the children a basic map of the area and explain that they have to use their map to find the ten coloured signs/markers hidden around the grounds. When they return, compare results together.

FOLLOW-UP

Repeat this activity several times during the programme to compare their performances. Ask the children to create their own courses for others to follow.

Games to play

Resources: small play equipment, e.g. balls, ropes, chalk, soft ball etc.

Discuss the children's favourite outdoor and playground games. When you have a list of simple traditional games that do not need lots of equipment, try playing some of them. For example:

Dodgeball – one player with a soft ball tries to hit the others on the leg below the knee – if hit, the player has to stand still until someone tags them and sets them free

Animal Transfer – players stand in a large circle with one person in the middle. Give each person in the circle one of five animal names. The person in the middle shouts out one of these and the 'animals' have to run clockwise around the outside of the circle till they get back to their own space. Reinforce learning in many different areas by repeating the game regularly using a different set of names such as domestic animals, colours, types of weather, flowers, trees etc.

Number Bundles – players run around in a specified space until the leader shouts out a number – players have to get into groups of that number as quickly as possible

Hide and Seek – two seekers close their eyes and count down from 30 while the rest of the players hide. Seekers try to find and tag the hiders before they manage to sneak back to 'home base'

FOLLOW-UP

In groups, ask the children to design their own simple game using a few pieces of equipment. Give each group a space in the grounds to create their game. Explain that they can use the chalk to draw a game space, shapes, numbers or letters. If there is no area of hard ground such as tarmac, use hoops, ropes or labels instead of chalk. Encourage the groups to try out their games as they go along to make sure they work, and invite them to teach their game to each other.

Activities to use for reflection and evaluation

At the end of sessions it is a good idea to use these ideas to encourage the children to reflect and evaluate what they have been doing.

Voting Pots

Resources: 3 large flowerpots, chalk, stones, sticks, leaves, daisies, petals – anything that can be used for voting

Draw a smiley face, a sad face and a neutral face on each pot. Ask questions to gauge the children's feelings, for example:
How do you feel about getting dirty?
Playing outdoors?

Discuss the question and then ask them to vote by placing a suitable object (e.g. stone, leaf, twig) in the pot which matches their feelings. Count the votes in each pot and discuss the results with the group.

FOLLOW-UP

Invite the children to design their own happy, sad and neutral faces on the voting pots. Capture the children's ideas by having a discussion about the kinds of outdoor activities they enjoy most. Encourage them to create a picture of their favourite activity, using the messy methods described in the section on creativity.

Pick a Place

Resources: evaluation statements, chalk

Prepare statements that you can use to evaluate the participants' attitudes to the session, such as what they think about getting dirty and messy. For examples, include:

- I like getting dirty
- I enjoyed being outdoors
- I hate being outside
- Getting dirty is cool
- It doesn't matter if I get my clothes get dirty
- I get told off for getting dirty
- I would rather be inside watching television/playing computer games than playing outdoors

On the ground, mark out four circles large enough to hold the group of children. Mark the centre of each circle to indicate a range of opinions from 'Strongly agree', 'Neutral', 'Don't know' to 'Strongly disagree'.

Explain the rules and have a practice. Read out the statement and then ask the children to run around the playground until you call an agreed signal to stop. They should then stop running and walk to stand still in the circle which reflects how they feel about the statement

FOLLOW-UP

Encourage the children to make up their own statements. Photograph the action and record the results.

FOR YOUNGER/OLDER CHILDREN

For younger children decrease the number of circles to two which invite a 'Yes' or 'No' response. For older children increase the number of options to six to include 'Agree' and 'Disagree'.

Another method of gathering children's opinions is the Bull's-Eye. This is more complicated and has a more mathematical slant so it might be more appropriate for older children.

Bull's-Eye

Resources: evaluation statements, chalk, stones or pebbles

Mark a target like a dartboard on the ground but with only five concentric circles. Mark each space from the centre out 5, 4, 3, 2 and 1. Read out or share a statement made by the children and invite each child to place a stone in the circle according to their opinion from the centre circle for 'Strongly agree' (5 points) to the outer circle for 'Strongly disagree' (1 point). Calculate the total score by adding the points for each stone.

FOLLOW-UP

Finding an average score can be useful when comparing the strength of feeling about a range of statements in connection with the evaluation of the programme as you will be able to include the children's opinions.

In the following section of this book you will find five planned activities that can be photo-copied. These include the games '1, 2, 3 Where Are You?', 'Water, Water Everywhere', 'Catch a Fallen Leaf' and 'Willow Weaving' (see Figures 9.1–9.4).

THE HEALTHY, ACTIVE AND OUTSIDE PROGRAMME SESSION PLAN

ACTIVITY 1: Safety Game: 1, 2, 3 Where Are You?

DATE 09.09.06 (Every session)	**GROUP** 10–12 children	**CONTEXT** Woodland area in grounds of setting	**LEADER/S** Jan/Lin

MAIN LEARNING INTENTION/POSSIBLE LEARNING OUTCOME
Listen to explanations (CLL)
To understand and remain within safe boundaries (PSED)
Count from 1 to 3 and 1 to 10 (MD)

RESOURCES Safe outside space Designated base Feature such as a tree, large stone, wall	**KEY VOCABULARY/QUESTIONS** Listen Stop Return Come back Immediately/ Straight away Explore Woodland Base Tree Trunk Feature Safety Touch/hold/contact with Can you hear the leader call? What is the safety signal to return to the safety tree/base? Why do you think we need a safety signal?

INTRODUCTION
Take children outside and explain the rules and why we need to have a safety signal. Explain that only the adult can call out the safety signal '1, 2 3 Where are you?' They need to listen and come back to base when they hear it.

STEP-BY-STEP CONTENT
Show the children the designated base and explain why it is always going to be the same place. Chose a memorable feature such as a specific tree to mark the area.
Practise touching/holding/keeping hands in contact with the tree trunk for increasing periods of time. Count out the time from 1 to 10 seconds.
Practise immediate response to the safety call '1, 2, 3 Where are you?' One adult at tree, One adult explore with the group. Repeat 3–4 times, responding immediately to call.

ADAPTING THE ACTIVITY FOR INDIVIDUAL CHILDREN		
Younger/less able children May need an adult to hold their hand May need another child to accompany them May need to stay close to the base May need to practise many times	**Older/more able children** Choose the feature to mark the base area. May count out the time to remain in contact with the tree. Explore larger area around base. May run off too far/over-stretch themselves.	**Children for whom this activity is particularly appropriate** Full time: Sam, Jake, Sonija Part time: Clem (a.m.) Jack (p.m.)

FOLLOW-UP ACTIVITIES/PROGRESSION/EXTENSION IDEAS
Respond to call without an adult accompanying group
Increase size of outside area children can go off to explore.
Increase time between safety calls to encourage children to explore independently for longer.
Randomly use the safety call at any time during the session to remind children of safety issues.

Figure 9.1 Example of planned safety activity '1, 2, 3 Where Are You?'

THE HEALTHY, ACTIVE AND OUTSIDE PROGRAMME SESSION PLAN

ACTIVITY Water, Water Everywhere!
An experience of wet, rainy conditions to learn about the changes that occur when it rains

DATE 09.09.06 (Every session)	**GROUP** 10–12 children	**CONTEXT** Outside area	**LEADER/S** Jan/Lin

MAIN LEARNING INTENTION/POSSIBLE LEARNING OUTCOME
To ask questions about why things happen (CLL)
To be familiar with and talk about features of the weather (KUW)
To look closely at the changes that occur when materials become wet (KUW)

RESOURCES	**KEY VOCABULARY/QUESTIONS**
Safe outside space with puddles Appropriate clothing Wellington boots	Wellingtons, Puddles, Rain, Rain drops, Sky, Rainbow, Water, Wet, Dry, Stiff, Soggy, Clouds, Splash, Change. What do we need to wear outside today? What do you think would happen if we didn't wear waterproof clothing? What can you see in the sky? What colour is it? Can you feel the rain? What does it feel or sound like? What do you think will happen to the tarmac, twig etc.

INTRODUCTION
Learn songs associated with rainy days such as 'I Hear Thunder', 'Incy, Wincy, Spider'. Gather all wet-weather clothing and dress for the outdoors. Go outside for a walk in the rain singing the songs you have learned together. Stop to observe the effects the rain has on the outdoor play space. (Link to Activity 1, Safety Game and Activity 2, Stop, Look, Listen.)

STEP-BY-STEP CONTENT
Take children outside on a rainy day or after it has rained to explore the changes that take place in the environment when it is wet. Go outside for a walk after or during a downpour of rain. Encourage the children to feel rain on their hands and faces, listen to it beating and watch it falling. Where it comes from and the changes it makes to the environment. Draw attention to the clouds and ask the children to describe the sky. Explain clouds are full of water drops, raindrops fall to the ground, make it wet and create puddles. Look around to see how things change in the rain (soil, tarmac, grass etc.). Check out natural resources to see how they change when they get wet, how they feel, look, change colour, change from stiff to soggy. Walk, jump, splash in the puddles to see what happens. Make rain footprints, push cars and drag sticks through puddles.

ADAPTING THE ACTIVITY FOR INDIVIDUAL CHILDREN

Younger/less able children	**Older/more able children**	**Children for whom this activity is particularly appropriate**
Need an adult to hold their hand. Listen to explanations. Stay close to the adult and observe others. Learn new vocabulary. Walk in puddles	Lead the activity. Give detailed explanations. Help organise the group. Lead other children by the hand. Jump and slash in puddles. Collect materials freely.	Full time: Part time:

FOLLOW-UP ACTIVITIES/PROGRESSION/EXTENSION IDEAS
Repeat on a sunny day, windy day and during different times of the day or year. Make comparisons. Talk about the differences in the way you dress/prepare/look after yourself in different weather conditions. Discuss the different effects of the weather, i.e. shadows on the ground, trees moving, leaves falling etc. Read stories about the weather.

Figure 9.2 Example of planned activity 'Water, Water Everywhere'

THE HEALTHY, ACTIVE AND OUTSIDE PROGRAMME SESSION PLAN

ACTIVITY Catch a Falling Leaf

Collecting leaves to use as resources

DATE	GROUP 10–12 children	CONTEXT Outside play space	LEADER/S

MAIN LEARNING INTENTION/POSSIBLE LEARNING OUTCOME

Encourage children to listen to each other's questions and to take turns (PSED).
Learn about the seasons and the effects of weather conditions, i.e. the wind on trees during autumn, how/why leaves fall to the ground (KUW). Allow to feel, touch, smell and see different leaves and the wind (KUW). Responding to significant experiences, having views about the activity and explaining them (CLL). Showing a range of feelings in response to catching/not catching a leaf and being out in the wind (PSED). Hand eye co-ordination, catching leaves (PD). Sort leaves and count them (MD).

RESOURCES	KEY VOCABULARY/QUESTIONS
Appropriate outdoor clothing Windy day Outdoor space with trees, with falling leaves Containers to collect the leaves	Trees, leaves, wind, autumn Falling, blowing, colours One, two, few, many, lots of

INTRODUCTION

Learn songs and read books about autumn and leaves to discuss with the children before going out. Look through the window on a windy day and watch the leaves falling and explain the activity before going outside. Dress appropriately for windy conditions.

STEP-BY-STEP CONTENT

Walk to the area in the grounds where there are trees or access to falling leaves or leaves blowing in the wind. Discuss the windy conditions and talk about why the leaves are falling off the trees and being blown around the outside area. Watch what happens when a gust of wind blows. Stand under or near a tree and take it in turns to try to catch a leaf as it falls. Discuss how it feels when you catch a leaf, do not catch a leaf or are the last one to catch a leaf, when you are waiting for your turn. Encourage children to watch patiently.

ADAPTING THE ACTIVITY FOR INDIVIDUAL CHILDREN		
Younger/less able children Observe others taking part Listen to explanations Learn new words Kick through piles of leaves Hold a leaf	**Older/more able children** Help others to catch leaves Jump up to catch leaves Make large collections and piles. Explain to others why leaves fall from trees.	**Children for whom this activity is particularly appropriate** Full time: Part time:

FOLLOW-UP ACTIVITIES/PROGRESSION/EXTENSION IDEAS

Make leaf collections. Use leaves as natural resources both inside and out. Sort leaves into colours, sizes, shapes or species. Share out leaves equally between children. Use leaves to make leaf prints or collages. Use piles of leaves for jumping in, on, over.

Figure 9.3 Example of planned activity 'Catch a Fallen Leaf'

THE HEALTHY, ACTIVE AND OUTSIDE PROGRAMME SESSION PLAN			

ACTIVITY Willow weaving

To learn how to use willow to weave a tapestry made of the natural resources found outdoors to make a fence to protect children from the wind. Demonstration of using real tools.

DATE	GROUP 3–4 children	CONTEXT Outside where there is soft ground	LEADER/S

MAIN LEARNING INTENTION/POSSIBLE LEARNING OUTCOME

Demonstrate an understanding of the names of the tools. Demonstrate an understanding of how to use the tools to make a frame (CLL). Use natural products to make a tapestry (CD). Large muscle development in handling, lifting, carrying, twisting, turning and hammering large sticks. hammering. Fine motor skills of weaving (PD)

RESOURCES	KEY VOCABULARY/QUESTIONS
Wooden mallet 6–8 strong sticks approximately 1 metre long, 4–6cm diameter. Long lengths of willow or similar pliable twigs. Leaves, flowers, twigs, feathers to decorate	Wood, willow, mallet, twist, turn, bendy Weave, in/out

INTRODUCTION

Explain that the play base outside needs some protection from the wind when the children sit down for circle time, have a snack or a rest. Explain that it is going to be an ongoing project that might take some time and that the children will be working in turn in small groups with an adult but that they will all have the opportunity to take part. Introduce techniques by demonstrating the process. Explain the properties of willow, demonstrate weaving in and out like a snake.

STEP-BY-STEP CONTENT

Choose a soft area of ground near the play base. Show the children the materials and let them handle them. Encourage them to feel and smell the different textures and odours of the wood. Explain the safety aspects of using tools, such as holding them down pointing towards the floor, only using them with an adult for the purpose for which they are designed to be used. Let the children take turns to hold the mallet and practise using it with the help of an adult. Put the mallet in a safe place. Take the strongest stick and show the children how to make a hole in the ground for it by twisting and turning it on the same spot on the ground. When a hole has been made, hold the stick in lace and use the mallet to hammer it firmly in place. Let the children take it in turns to hammer it. Repeat using all the sticks in a row at intervals to make the frame. Using the willow, weave it between the sticks to make the natural tapestry which will act as a shelter from the wind.

ADAPTING THE ACTIVITY FOR INDIVIDUAL CHILDREN		
Younger/less able children Watch the activity Help the adult to look after tools and resources Learn new words and safety procedures Use tools with hand over or under adult's hand	**Older/more able children** Use tools independently Push large sticks into the ground Help others to engage in the activity Lead the activity	**Children for whom this activity is particularly appropriate** Full time: Part time:

FOLLOW-UP ACTIVITIES/PROGRESSION/EXTENSION IDEAS

Collect natural materials such as twigs, sprigs of foliage, feathers, flower heads and fir cones and weave them into the basic tapestry to decorate it. Make several tapestry fences to make an enclosure for the play base. Make smaller individual tapestries. Make a dream catcher by bending a piece of willow into a circle and attaching natural objects to it such as twigs, leaves and feathers; hang it in the shelter or den as a decoration.

Figure 9.4 Example of planned activity 'Willow Weaving'

The safety game '1, 2, 3 Where Are You?' is the one activity that all children must learn and take part in before they are allowed to go off alone to explore and engage in free play in the woodland under 'remote supervision' once the leaders are sure that the children respond to the safety procedures practised at the start of each session and stay within the agreed boundaries set by the group.

Easy-to-organise ideas

In this section you will find a range of easy to organise ideas for activities that can be easily adapted to suit various age groups and the equipment you have available in your setting. Use the planning sheet on pages 110–11 and follow the examples of the plans above to record the ideas you want to use in your outdoor session. The activities are grouped in the areas of the Early Years Foundation Stage curriculum to help you choose.

How to use this section of the book

This section of the book is organised into the six areas of learning for the under-fives that have been identified by the School Curriculum and Assessment Authority. All the outdoor play activities described in this book are directly linked to the six areas of learning, which are 1 – Personal, Social and Emotional, 2 – Communication, Language and Literacy, 3 – Problem Solving, Reasoning and Numeracy, 4 – Knowledge and Understanding of the World, 5 – Physical Development, and 6 – Creative Development.

The activities are practical ideas which are designed to take place in a variety of outdoor play settings. Many of them can be adapted for use in many other areas including the indoor play space. Each outdoor activity is based around a key learning objective and is planned to stimulate and develop young children's outdoor play experiences in a safe enjoyable way.

For each activity, advice is given about what resources are required, and how to set up and carry out the activity with the children. Ideas are suggested to help you adapt the main activity to meet the needs of older or younger children or to add differentiation for children with different abilities or prior experiences. Each activity includes follow-up ideas and shows cross-curricular links where appropriate. There are suggestions for questions to ask relating to the activity.

Personal, social and emotional development

The following ideas are based upon the personal and social aspects of children's development. Children will be encouraged to play cooperatively, to understand the difference between right and wrong, to take turns, to share, to be aware of personal hygiene, to develop independence, to respect themselves, each other and property.

Dens, Bases and Secret Places

Learning objective: to play cooperatively to create dens and secret places to be used as bases for imaginative role play
Resources: a table, a groundsheet, 3–4 old blankets, some string

Set the scene by making an outdoor den. Cover a table with an old blanket. Encourage the children to use the den during outdoor play times. Explain to the children that they are going to make their own outdoor den in a hidden corner of the outdoor play space. The den will be their secret place to play in. Tie the blankets onto a fence, drape them over a table or hang them from trees according to what is available in the play space where this activity is taking place. Challenge the children to design and build the dens of their dreams. Find props to accompany their imaginary play. For example, use a picnic set and food to have a picnic inside the den.

Ask the children where they would like to build the den. Discuss the resources they will need. Consider the feasibility of making the den of their dreams. Talk about the reasons for building dens and find ways of making them safe, comfortable, secret, dark, light and so on.

QUESTIONS TO ASK

Where do you want to build your den? What will you use to build it? How can you make your den a secret place? Have you ever had a den before? What is it like inside your den? What could you do inside the den?

FOR YOUNGER/OLDER CHILDREN

Help younger children to create their den. When it is finished, let them place domestic role play props inside to pretend playing at home. Ask older children to think of a theme to go with their den. Invite them to make their own props to use inside it.

FOLLOW-UP ACTIVITIES

- Invite some friends to a picnic inside the den.
- Set up a historical den with crafts and clothes from times past.
- Hide things inside the den.

Figure 9.5 Building our den

Traffic Lights

Learning objective: to learn how to stop on the command of a signal
Resources: a photograph of a set of traffic lights; 3 pieces of card; scissors; a red, amber and green marker pen; a circular object to draw around such as a small saucer; a flat, safe outdoor play space

SETTING UP

Draw around the saucer three times on the piece of card. Colour the circles red, amber and green. Cut out the circles and use them to represent the traffic lights.

WHAT TO DO

Talk about traffic lights. Ask the children to name the colours of a set of traffic lights and invite them to recall what happens when the lights change colour. Discuss the purpose of using signs rather than language. Talk about the ways people communicate with each other when they cannot see or hear.

Explain the boundaries of the game to the children. Discuss all safety aspects such as looking where you are going when you run, and stopping or sitting down on the ground in a controlled manner. Explain to the children that the coloured circles represent the traffic lights. Hold up a green circle as a sign for the children to run around. Hold up the red circle, explaining that it is a signal for them to stop running and stand still. An amber signal indicates to the children to sit down. If the red circle is held up after the amber one, the children remain in a sitting position. Hold up the signals in random order for the children to carry out the corresponding action. The last child to respond to the signals each time sits out. The last child to be caught takes over the role of the traffic controller, holding up the cards to restart the game.

QUESTIONS TO ASK

Have you ever watched the traffic lights changing colour? What does the red light mean? Have you noticed any other signs? What do you think it would be like if you could not see? What do you think it would be like if you could not hear?

FOR YOUNGER/OLDER CHILDREN

Play the game using only the red and green circles as stop and go signs. Introduce the element of body awareness into the game. For example, the green circle indicates to the children to run quietly on their toes, the amber circle is the sign to sit up straight, the red one is the sign for the children to stand with feet together and arms by their sides.

FOLLOW-UP ACTIVITIES

- Take the children to a safe site to watch the traffic lights changing colours.
- Play the game by calling out the colours.
- Invite children to cover their eyes to listen to a spoken command. Challenge them to communicate to each other using gesture instead of words.
- Dance around to music played on a percussion instrument; when the music stops, the children stop dancing and stand or sit still.
- Play instruments when the green card is held up, put them down for red, hold them still for amber.

Where's My Hat?

Learning objective: to encourage children to look after their own property by playing a searching game to find a hat

Resources: a straw hat, some ribbon and the book *Where's My Hat?* by Neil Morris (Hodder & Stoughton, 1982)

Tie the ribbon around the brim of the hat. Read the story 'Where's My Hat?' to the children before going outdoors. This is a story about a little girl who loses her new hat. Her friend plays tricks on her by pretending to steal it. The chase begins and the mystery unfolds as the hat is spotted in many different locations. Discuss the importance of looking after our own possessions and helping each other to find them when they become lost. Hide the hat in the outdoor play space before going outdoors with the children.

Before going outside explain to the children that while you were out walking the wind blew your hat off and you lost it. Explain that you cannot find your hat anywhere and that they are going to help you find it. Invite the children outdoors to help you to look for your hat. When the hat is found, the child who finds it restarts the game by hiding it again.

QUESTIONS TO ASK

Have you ever lost anything special? How did you feel about it? Did you find it? When you find something that has been lost, how do you feel?

FOR YOUNGER/OLDER CHILDREN

Wear the hat on a walk around the outdoor play space with the younger children. Let it secretly slip off your head. When the children notice you are no longer wearing the hat, retrace your steps so that they can find the hat. For older children, hide the hat so that there is no sign of the red ribbon as a clue.

FOLLOW-UP ACTIVITIES

- Hide a funny hat in the outside play space and send the children off to retrieve it. The child who finds it has to make up a funny dance, sketch or make a funny face.
- Hide all the children's own hats outdoors. Invite the children to search for them.
- Set up an outdoor hat shop.
- Design and make a hat to wear outdoors.
- Make a pirate's hat to wear outdoors by folding a large sheet of newspaper.

Dress Up Warm

Learning objective: to encourage independence by playing an outdoor dressing-up game

Resources: four sets of outdoor winter clothes made up of a hat, a scarf and a coat, large enough to go on top of the clothes the children are already wearing

Mark out a start and finishing line in a suitable outdoor play area. Space out the clothes between them so that you have four hats in a row, four scarves in a row, and four coats in a row. Ask the children to practise doing up and undoing the fasteners on their outdoor clothing. Talk about the order in which they dress themselves in the morning and at bedtimes.

Take the children outdoors to the start line. Explain that each child has to run to the first row of clothes to put on a hat, to the second row of clothes to put on a scarf, to the third row of clothes to put on a topcoat. When the children have put on all the clothing, they must run to the finishing line. At the finishing line each child removes the outdoor clothes and folds them up neatly in a pile. Repeat the game several times to give the children plenty of practice in dressing, undressing and folding up their clothes.

QUESTIONS TO ASK

Can you dress and undress yourself? What do you put on first? Can you do up the fasteners on your clothes? Can you put you own shoes on? What do you do with your clothes when you take them off?

FOR YOUNGER/OLDER CHILDREN

Ask an adult to play the game with each child, helping them to put on the clothes and do up fasteners. Older children could play the game in the form of an obstacle race. Increase the amount of clothes they have to put on.

FOLLOW-UP ACTIVITIES

- Sort piles of clothing into indoor and outdoor wear, summer and winter clothes or day and night clothes.
- Base the game upon a theme. The children could dress up like clowns, scarecrows, pirates or knights.
- Make a display of the clothes you wear in the rain, on the beach or to bed.
- Have a multicultural theme to the game.

Windy, Windy Weather

Learning objective: to encourage cooperation and sensitivity to the needs of others

Take the children outside on a windy day to experience the wind blowing. Invite the children to walk all around the outdoor area, feeling the wind as it blows through their hair and into their faces. Explain to the children that you are going to play a game called 'Windy, Windy Weather'. Gather the children into a little huddle to demonstrate how it is much warmer when you get close to each other. Ask the children to hold hands in a long line. The adult stands in the middle, holding the children's hands on either side. Walk together in a long line, face to the wind. Chant the words 'windy, windy weather' several times. Then, unexpectedly call out 'windy windy weather we all come together' which is the cue to swing round into a huddle, still holding hands. After a few moments, repeat the above activity. Ask the children how they can escape from the wind. Ask them to walk in different ways to avoid its force. Ask the children to walk with their backs to the wind, with their face down or with it partially covered with their hands. Encourage them to protect one another from the wind by standing behind each other in a row. Find out what it is like to walk towards the wind or away from it.

QUESTIONS TO ASK

What do you feel like on a windy day? Do you like the wind? What do you see happening outdoors when it's windy? Have you ever watched things blowing in the wind? How can you tell which way the wind is blowing? How can the wind help us?

FOR YOUNGER/OLDER CHILDREN

Play the game with only two children at a time. Encourage older children to group into threes to play the game by themselves.

FOLLOW-UP ACTIVITIES

- Listen to the sound of the wind. Make up dances and chants to match the sounds you hear on a windy day.
- Chase leaves as they swirl round and round in corners of the outside play area.
- Watch the wind blowing in the trees.
- Make a simple kite to fly in the wind.

Communication, language and literacy

The following outdoor activities provide ways to encourage the development of children's language and literacy skills. Some of the activities extend talking and listening skills whilst others support stories, rhymes and role play.

Bird Charts

Learning objective: to build upon children's vocabulary through observing, recording and talking about the birds they see outdoors
Resources: clipboards (1 for each child), drawing paper, marker pens, reference book of birds

Make a simple tally chart for each child. Ask the children to draw bird shapes at the top of the chart to represent different birds. Give each child a clipboard, drawing paper and some marker pens. Discuss the birds you see outdoors. Use the reference book to point out the individual markings which distinguish one species of bird from another, for example the red breast of the robin or the black and white plumage of the magpie. You could entice the birds into the outdoor play area by scattering some birdseed around the ground. Throughout the session, watch and record the birds that come into the outdoor play space by making the appropriate symbol on the tally chart. Name birds as they fly by and encourage the children to repeat and join in the naming process to help them learn new vocabulary. Describe the distinctive features of each bird, noticing different sizes, colours and shapes. Look at similarities, pointing out that all birds have wings, feathers and beaks. Use the correct terminology so that the children hear new vocabulary in the right context to give them the confidence to repeat new words and use them.

Count the numbers of each species recorded on the chart. Discuss and display the chart with pictures of all the birds recorded. Encourage the children to describe and recite the names of the birds they have seen. Help them understand why the birds have come into the play area.

QUESTIONS TO ASK

Which birds have you seen? What do they look like? Why do you think the birds have come into the garden? How many different types of birds have you spotted? How many birds have you counted?

FOR YOUNGER/OLDER CHILDREN

Younger children may be able to distinguish between big birds and little birds, blackbirds and brightly coloured birds, or choose just two or three common birds to look out for. The children could count and name the birds as they see them. Encourage older children to make their own charts. Ask them to use the reference book to identify the birds. They could make observations and recordings over a week or a month, listing only birds that land in the outdoor play space or visit a bird table to feed.

FOLLOW-UP ACTIVITIES

- Make dough models of birds.
- Make a simple bird hide.
- Make some binoculars to watch birds from inside the hide.
- Sing the nursery rhymes 'Four and Twenty Blackbirds' and 'Two Little Dicky Birds'.
- Make a bird mobile.
- Make some bird food by mixing melted lard, biscuit crumbs, nuts and dried fruit. Put the mixture into empty yoghurt pots, hang from a tree and watch the birds feeding.

Scribbling in Sand

Learning objective: to convey meaning through drawing pictures in sand
Resources: two large shallow trays, silver sand and a jug of water

Put a fine layer of sand to cover the surface of both trays. Place trays outside on an even surface.

Tell the children that they are going to make marks in the sand with their fingers. Ask them to take it in turns to guess what the other has drawn. Challenge the children to experiment with drawing and writing, using their fingers in different ways. Encourage them to make marks in the sand by using the index finger as a pencil, using two fingers together, making thumbprints or using a fist to make larger marks. The children could pretend to make secret messages and codes for each other to decipher. Help them to understand that words and pictures can convey meaning to others by pretending to write simple messages in the sand. After a while, pour a little water into one of the trays to dampen the sand. They will be able to make deeper impressions in the damp sand. Repeat the activity using wet sand. Discuss the difference between drawing in wet sand and drawing in dry sand.

Ask the children to search around the outdoor play area for objects to use for scribing in the sand. Encourage them to experiment with feathers, small twigs, stones or lolly sticks.

QUESTIONS TO ASK

Can you make a mark in the sand? What does the sand feel like? Can you make lines, squiggles or fingerprints in the sand? Can you copy what I have drawn in the sand? Can you guess what your friend has drawn in the sand? What things can you find around the outdoor play area to make marks in the sand? What else can you do?

FOR YOUNGER/OLDER CHILDREN

Younger children could just make patterns and marks in the sand with their fingers, experiencing the difference between wet and dry sand. Older children could practise making marks in the sand to represent the letters of their names or write their names by going over the shape you have already marked out.

FOLLOW-UP ACTIVITIES

- The children could take it in turns to draw with a finger on each other's back, and then guess what has been drawn. After three guesses the symbol is revealed.
- Repeat the activity using a mixture of cornflour and water.
- Repeat the activity, using finger paints.

Marks in Mud

Learning objective: to encourage communication through writing by leaving messages in mud
Resources: a garden area with mud, a jug of water, a notebook, a pen; for each child you also need 1 twig, 1 lollipop stick, 1 piece of card (12cm × 6cm), glue, some marker pens

Decide upon a short, winding route within the outdoor space you have available. Find or create patches of mud for the children to make their messages. Use the water to dampen down the earth patches to ensure a certain amount of success. Ask each child to make a marker flag by drawing a bold design on the piece of card and gluing it to the lollipop stick. Explain that the markers will indicate the areas in the garden where they are going to make a trail and leave messages for the other group to follow. Explain the purpose of the trail. It could lead to a place of interest, to lost treasure or to a picnic spot. Give each child a twig. Tell the children to make marks in the damp soil for their message. The adult leading the group needs to carry a notebook and pen to record the message for future use. Complete the trail by writing a message and pushing a marker flag into the ground at regular intervals along the route. Invite the other group to follow the trail by searching for the markers and reading the messages left in the mud. Repeat the activity to give all children the experience of setting and following a trail.

QUESTIONS TO ASK

What does your message say? How will the people following the trail know what your message means? Do you know of any other ways people leave messages for each other? Have you noticed any signs around you? What do the signs mean?

FOR YOUNGER/OLDER CHILDREN

Younger children could use their fingers to make marks in the mud. They could hide the marker flags to play a hunting game. Older children could plan their own activity; they could clear their own patches of earth, and use a variety of scribing tools, such as feathers, sticks and carving tools to create different marks and symbols with specific meanings.

FOLLOW-UP ACTIVITIES

- Set up trays of wet soil outdoors for children to practise writing and drawing.
- Make marks in different mediums such as plasticine, dough or clay, using a range of mark-making tools, some conventional, some improvised.
- Make a map to record the activity.
- Make and follow footprints in the mud.
- Go on a sign-spotting walk around the local environment.

'We're Going on a Bear Hunt'

Learning objective: to respond to a story to develop an understanding of some positional language

Check out the area you are using to ensure safety; make sure there are no dangerous objects lying around and that the children cannot get out. Take a copy of *We're Going on a Bear Hunt* by Michael Rosen and Helen Oxenbury (Walker Books, 1993), a large teddy bear, two or three old blankets and a variety of outdoor play equipment for setting up an obstacle course. Read the story 'We're Going on a Bear Hunt' to the children. This is a story about five prospective hunters who cross fields, wade in a river, drag themselves through mud, through a forest, through a snowstorm, into a cave where the bear scares them into running all the way back home again. Set up an obstacle trail to correspond to the actions in the story. The children could go through a tunnel, crawl under a sheet or over a bench. Make a 'cave' with the blankets at the end of the course. Hide the teddy bear inside it.

WHAT TO DO

Explain that you are going on a bear hunt in the garden. Refer them back to the pictures in the story and demonstrate the actions. Focus on the positional language under, over, through and back as used in the story to describe the bear hunt. Practise the actions of going over, under, through and back. Encourage the children to chant the appropriate positional words as they travel along the course. At the end, challenge the children to find the hidden teddy. When they find the teddy they have to go back along the obstacle course to home. Ask the children to recall the sequence of events on the way to find the bear. Make a game by saying, 'the bear is coming...crawl back under...walk back through...jump back over...crawl back under...walk back through...jump back over'.

QUESTIONS TO ASK

How many of the actions can you remember? Can you do actions to match the words in the story? What would you do if you met a real bear? Have you ever felt scared? What is it like?

FOR YOUNGER/OLDER CHILDREN

Play going on a bear hunt in the garden with younger children. When the children meet the 'scary' teddy they must run back to a predetermined place of safety. Encourage older children to set up their own bear hunt and take it in turns to hide the teddy bear at the end. Give them the blankets to make their own cave.

FOLLOW-UP ACTIVITIES

- Hunt for other 'beasts' in the garden.
- Set up more complex routes to the cave. Encourage the children to include the positional language over, under, through and back to recall the activity.
- Ask the children to climb over or crawl through or under objects they find in the garden. Hide a small teddy in the garden and help the children to find it by giving positional clues as to its whereabouts.

Weather Watch

Learning objective: to encourage communication of meaning through recording observation of the weather
Resources: examples of weather charts and weather symbols, a large sheet of card, several sheets of white A4 paper, felt pens, scissors and Blu-Tack

Show the children some conventional weather charts and symbols to encourage discussion about symbols conveying meaning. Discuss different types of weather. Ask the children to name the different combinations of weather; for example, sometimes it is wet and windy, or sunny and windy. Take it in turns to suggest a different description of the weather that day. Make a chart with the days of the week at the top, using the large sheet of card. Give each child some card, scissors and felt pens to design their own weather symbol. Ask each child to make a different symbol. Make several copies of each symbol. Display the chart in a prominent, reachable position. Ask the children to put Blu-Tack on the back of each symbol. Go outdoors to see what the weather is like. Talk about the weather and use the appropriate symbol to record daily weather conditions throughout the programme.

QUESTIONS TO ASK

What is the weather like today? What kind of weather do you like best? What do you feel on a rainy day? What do you do when it rains? What do you do when it is sunny?

FOR YOUNGER/OLDER CHILDREN

Take younger children outside regularly to feel and see what the weather is like for themselves. Talk to them and point out the different weather conditions as they are playing outdoors. Encourage older children to develop their own ways of recording the weather, making their own charts and symbols to use on a regular basis. Get them to listen to weather forecasts.

FOLLOW-UP ACTIVITIES

- Make a display of all the clothes you might wear in the summer or winter.
- Discuss what sort of activities you might do on a dry day, a rainy day, a cold day, a windy day, a sunny day and so on.

- Ask them to draw or paint a picture to depict the weather, explaining about warm and cold colours.
- Make a weather mobile using the symbols made for the weather chart; suspend it from a tree or a fence to watch it moving in the wind.

Lift Some Litter

Learning objective: to develop an understanding of the way writing is used for classification purposes through collecting and sorting litter
Resources: a plastic container and a pair of rubber gloves for each child, a large sheet of sugar paper, some marker pens and some scissors

Prepare a litter analysis chart by drawing two columns on the sugar paper. Give each child a pair of rubber gloves and a container for litter. Take care! Ensure that an adult checks the outdoor area being used to remove any dangerous objects. Explain any ground rules, boundaries and safety issues, telling the children to check with an adult if they come across any objects they are not sure about. Give each child a container. Tell them to wear the rubber gloves to pick up the discarded litter in the garden. Gather the children together to look at the litter they have collected. Decide upon two categories into which the litter can be sorted. These could be natural objects and manufactured ones or all the brightly coloured objects and all the dull-coloured objects. Make a chart by drawing the two categories at the top of a piece of paper. Sort the litter, making a tick on the chart underneath the relevant category. Discuss and compare what has been found. Tot up all the marks to discover what kind of litter is the most common.

QUESTIONS TO ASK

How did the litter get into the outdoor play area? What can you do with all the litter you have found? What do you do with your litter? What happens to all the litter lying around?

FOR YOUNGER/OLDER CHILDREN

Help younger children to sort the litter according to simple criteria such as small pieces and large pieces. Ask the children to make a mark on the chart for each piece of litter found. Count and recite the marks together. Let the older children decide for themselves ways to display and record their findings.

FOLLOW-UP ACTIVITIES

- Encourage the children to find creative ways of displaying the litter.
- Go litter lifting in the same area regularly over a period of time. Compare and record the different types of litter found. Make a note of any changes. There could be less litter due to the litter-lifting activity.
- Make posters to deter litter dropping. Fix them to some containers and place them outside. Encourage children to use them as litter bins. Explain that the marks and writing on the posters will inform others that they should use the containers as litter bins.

Pick Up a Rainbow

Resources: coloured card or paint charts, small bags, chalk or large sheets of paper, pens, rope/string

Give each pair or group a colour palette made up from different colours of card or use commercial paint charts. Invite the children to search for objects that roughly match each colour and collect them in their bag. Emphasise they must not take any living items, such as leaves still on trees, plants or insects, and remind them to use gloves if collecting litter. Ask the groups to sort their own items according to colour. Using a printed tally sheet, or one chalked on the tarmac, collate the number of objects of each colour from each group.

Discuss which colours are the most common and why they think this is. Try this activity at different times of the year and compare the difference (if any) in seasonal colour and the possible reasons for this.

EXTENSION ACTIVITIES

Natural or manufactured?   Ask the children to put their objects in the appropriate circle and discuss which circle has the most items and why they think this is. Which is the most common colour in each circle? Discuss why this might be. Discuss the difference between natural and manufactured items. Ask each group to separate their items into those they think occur naturally and those that do not. Draw two large circles with chalk on tarmac, or use hoops or make them using rope. Label one 'natural' and one 'manufactured'. Depending on the items found, an overlap between the two circles might be necessary. Follow up this activity with a discussion about litter in the area.

Word Map

Give each group a card with two contrasting words on it – e.g. light/dark, smooth/rough, a long/short, shiny/dull. Ask the groups to explore the grounds and find spaces or features that illustrate their words. Label the space on a simple blank map of the site. Alternatively, mark the place with a word card or with chalk. Bring the groups back together and go on a tour of the grounds, discussing how the shapes/textures/light of different parts of the grounds affects how they use and feel about it.

QUESTIONS TO ASK DURING DISCUSSIONS

Which games are played in certain areas? Where are good hiding places? Which areas are good for sitting and talking? Which spaces/features are safe/fun/exciting? Which are scary/dangerous/dirty?

Natural Designs

Resources: digital camera

Using the contrasting word cards from the activity 'Word Map' above, ask each group to collect a selection of materials which illustrate their two words. Explain that they are going to create a design which illustrates the contrast of their words. In the spirit of environmental art, these should be created outside in; for example, a 'rough/smooth' design will be created in a smooth or flat area of the grounds. When the designs are finished, allow the children to circulate and appreciate each other's work and give everyone the opportunity to present their design to the rest of the group. Take digital photos of the finished designs and display them.

Scavenger's Letter Links

Learning objective: to look for objects in the garden with the same letter as the children's initial
Resources: a piece of paper for each child playing the game and some marker pens

Write the initial letter of each child's name on separate sheets of paper and give it to them. Discuss the initials and their letter sounds. Tell the children how other objects may start with the same letter. Give them plenty of examples to help them grasp the concept. Take the children on a hunt around the garden to discover what objects can be found starting with the same letter as their own initial. Write the words of the objects down, emphasising that the first letters are all the same. Compare the sounds as well as the shapes of the letters. Count the lists of words to find out whose name has the longest list of objects to find out which letter is the most popular one. Encourage an awareness of letter links by asking the children to look for similar letters in the writing they see around them.

QUESTIONS TO ASK

What is the first letter of your name? Do you know anything else which starts with the same letter? Can you write the first letter of your name? Have you seen the letter anywhere else?

FOR YOUNGER/OLDER CHILDREN

Write each young child's name out in full. Point out any similarities between their initials and the lists of the objects you have recorded for them. Encourage the older children to make a list of the first symbol of their name several times on a sheet of paper. Add the rest of the word when you find an object starting with the same symbol.

FOLLOW-UP ACTIVITIES

- Encourage children to look for their initial in written signs.
- Print notices to display in the garden. Send the children off to find and count how many times the first letter of their name appears in the printed notices.
- Look for the children's initials in print when you are looking at books together.
- Look for the children's initials in signs around the neighbourhood.

Market Stalls

Learning objective: to increase vocabulary and competence in using language through role playing at the market place
Resources: a table for each stall, money containers, recycled materials to represent produce, large sheets of paper, marker pens, sturdy cardboard, scissors and pretend money

Ensure that the resources used to stock the market reflect a range of foods, artefacts etc. from different cultures. Arrange the tables according to a market set-up. Make signs for all the stalls and fix them to the tables. Give each child a piece of paper and some marker pens to make their own stall signs. Place a variety of goods and some pretend money in the containers on each table.

Arrange a visit to a local market place as preparation for this activity. Encourage children to watch and listen to the way people buy and sell things to each other. Point out some of the new vocabulary for them to repeat and learn. Start the activity with discussion about what markets are, reminding the children of their visit to the market. Discuss the idea of setting up a market in the outdoor play space. Allow the children to decide what type of stalls they will have in the market. These may differ according to the geographical area or the time of year. A busy city might have a market place with food, clothes and antique stalls; a country market might have animal, craft and flower stalls; a seaside market might sell fish. Base the ideas on the children's own experiences of markets.

Ask the children to search through their belongings for items to pretend to sell. They could make items for sale by cutting out shapes from sturdy card or using recycled materials such as empty plastic bottles, boxes and cardboard tubes. Invite the children to arrange the goods for sale on the tables as you would for a market. Give each child some plastic money. Encourage the children to role-play the scenes of a busy market place. Challenge them to buy and sell goods to each other.

QUESTIONS TO ASK

Have you ever been to a market? What was it like? What did you buy? What do you have for sale on your market stall? How much does it cost to buy?

FOR YOUNGER/OLDER CHILDREN

Set up one stall using some of the children's toys. Give the younger children some pretend money and invite them to pretend to be the stallholder. Encourage the other children to visit the market stall to buy back their toys. Encourage older children to plan their own outdoor market. Ask them to decorate and set up their own stalls to recreate the atmosphere of a busy market place. Encourage them to use market banter during their role play. Leave the stalls set up for several days/weeks for the children to develop the play according to their own needs.

FOLLOW-UP ACTIVITIES

- Set up different types of stalls on different days of the week. You could have a fish market, a craft market or flower market.
- Make some real things to sell. The children could sell plants they have grown, pictures they have drawn, squash and cakes they have made.
- Use real money.
- Have a multicultural market theme displaying articles from different countries.

Problem solving, reasoning and numeracy

Outdoor play can provide opportunities for children to take part in practical mathematical activities. The following ideas help to develop the children's knowledge of quantity, capacity, volume, shape, matching pattern, sequence, time, counting, size, sorting and grading.

Scooping Conkers

Learning objective: to develop an understanding of quantity through scooping and weighing conkers
Resources: a deep outdoor tray, enough conkers to fill the tray, 6 scoops, and 6 plastic containers such as ice cream tubs

If possible, collect the conkers with the children during the autumn. Talk about the conkers as you collect them, counting how many each child has found. Store until use. Position the tray outdoors and fill with conkers. Remind the children of the time they went conker collecting. Give each child a scoop and a container. Let them experiment. Invite the children to scoop up the conkers in the tray. Suggest that they fill their plastic container with conkers. Count the number of conkers each child has scooped into the container. Return all conkers to the tray and repeat the activity several times. Compare and discuss the different quantities of conkers used throughout the activity. Point out the number of conkers in the tray. Reinforce mathematical language such as add more, take away a few, many, a couple, full, half-full, empty. Ask the children to compare the quantity of conkers there are in a flat scoop with the quantity in a heaped scoopful.

Where did the conkers come from? Have you ever been conker picking? What time of the year do you look for conkers? How many conkers do you think there are in the tray? How many little conkers fit into the container? How many large conkers fit into it?

FOR YOUNGER/OLDER CHILDREN

Ask an adult to work with the younger children to encourage them to count the conkers as they play with them. Older children could work cooperatively in pairs to estimate and compare the quantities of conkers they are using.

FOLLOW-UP ACTIVITIES

- Repeat the activity using different-sized scoops and containers to increase understanding of quantity, capacity and volume.
- Draw mathematical shapes on the ground with chalk. Fill the outlines with conkers. Count the conkers in each shape.
- Draw several chalk lines on the ground. Place conkers along the lines. Compare the quantities you have used.
- Make a trail of conkers for others to follow.
- Hide the quantity of conkers required to fill a container. Tell the children to find the conkers to fill it up again.
- Use the conkers for threading activities. Compare the difference between the longest and the shortest string of conkers.

Sorting Shapes

Learning objective: to recognise the two-dimensional shapes occurring in patterns found outdoors
Resources: templates (approximately 8cm × 8cm) of the two-dimensional shapes of a square, a triangle, a circle and a rectangle, some card, a marker pen, scissors

Use the templates to make a set of shapes for each child. Show the shapes to the children. Ask the children to name the shapes they know. Reinforce the children's knowledge of the shapes by asking them to name each shape in turn. Explain to the children that they are going to go outside to look for the shapes they have been talking about. Give each child a set of the shapes you made in advance. Challenge them to search around the outdoor area to find a shape to match it. Ask the children to point out the shapes they find. Repeat the activity until each child has had the opportunity to find a square, a triangle, a circle and a rectangle.

QUESTIONS TO ASK

Can you name the shapes you found in the outdoor play space? Can you match them to the set of shapes you have with you? Can you describe the difference between a square and a rectangle? What shape did you see most often? Did you find any patterns outdoors which use the same shapes over and over again?

FOR YOUNGER/OLDER CHILDREN

Ask an adult to accompany the younger children on a shape-spotting walk around the grounds. Point out and name the shapes you see. Encourage the children to do the same. Give older children an assortment of shapes. Send them off on their own to match up the shapes with anything they can find outside. Encourage older children to make comparisons and to articulate their discoveries using mathematical language.

FOLLOW-UP ACTIVITIES

- Search for patterns in brickwork, on walls, fences and doors. Ask the children to draw the patterns they see.
- Go on an outdoor walk to search for other mathematical connections. Look out for straight lines, curves, symmetrical or asymmetrical patterns.
- Draw large circles, triangles, squares and rectangles on the ground with chalk. Hold up a triangle card as a cue to the children to stand on the triangle shapes. Repeat the activity several times revealing different-shaped cue cards.

'What's the Time, Big Bad Wolf?'

Learning objective: to play an action game to develop an understanding of the sequence of time
Resources: some chalk, a picture of a wolf, a large, safe outdoor play space

Draw a chalk line on the ground in the outdoor play space to represent the wolf's home. Draw another chalk line 20 metres from the first line. Show the children the picture of the wolf. Explain that the wolf is hungry. Stand on the first line with your back to the children pretending to be the hungry wolf. Invite the children to stand behind the other line. The children taunt the wolf by chanting, 'what's the time, Mr Wolf?' When the wolf replies 'two o'clock', the children move two steps forward. When the wolf replies 'three o'clock', they take three steps forward, and so on. The wolf turns around to try to catch the children moving towards him. Anyone caught moving goes back to the base line to start again. The chanting continues until the wolf calls out 'dinner time'. He then chases the children back to the line, hopefully catching one of them for his dinner. The children are out when they are touched by the wolf. The last child caught becomes the wolf. Any child who creeps up to the wolf's back before 'dinner time' also becomes 'Mr Wolf'.

QUESTIONS TO ASK

Do you know any stories about a hungry wolf? What time do you get up in the morning? What time do you have your dinner? What time do you go to bed? What do you do when you feel hungry?

FOR YOUNGER/OLDER CHILDREN

An adult could be Mr Wolf every time the game is played. Use only the commands 'one o'clock' and 'two o'clock' and 'dinner time'. Walk with the younger children as they take footsteps towards the wolf. With older children increase the difficulty of the game by using all the hourly times to represent a different activity in the wolf's daily life cycle. For example, eight o'clock could be bedtime, the cue for the children to pretend to sleep.

FOLLOW-UP ACTIVITIES

- Count the number of footsteps it takes to reach certain destinations.
- Play 'Grandma's Footsteps'. Children creep up behind an adult while her back is turned. When she turns round and looks, they must stop. The child to touch her back becomes Grandma.
- Re-enact some of the story lines of traditional wolf stories such as 'Little Red Riding Hood' and 'The Three Little Pigs'.
- Use photographs to record the sequence of events in the children's day.

Skeletons in the Shed

Learning objective: to encourage an understanding of addition and subtraction by making a whole flowerpot man from separate parts
Resources: 1 flowerpot (90mm/3.5in), 10 cardboard or plastic tubes (11cm), 2 pieces of string (130cm and 60cm long) for each child, a large cloth and some marker pens

Put the flowerpots, tubes and string in a pile on the cloth outside. Show the children a sample skeleton. Draw a face on the flowerpot. Make a hole on both sides of the cardboard tube representing the shoulders. Secure the longest piece of string to another tube and thread it through three tubes, into the holes made in the shoulder piece, up through the flowerpot head. Tie to make a loop. Thread the string back down through the tubes representing the shoulders and body, into two more tubes to make the other leg. Secure the string. Take the short length of string, using the remaining tubes to make the arms. Secure the string at both ends. Show the children a sample of a skeleton. Explain about bones and name the body parts; the head, the shoulders, the two arms and two legs. Tell the children the pile of tubes and flowerpots represent the head and bones of the body. Let them choose one flowerpot and ten tubes to make the skeleton. Count the parts as you demonstrate the activity, adding or subtracting the tubes one at a time. Explain that the number of bones used to make the skeleton remains the same whether they are piled up together or spaced apart, even though they look different.

QUESTIONS TO ASK

How many bones do you need to make the skeleton? Which looks the biggest, the pile of bones or the whole skeleton? Can you feel your own bones through your skin? What do they feel like?

FOR YOUNGER/OLDER CHILDREN

With younger children make a simple model using six tubes instead of ten. Name and count the bones. Match the skeleton's bones to the corresponding parts of their own body. With older children complete the activity as a team game. Tell them to run, one at a time, to collect a tube or flowerpot to take back to make up the whole skeleton. Decorate the model to make it look more realistic.

FOLLOW-UP ACTIVITIES

- Make life-sized or more detailed skeletons by using large flowerpots and pieces of drainpipes and make them elbows and knees or hands and feet.
- Use the characters as puppets to dramatise scary stories.
- Make up a movement activity. Invite the children to lie on the floor like a pile of bones. The skeleton of the flowerpot man gradually comes to life as each bone is put back into place. Dance around, pretending to be skeletons.
- Learn the song 'Dem Bones'.
- Make a dark den in the garden with an old blanket. Tell scary stories such as 'Funny Bones' to each other using the skeletons as props.

Targets of Ten

Learning objective: to encourage counting up to ten by playing an outdoor target game
Resources: a large bucket, ten beanbags and chalk

Place the bucket in a space in the outdoor area. Draw a chalk circle around the bucket, approximately 4 metres in diameter. Hide the beanbags all around the area you are going to use to play the game. Challenge the children to find the beanbags. Count the number of beanbags each child finds. Invite the children to stand on the outer edge of the circle to throw the beanbags into the bucket. Count the number of beanbags that each child throws into the bucket. The child who throws the most beanbags into the bucket hides them all around the outdoor play space ready to restart the game. Repeat the game several times to give all children the opportunity to hide and count the beanbags.

QUESTIONS TO ASK

Can you find all the beanbags? How many beanbags can you find? Can you count the number of beanbags in the bucket? Can you throw the beanbags underarm? Can you throw them overarm? Can you throw the beanbags with one hand? Can you throw the beanbags with two hands?

FOR YOUNGER/OLDER CHILDREN

With younger children match the number of beanbags you hide to the counting ability of the children involved. Count the beanbags with the children as they place them in the bucket. Increase the degree of difficulty for older children. Use a smaller bucket. Increase the distance between the chalk line and the bucket. Give older children a set amount of time to throw all the beanbags back into the bucket.

FOLLOW-UP ACTIVITIES

- Try hiding and throwing different objects such as quoits, skittles, batons and balls.
- Throw the beanbags into a hole in a piece of card decorated as a person with an open mouth.
- Record scores by marking a line on a piece of paper each time the child gets a beanbag into the bucket.
- Hide ten different objects around the ground. Let the children take it in turns to find and count the ten objects they find.
- Learn the song 'Ten Green Bottles'. Fill ten small plastic bottles with water coloured green. Play skittles by knocking the bottles down with the beanbags.

Finding Families

Learning objective: to grade objects found in the garden into small, medium and large
Resources: three cardboard boxes, three sheets of paper, some butterfly clips, scissors, glue and a marker pen

Fix the boxes together with the butterfly clips to make a house or block of flats to house the objects the children are to find. Cut the paper to fit inside each box. Write the headings 'small', 'medium' and 'large' separately on the three sheets of paper. Glue the paper as carpets inside the boxes. There is now a room for large objects, a room for medium objects and a room for small objects. Explain to the children that they are going outdoors to look for families of objects. These should be objects that are the same apart from size, such as a large, a medium and a small stone. Explain to the children that there is a room in the house for all the small objects, another room for all the medium-sized objects and a third room for all the large objects. Invite the children to sort the objects they collect by putting them into the rooms in the house according to their size. Challenge the children to find and sort at least three sets of objects. They could find three different-sized stones, leaves or twigs. Compare the sizes of the objects to reinforce the idea of grading according to size.

QUESTIONS TO ASK

Can you point to all the small objects? Can you show me all the medium objects? Where are all the large objects? Why are the objects different? Can you see any objects of the same family? Can you count all the small objects? Can you count all the medium objects and all the large objects? Do you know any stories about small, middle-sized and large animals?

For younger children use two boxes and grade objects into big and little. Point out similarities and differences. For older children increase the number of objects the children need to find. Encourage them to find their own way of recording the activity, or to take the lead in hiding objects around the ground.

FOLLOW-UP ACTIVITIES

- Find sets of objects which are exactly the same size. Grade them according to size.
- Read traditional stories about graded sizes, such as 'Goldilocks and the Three Bears' and 'The Three Billy Goats Gruff'.
- Group the children according to height. Who is the tallest? Which children are the same height? Who is the shortest?
- Display collections of 'families' such as Russian dolls.
- Walk around the outdoor area. Look for objects to grade according to size, such as flowerpots, trees, flowers or chimney pots.

Fill It Up

Learning objective: to discover how many objects can be crammed into an empty tube
Resources: 6 small empty, identical containers with lids; a variety of tiny outdoor objects such as seeds, stones, leaves; a sheet of writing paper, a marker pen

Fill one of the tubes with as many tiny outdoor objects as possible. Spread the articles out on a piece of paper. Demonstrate how they all fit into the empty sweet tube. Prepare a list of the children's names. Invite the children to go outdoors. Explain that they are going outside on a scavenger hunt to look for tiny outdoor objects to fill up the empty sweet tube. Warn the children not to put any little objects in their mouth. Explain the concept of a scavenger hunt. Explain the boundaries and give the children a set time of approximately 15 minutes to look for things to put in their empty tubes. When the time is up, count the objects in each child's tube to see who has collected the most. After the count, challenge the children to put the objects back into their tubes. Discuss the activity with the children, focusing on quantity and size. Before the hunt begins, ask the children to make estimates about how many things they think will fit into the tubes. Record each child's estimate on a piece of paper. Compare the estimates with the final scores.

QUESTIONS TO ASK

What was in the tube before? What size objects will fit into the empty tube? Where did you find the small objects that fit into your tube? Can you squeeze any more objects into the tube? Can you guess how many objects there are in your tube? Can you count them?

FOR YOUNGER/OLDER CHILDREN

Hunt for a specified number of objects within the younger children's counting ability. For example, challenge the children to find five small objects to put into their tube. Older children can work together in pairs to fill the tubes. They can count and record the number of objects they have fitted into the tube. They can find creative ways to display the small objects or make a collage with them.

FOLLOW-UP ACTIVITIES

- Go on a scavenger hunt to look for specific things. Look for green objects, different kinds of leaves or different types of stones.
- Hide objects around the outdoor area. Invite the children to search for the objects you have hidden.
- Play treasure hunts. Choose ten items to be the treasure. Allow children to take it in turns to hide and hunt for the treasure around the outdoor play space.
- Play a game of hide and seek.

Captain's Calling

Learning objective: to play a nautical game using mathematical language
Resources: some pictures illustrating sailors, ships and nautical scenes, chalk, a large outdoor space

Set the scene by showing the children pictures of ships and sailors. Tell the children that they are going to play a game called 'Captain's Calling'. Chalk a large boat shape on the ground to represent the deck of a ship. Explain that a captain is in charge of the ship. The captain gives orders to the crew, who always do exactly what he tells them to do. Explain that the deck shape you have marked out on the ground is a ship in the game. Invite the children to stand on the deck, which is inside the outline of the ship you have marked out in chalk. The adult pretends to be the ship's captain. The children pretend to be the crew. The captain calls out commands to keep the sailors in order as the ship sails upon the sea. On the cue 'Captain's coming' the sailors stand to attention, saluting the captain. The captain then gives his orders to the crew. He commands them to take two steps to the left and so on. Use five directional commands according to the children's knowledge and ability. For example, the captain could call out, 'forwards', 'backwards', 'to the left', 'to the right', 'turn round in circles'. Make up actions to match the orders called out by the captain. Before the game starts, help the children to practise responding to the commands with the corresponding actions until they grasp the idea of the game. Remind the children to use the whole space and not to touch each other or move outside the boundary lines of the ship. Invite the children to move according to the instructions the captain calls out. Anyone who gets the actions wrong or who responds too slowly is called out to sit on the sidelines. The game is over when every child has been called out.

QUESTIONS TO ASK

Can you hold up your left hand? Can you hold up your right hand? How do you walk backwards? Can you turn around on the same spot? Do you know any songs about sailors or ships? Have you ever seen a big ship? Have you ever been on a boat?

FOR YOUNGER CHILDREN

For younger children reduce the number of commands to three and keep them simple. For older children increase the commands in number and difficulty. Call out commands in quick succession to catch the children out. Encourage them to make up their own commands and take it in turns to be the captain.

FOLLOW-UP ACTIVITIES

- Repeat the game using commands and actions associated with life at sea, such as 'person overboard', 'climb the rigging', 'walk the plank', 'hoist the flag', 'scrub the decks', 'as the crow flies'.
- Use comical commands such as 'jelly wobble', 'seasick sailor', 'chicken tonight'.
- Use scary commands such as 'storm brewing', 'shipwreck', 'shark aboard' and 'pirates landed'.
- Learn songs about the sea, for example 'I Like to Sail in My Big Blue Boat', 'The Big Ship Sails', 'Row, Row, Row Your Boat', 'Bobby Shaftoe'.

Knowledge and understanding of the world

The outdoor activities in this section of the book will encourage the development of children's understanding of their environment and of other people, and the skills necessary for future work in history, geography, science and technology are introduced. The school grounds provide the perfect opportunity for children to have first-hand experience of wildlife, and studies of the natural environment can be linked to all areas of the curriculum. Some wildlife will be present in all outside spaces, whether you have a concrete jungle or a leafy green desert.

If you have trees in your grounds, try this activity as a starting point to gain the children's interest and to determine what ecological relationships are present in your outside space.

Figure 9.6 Looking at minibeasts

What Lives in a Place Like This?

Resources: a large white sheet, collecting trays, recording materials

Place a large sheet under a tree. Carefully shake the lower branches of the tree until there is a collection of leaves, flowers, seed pods, fruits and insects on the sheet. Gather up the sheet and empty the contents into a collecting tray. Working in small groups, ask the children to sort the items into different categories and to identify any creatures. What are the relationships between the different organisms, and between the organisms and the tree? What is missing? What creatures, e.g. mammals, birds, creatures in the wood, are required to complete the web? Count the frequency of different creatures and repeat for different trees to compare the communities supported by different trees.

Wildlife Treasure Hunt

Resources: collecting baskets, laminated pictures of 'treasure' to find

Get the children to work in pairs and walk around the outdoor area on a treasure hunt, collecting what they find in their basket. Challenge them to find things in a chosen category such as:

- Size – find a twig as small as your finger, a stick as long as your arm/leg etc.
- Numbers – find leaves with 1/2/3/4/5/6/7 points
- Colours – find an example of all the colours in the rainbow, or try to match the colours of their clothing
- Alphabet – find something beginning with each letter of the alphabet
- Shapes – find an example of a circle, square, triangle, rectangle, oval, diamond, star and spiral.

Remind them not to pick any living plants and to handle living creatures with care.

FOR YOUNGER CHILDREN

Provide younger children with laminated pictures of the creatures/artefacts they are looking for.

Minibeast Habitats

It is very easy to make habitats for minibeasts to measure the biodiversity of your grounds.
Resources: potatoes and other vegetables/fruit, magnifying glasses, collecting trays and recording materials

Hollow out half a potato with a teaspoon, making a hole at each end. Lay the potato flat on the ground so that the entrance is level with the surface. Experiment by leaving the potato in different places to see how the wildlife diversity differs in different places and at different times of day. Use different fruits and vegetables to find out how they affect the creatures that decide to live in them.

OLDER CHILDREN

Older children could be encouraged to examine the creatures using microscopes or magnifying glasses and classify them into different types by looking at numbers of legs, presence/absence of wings or antennae.

FOLLOW-UP

Draw/paint the creatures and then return them to where they were found.
Create a display of the artwork made explaining where each creature was found.

Puddle Play

Learning objective: to respond to the rhyme 'Doctor Foster' to increase the children's knowledge and understanding of how the rain creates puddles.
Resources: wet weather clothing, Wellington boots, and an outdoor play area after it has rained. A copy of the rhyme 'Doctor Foster went to Gloucester'.

Learn the rhyme 'Doctor Foster'. Get dressed in outdoor clothing and Wellington boots. Go outdoors and search for some puddles. Sing the rhyme with the children as you are walking outdoors. When you come to a suitable puddle encourage the children to paddle carefully until they are standing in the middle. Ask the children why Doctor Foster stepped in the puddle. Ask them why he never went to Gloucester again. Ask the children to look for puddles in the garden, allowing them plenty of time to explore and experiment. They could jump in puddles or over them. They could wade through puddles on tiptoe. They could splash through them with heavy footsteps. Talk about the weather and where the puddles have come from and why they are in the places they are in. Talk about what it feels like to be wet.

QUESTIONS TO ASK

Where do puddles come from? Why do you think there are puddles left on the ground after it has rained? Why did Doctor Foster step in a puddle? How did he feel when the water came up to his middle? What happens when you splash in the puddles? What happens to puddles when the sun comes out?

FOR YOUNGER/OLDER CHILDREN

Take younger children out for a walk in the rain to watch it falling and making puddles.
Challenge older children to jump over large puddles. Compare the amount of water in different-sized puddles.

FOLLOW-UP ACTIVITIES

- Make footprints after walking through puddles.
- Push wheeled toys through puddles to make tracks.
- Look at reflections in puddles.
- Find small objects in the outdoor play space to sink or float in the puddle.
- Make a paper boat to sail in the puddle.

Bottle Banks

Resources: for each child, you need 1 large plastic bottle, scissors, 40cm lengths of string, a label and a permanent marker pen

Place all materials outdoors on a flat surface. Begin by talking to children about the need to save rainwater. Give each child a plastic bottle and a marker pen. Explain that you are going to make a rain gauge to collect and measure the amount of rain that falls during a period of one week. (Choose a time when there is likely to be some rain.) Help the children to make their own rain gauges. Ask an adult to cut off the top of the plastic bottle and cover sharp edges with masking tape. Invert it back into place to make a funnel through which the rain can collect and drip into the bottle. Use strong adhesive tape to attach the funnel to the bottle. Tape a length of string onto either side of the bottle to make a handle. Write each child's name on a sticky label and stick it to their bottle. Mark lines the width of thumb spaces from the bottom of the bottle to its neck. Hang the bottles up outdoors, either from a tree or on a fence. Go outside regularly to check how much rain has collected in each bottle.

QUESTIONS TO ASK

Where does the rain come from? How much rain will collect in the bottle during the time between sessions? How can the water be measured? How long will it take to fill the bottle up to the top? What can you do with the water? Are there any other ways you can save water?

FOR YOUNGER/OLDER CHILDREN

Younger children will be fascinated by watching rainwater collecting in the bottles as it falls.
    Let the older children make their own rain gauge. Each child can write a name label to go on their bottle. They can check the amount of rainfall at a set time each day and record their findings.

FOLLOW-UP ACTIVITIES

- Use the water collected in a safe, useful way, perhaps to water plants. Warn the children not to drink it.
- Compare the levels of rainfall collected in different-sized bottles.
- Make a tally chart of how much rain falls in the week by making thumbprints on a piece of paper to correspond to the thumb measures marked on the bottles.

Playful Shadows

Learning objective: to develop an awareness of the features of living things by exploring shadows
Resources: a piece of chalk for each child

Explain to the children the way the sun creates shadows on a sunny day. Inform the children that, on a sunny day, shadows out of doors are different lengths at different times of the day because of the way the sun moves across the sky. Explain to the children that shadows touch them where they touch the ground, which is usually at their feet. Explain that shadows copy everything that they do. When the sun is high in the sky, shadows are short. When the sun is low in the sky, shadows are long. Invite the children to go outside with you on a sunny day. Point out some of the shadows on the ground. Ask the children to make their own shadows by standing in a sunny spot. Indicate to them to stand in a space away from each other. Ask them to stand still so that they can identify their own shadow. Ask the children to move around the outdoor space watching their shadow as it follows them. Challenge the children to find ways of making sure they can retain their whole shadow so that it is easily recognisable. Give them time to experiment. Encourage them to discover ways of moving so that the shadow seems to grow taller or smaller, so that it disappears altogether. Take it in turns to play stepping on each other's shadows.

QUESTIONS TO ASK

How many shadows can you see in the outdoor space around you? When the sun goes in, what will happen to the shadows? Can you make your shadow move? If you jump into the air, what happens to your shadow? Can you lose your shadow?

FOR YOUNGER/OLDER CHILDREN

Walk around the outdoor play space looking for shadows. Point out the way the children's shadows move with them as they walk. Ask younger children to touch their shadow.

Ask older children to make different-shaped shadows by moving their bodies in different ways. Challenge them to make their shadow join them at different parts of their body other than their feet.

FOLLOW-UP ACTIVITIES

- Play shadow games. Chase a friend around the outdoor play space. Shout 'stop', stand still and try to touch your friend's shadow with your foot. If you succeed, swap roles and repeat the chase as before.
- Make a sundial by standing a pencil on top of a cotton reel. Glue the cotton reel to a piece of white paper. Leave the sundial outdoors on a sunny day and mark where the shadow falls at hourly intervals.
- Show the children how to make animal shadows with their hands. Try to make a butterfly, a cat, a crocodile, a rabbit or a fox.

A Bowlful of Bubbles

Learning objective: to explore how bubbles are made and how they float in the air
Resources: a large bowl, a jug of water, a tablespoon, 4 tablespoons of washing-up liquid, 12 tablespoons of water, a few drops of glycerine and a large drinking straw for each child taking part.

As this is a messy activity, ensure all children wear aprons. Place some plastic sheeting or spread out newspaper on the ground before you start. Encourage the children to talk about the materials they are going to use. Allow the children to handle them carefully for a few moments, encouraging discussion.

Explain that you are going to make a bubble mixture. Help the children to measure out four table-spoonfuls of washing-up liquid. Put the liquid into the bowl. Help the children to pour 12 tablespoons of water into the bowl. Pour three or four drops of glycerine into the soapy mixture. Give the children a straw each. Encourage them to mix the liquids together with the straws. Ask the children to use the straws to blow bubbles. Ensure that the children do not try to drink the liquid. Encourage them to continue blowing until they have made a bowlful of bubbles. Ask the children to find ways of making the bubbles float in the air, perhaps by scooping up handfuls and flicking or shaking them off into the air.

QUESTIONS TO ASK

Ask the children to touch the different liquids as they mix them. How do they feel? Which ones do they like to touch? What happens to the mixture when they blow air into it? What happens to the bubbles when they flick them into the air? What happens when a bubble bursts? What happens when the bubble bumps into an object or touches the ground?

FOR YOUNGER/OLDER CHILDREN

Give younger children their own pot of bubbles with a bubble blower and show them how to blow bubbles.

Give older children the materials and ask them to experiment with them until they make their own bubble liquid. Challenge them to cover the whole surface area being used with a mound of bubbles.

FOLLOW-UP ACTIVITIES

- Buy some conventional bubble mixture and a range of bubble blowers to create different-sized bubbles.
- Blow bubbles using your fingers to form a circle.
- Use other things to create bubbles such as sponges, whisks and brushes.
- Spray a deep layer of shaving foam into the bowl. Encourage children to explore the medium and try to make the foam float in the air by blowing it off their fingers.
- Try to make feathers or balloons float in the air by blowing them.

Patchwork Plot

Growing a small garden in your outdoor space should be perfectly possible. This simple activity aims to give your school a small plot with as many different plants as possible.

Learning objective: to develop an awareness of the passage of time through creating a garden patch

Resources: plans of your grounds and a patch of ground in the outdoor play space which can be dug up to create a small garden, pictures of gardens, tape measures, rulers, wood, hammer, some nails and string, small gardening tools, plants, seeds, a watering can and some water

Go outside and search for a suitable small plot of land to create a garden patch. If there is no suit-able ground in the outdoor play space, put some soil in a deep tray or use a commercial growbag for this activity.

Look at the pictures of gardens and discuss them. Decide where would be the best place to put the garden. A sunny position is best. Explain that they are going to create their own garden. It could be a vegetable patch, a flower garden, a mixture of both, a fragrant garden of perfumed flowers or a wild area to attract the butterflies and bugs. Visit a garden centre or ask parents to donate a plant for the plot from their own garden. Decide what kinds of plants you might like. Choose fast-growing varieties of plants such as lettuce or radish to avoid disappointment. You could also try strawberries, marigolds, herbs, mini sweetcorn, mini cauliflower or French beans. Prepare the plants in advance, either by growing them from seed beforehand or by buying them. Measure a plot that is 120cm × 120cm, marking the corners with pegs. Make the edges of your plot with old wood (120cm × 10cm × 3cm). Dig over the area with a fork and rake it flat. Remove any large stones. Subdivide the large square into 16 smaller squares by marking them out with stones or by banging nails into the wooden edging every 30cm, tie string to the nails and use the string to divide the plot.

Give the children some small garden tools and ask them to make holes for the plants. Put the plants into the holes, cover the roots with soil and water them. Watch the plants as they grow. Encourage the children to care for the garden patch throughout the year. Observe the changes throughout the seasons and watch the wildlife visiting or hiding in the patch.

QUESTIONS TO ASK

What would you like to grow in the garden patch? What do you need to do to help the plants grow? What happens to the plants when they grow? What happens when the plants have finished growing? How do you grow? What do you need to help you grow?

FOR YOUNGER/OLDER CHILDREN

Plant seeds in pots. Encourage the children to water the plants and watch them grow.
Give older children sole responsibility for looking after their own patch of garden.

FOLLOW-UP ACTIVITIES

- Grow tomato plants in a growbag outside. Harvest the tomatoes and eat them when they are ready.
- Take children to visit different types of gardens.
- Take children to a garden centre to buy their own seeds or plants.

Blowing in the Wind

Learning objective: to develop an understanding of how the wind blows
Resources: a piece of lightweight material such as nylon or parachute material, a pipe cleaner, a straw, scissors, a conventional windsock or a picture of a windsock

Take all the materials outdoors and place on a groundsheet. Tie the example of a windsock in a suitable place to catch the wind, such as in a tree or on the fence. Go outside with the children. Show them pictures of windsocks and discuss them. Explain that the children are going to make their own windsocks. Demonstrate step by step how to make the windsock. Encourage the children to try to make their own versions of the windsock. Cut a piece of material the same length as the pipe cleaner and cut small holes 1 centimetre apart along the top edge. Thread the pipe cleaner through the holes and mould it into a ring shape. Twist the end of the pipe cleaner together. Using a second pipe cleaner, fix the sock onto a place where it will catch the wind. Observe what happens as it blows in the wind.

QUESTIONS TO ASK

Which way is the wind blowing? What happens to the windsock when the wind changes direction? Look around you; what else can you see blowing in the wind? Have you ever seen a weather vane? What is it for?

Hang up a windsock outdoors and take the children outside to watch it blowing in the wind. Give the children a windmill to play with outdoors. Older children could work together in pairs or small groups to design and make their own windsocks, experimenting with a variety of materials to come up with the most efficient design.

FOLLOW-UP ACTIVITIES

- Make a wind flower in the same way as you would make a windmill by curving the edges of the card when you cut it into shape.
- Go outdoors to watch the clouds blowing across the sky.
- Watch washing blowing on a washing line.

Nature Search

Learning objective: to observe the creatures living in the outdoor environment
Resources: natural features such as plants, trees, bushes, branches or logs lying around, stones to overturn etc., a plastic container and a magnifying glass for each child taking part in the activity

Before starting the search, remind the children of all safety issues, boundaries and ground rules.

Go outdoors with the children, talking to them as you walk about safety issues and caring for all the little creatures they see in the outdoor environment. Show them how to handle the little creatures they find, reminding them that all living things must be treated with care. Return the insects to their homes when they have finished observing them. Allow the children to investigate the creatures they find by looking at them through the magnifying glass. Look out for spiders in dark corners, woodlice along walls and near doors, slugs and snails behind flowerpots, ladybirds and caterpillars, butterflies and moths among the leaves of trees and bushes. Ask the children to describe the insects they find and name them if they can.

QUESTIONS TO ASK

What insects live in the outdoors? Where will you look to find minibeasts? How many legs does a spider have? How many legs can you see on the insects you find? Where will you find woodlice? When are you most likely to see slugs and snails?

FOR YOUNGER/OLDER CHILDREN

Take younger children on a walk outdoors to look for minibeasts, talking about the way we need to care for the insects they see. Point out the creatures and name them to the children as you walk along. Encourage older children to classify the insects they find by comparing them with pictures in reference books. Encourage older children to record their observations by drawing the insects and spiders they find (see Figure 9.7).

FOLLOW-UP ACTIVITIES

- Make a wormery by collecting some worms and placing them in a plastic container with some damp compost. Place some leaves on top and put the container in a safe place to watch.
- Draw pictures of the insects found outdoors.
- Create a mini stone pile; leave undisturbed for a few weeks to attract insects.
- Count the number of butterflies you see outdoors on a summer's day.

Figure 9.7 Finding spiders

Magic Water Painting

Learning objective: to observe and begin to understand what happens when water covering a surface dries up

Resources: an outdoor pavement or wall space, water in plastic buckets, decorating brushes and waterproof aprons

This is a messy, outdoor activity so the children will need to wear protective aprons. Give each child a bucket full of water and a large decorating brush. Indicate the wall or ground space on which they can paint with the water. Explain to the children that they are going to paint pictures or patterns on the wall or ground. When they have finished, leave the pictures and spend some time discussing what they have been doing, giving them the opportunity to predict what they think might be happening to their pictures while they are talking. Return to the pictures. As if by magic the water marks will have dried up and the pictures will have disappeared. Explain that the water marks will dry up on a sunny day but that they do not really disappear but turn into drops, too small to see, which rise up into the air to make clouds.

QUESTIONS TO ASK

Ask the children to describe what has happened to the water marks. Why do you think they have dried up? What would happen if was raining? What would happen to the picture on a hot, sunny day? Where does the water go?

FOR YOUNGER/OLDER CHILDREN

Younger children could paint over whole paving slabs or bricks. Point out the difference between wet and dry patches in the garden. Help them to describe the difference between wet and dry. Encourage older children to observe their water paintings at regular intervals. Give them the opportunity to record what is happening. Extend their discussions so that they begin to understand the concept of evaporation.

FOLLOW-UP ACTIVITIES

* Use a variety of brushes; compare the time it takes for broad brushstrokes to dry as opposed to fine ones.
* Paint different-sized areas of wall or ground space with water; compare drying times.
* Make water pictures in shady patches, in sunny places, on the ground, on the wall. Compare drying times.

Physical development

Be active – get fit and healthy by getting outside more. The outdoors is the perfect place for children to play and the aim is to use the outside space to get them as active as possible through play and games which will get their bodies working and burn off some energy at the same time as lifting their spirits by letting them have fun. All the following outdoor activities and action games will help children to develop physical skills and improve their gross and fine motor skills as they get used to using their bodies and handling different tools, materials and equipment.

Heffalump

Learning objective: to develop imagination and increase mobility by playing an action game
Resources: a copy of the book *Winnie-the-Pooh* by A.A. Milne, a safe outdoor play space and some white chalk

Mark two chalk lines approximately 20 metres apart. Talk to the children about the character Heffalump in *Winnie-the-Pooh*. Read them the extract where Pooh is scared when he looks in the mirror and sees another Pooh, dreaming that there is a Heffalump under his bed. Invite the children to go outside to where you have chalked the lines for the game. Explain that Heffalump is an enjoyable action game. One child is chosen to be the 'Heffalump' and stands behind one of the chalk lines with his back to the others. Heffalump is dreaming about all the clever actions he can do. He talks in his sleep, calling out an action such as 'hopping'. The children standing on the other chalk line must start to hop around the space being used for the game. When he calls out another action such as 'jumping', the children change actions from hopping to jumping. Different actions are called out until Heffalump wakes up. He yawns loudly and all the children 'freeze'. Then Heffalump calls out, 'I'm hungry. I want a bun.' On the word 'bun' he chases the children, thinking they have something for him to eat. The first child to be caught takes on the role of Heffalump.

QUESTIONS TO ASK

What actions can you do? Can you jump with two feet together? Can you hop on one leg? Can you hop on the other leg? Can you skip? Can you run with little tiny steps? Can you walk with long strides? What do you think Heffalump would like to eat for his dinner? Do elephants really like buns? Have you ever seen a real, live elephant? Can you imitate an elephant walk?

FOR YOUNGER/OLDER CHILDREN

Play the game with an adult taking on the role of Heffalump. Choose actions within the capabilities of young children, perhaps having only three choices of actions such as walk, jump and run. Increase the difficulty of the actions for older children to carry out. They could do bunny hops, jump high, walk with straight legs or walk keeping their knees together and so on.

FOLLOW-UP ACTIVITIES

* Play other action games such as 'Tag', 'Off-ground Touch' and 'Bulldog'.
* Create a dance around the elephant's dream, using all the actions he would like to be able to do.
* Play the game 'The Wolf and the Sheep'. Put some hoops on the ground. One child is the wolf and the others are the sheep. The wolf says, 'I am a wolf and I live here. I will eat you if you come too near.' Fill the gap with an action such as hop or skip. The children hop all around the outdoor space apart from in the hoops. The wolf calls out different varieties of food until he calls 'lamb chops', which is the cue to run to a hoop. An adult gradually takes away the hoops and any child left outside a hoop is out. The last child in becomes the wolf.

Footprints All Around

Learning objective: to encourage increasing control and confidence by making and following footprints
Resources: a mud patch, a jug of water, Wellington boots or similar for each child taking part in the activity and an outdoor brush

Find a patch of mud or create one by pouring water onto a patch of earth. Ask the children to put on their Wellington boots. Go outside to the mud patch. Talk to the children about the way animals leave trails of muddy footprints. Invite the children to step into the muddy patch one at a time. Ask each child to make a trail of footprints. Encourage the children to follow each other's trails by stepping carefully on top of each footprint already made. Discuss the different footprints, comparing patterns and size. Ask the children to look at the patterns on the bottoms of each other's boots. Challenge them to match the footprints to the right boots. Make long trails, straight trails, trails with many footprints, trails with spaced-out footprints and so on. When the children have finished, pour some water onto the footprints and brush all the mud away, leaving the pavement area clean. Ensure that the children wash their hands after touching mud.

QUESTIONS TO ASK

How can you tell which animal has visited the outdoor play space? How many clear footprints can you make after standing in the muddy patch? How can you make different patterns with your footprints? How can you find out who or what made the footprints?

FOR YOUNGER/OLDER CHILDREN

Take only two children out at a time to make muddy footprints. Ask an adult to make footprints for the children to follow. Challenge older children to discover ways of disguising their footprints. Encourage them to track each other around the outdoor play space by searching for evidence of these secret trails.

FOLLOW-UP ACTIVITIES

* Look for evidence of animal footprints around the outdoor play area. Use reference books to identify them.

Fruit Shop

Learning objective: to develop physical control and awareness of space whilst encouraging children to adopt a healthy lifestyle through this action game of visiting a fruit shop
Resources: a large outdoor play space, some chalk, an apple, a banana and another piece of fruit depending on the season, for example a pear or star fruit

Buy some fruit to use as a stimulus for the activity. Draw a circle large enough to contain up to eight children in the middle of the outdoor play space where the game is taking place. Give the children the opportunity to handle and talk about the fruit. Discuss the shapes, talking about the roundness of the apple, the long, curved banana shape and the odd-shaped pear.

Take the children to a suitable outdoor space to play an action game. Define the boundaries and point out safety issues. Think up appropriate movements or shapes to represent each piece of fruit you use to play the game. An apple could be a small, tucked shape, a banana could be a long, stretched shape, a star fruit could be a wide body shape, and a pear could be a bunny hop and so on. The circle chalked in the middle of the space represents the fruit bowl. Explain to the children that they are going to be moving around the space quickly and that they need to listen to the commands called out by the adult in order to play the game. Practise the actions used to represent the different fruits the adult calls out. When the game begins, the children are running around the outdoor space as if on their way to the fruit shop to buy some fruit. The adult calls out the name of a fruit. For example, on the cue 'apple', the children run to the 'fruit bowl' and curl up in a ball as if they are an apple. The last child to respond is out and becomes the piece of fruit eaten by the adult. The children run off to the fruit shop again. When the word 'banana' is called out, the children lie in the fruit bowl in a long, thin banana shape. On hearing the word 'pear' the children have to stop running and go to the fruit bowl to do bunny hops. The game continues until all the fruit has been eaten.

QUESTIONS TO ASK

What kind of fruit do you like to eat? What shape does the fruit look like? Can you make a shape with your body that looks like a piece of fruit? Where do you buy fruit? Where do you put the fruit you buy when you get back home? Why do you eat fruit?

FOR YOUNGER/OLDER CHILDREN

Reduce the number of commands for younger children. Ask them to run to the fruit shop to buy just apples or bananas. Younger children can make the shape you call out on the spot where they stop running. Increase the difficulty of the game by increasing the number of 'fruit' actions the children need to remember. Use five varieties of fruit as cues for action. Call out different fruits in quick succession to encourage older children to respond quickly.

FOLLOW-UP ACTIVITIES

- Cut the fruit into halves and quarters to share as refreshments after the game.
- Take the children to a fruit shop to buy some fruit.
- Slice the fruit and use to make prints with paint.
- Buy exotic fruit from different countries. Choose pineapple, mango, passion fruit and kiwi to extend children's knowledge and vocabulary.
- Use the fruit to feel, touch, smell, dissect and taste.

Clear the Decks

Learning objective: to develop manipulative skills and encourage an awareness of space and direction by playing this collection game
Resources: a safe outdoor space, a large collection of small outdoor objects such as quoits, balls, skittles, beanbags, spades and so on (enough for each child to collect at least 10 items)

Collect together the equipment needed to play this game. Place the items at random all around the outdoor play space. Take the children outdoors. Discuss the boundaries and safety issues before the game starts by reminding the children where they can go and what they can do. Point out all the items scattered around the ground. Explain that the children are going to try to collect them all together to clear the decks. The child who manages to collect the most items has a turn at scattering them all around the outdoor play area in order for the game to start again. Invite each child to choose a base where they can safely store their items until they count them at the end of the game. Ensure all the children are aware of each other's home base so that there is no confusion about which items they pick up. Repeat the game several times.

QUESTIONS TO ASK

How can you clear up the toys scattered all around the outdoor play space? How can you collect lots of items in one go? Where are you going to put the toys to count them? How many toys have you collected?

FOR YOUNGER/OLDER CHILDREN

Scatter fewer toys around a smaller space for younger children to collect. Give them a container to carry them back to the counting spot. Increase the number of items they have to collect and try to hide them around the outdoor play area to increase the difficulty of the game. Encourage older children to work in pairs or small groups.

FOLLOW-UP ACTIVITIES

- Sort the items collected.
- Talk about clearing up toys after the children have played with them.
- Play the game using small items such as marbles.
- Play the game with playing cards; give five points for an ace, four points for a king and three points for a queen and so on. When the children have collected all the cards, encourage them to count up their individual scores.

Follow Me

Learning objective: to have fun developing physical control and coordination by following a leader
Resources: a safe outdoor area suitable for an action game

Remind children of the safety issues and boundaries involved in playing an action game out of doors. Take the children outdoors and position them behind the adult's back. Ensure that two adults are present as one adult will have their back to the children. The adult is going to lead the game to start. Invite the children to copy every move the adult makes. The adult moves around the outdoor play space, encouraging the children to follow, copying the actions made by the leader. The adult tries to vary the type of movement by running, skipping, hopping, jumping and walking in random order for several minutes. As the children follow say STOP! LOOK! LISTEN! Ask them what they can see or hear. Extend by encouraging children to stop, look, listen, THINK! AND check!

QUESTIONS TO ASK

Can you copy every move your friend makes? Can you follow the leader? Do you ever copy anyone else? What is it like when someone copies you?

FOR YOUNGER/OLDER CHILDREN

Choose simple actions within the experience of young children. The adult needs to face the children as they are following the leader to give them encouragement. Increase the difficulty of the actions. Change from one movement to another in quick succession. Give older children the opportunity to be the leader.

FOLLOW-UP ACTIVITIES

- In pairs, copy each other's movements. Pretend to be looking in a mirror, matching each other's movements face on.
- Copy facial expressions.
- Copy difficult, funny words and try copying tongue-twisters.
- Play secret whispers. Each child whispers a phrase into the next child's ear until all the children have had a turn. The last child repeats the phrase out loud to see if it is still the same as when the whispers began.
- Play the game 'Simon Says'.

Through the Tunnel

Learning objective: to develop an awareness of space and others by playing this outdoor action game

Take the children outdoors. Define the area and remind the children of any safety or ground rules. Explain that the game they are to play is an action game whereby the leader chases them around the outdoor play space to try to touch them. When they are touched, they have to stand with their legs apart to make a tunnel through which one of the other children will crawl to release them from captivity. They have three lives. When they are caught for the third time they are out of the game. The last child to be touched takes over the role of leader for the next game. If all the children are caught out and there is no one left to crawl through the tunnels, the leader can opt to start the game again or nominate a new leader.

QUESTIONS TO ASK

Can you make a tunnel with your legs? Have you ever been through a tunnel? What is it like going through a tunnel? Where do you see tunnels? What animals make tunnels in the ground?

FOR YOUNGER/OLDER CHILDREN

Decrease the number of chances so that younger children are out on the first touch. They could make the tunnel shape with their legs to indicate when they are out. Older children could have two leaders in the game to increase the level of difficulty for the children being chased. They could make the tunnels with their arms and legs instead of making them with just their legs.

FOLLOW-UP ACTIVITIES

- Take the children to visit a dark tunnel.
- Make a long people tunnel by asking the children to stand with their legs apart or on their hands and knees next to each other. Take it in turns to crawl through the tunnel.
- Try to dig a small tunnel in an outdoor sandpit.

Collecting Tails

Learning objective: to move confidently with increasing control
Resources: some strips of parachute material approximately 5cm wide by 50cm long

Take the children outdoors. Remind them of any safety rules and set the boundaries for the game. Explain to the children that they are going to pretend to be animals running away from a hunter who is trying to catch their tails. Give them a strip of parachute material and tell them to tuck it down the back of their shorts or into their waistband so that it hangs down the back like a tail. An adult chases the children around the outdoor play area, trying to catch hold of the tails. The game is over when all the tails have been retrieved. Talk to the children about taking care not to bump into one another by looking where they are going. Encourage the children to use all the space. Remind them not to hold onto their tails or tuck them too far down their shorts.

QUESTIONS TO ASK

What animals have long tails? Have you ever seen any animals with long tails? Where have you seen animals with long tails? What happens to the tails when the animal runs? What happens to the tail when the animal is sad or happy?

FOR YOUNGER/OLDER CHILDREN

Play the game at a slower pace by asking younger children to walk around like animals. Have smaller groups of three or four children playing at a time. Demonstrate how gentle you have to be when you take the tail. Older children will enjoy taking it in turns to be the hunter as well as the animals. Have a time limit to see who can collect the most tails during the time set.

FOLLOW-UP ACTIVITIES

- Play cat and mouse chase games around the outdoor play area.
- Talk to children about kindness and care of animals and of each other.
- Talk about the use animals have for their tails, how some monkeys have prehensile tails, how cows flick flies off their backs with their tail and so on.

Creative development

Outdoor play can provide many situations to encourage creative development and for children to use their imaginations. These activities help children to express ideas and feelings in a variety of ways. These activities will help you to think about creating pieces of artwork outside.

Make Your Mark

Drawing is about making marks. There are many different ways of making marks which you can experiment with outside.
Resources: a range of different types, colours, rolls of paper, sticks, stones, ribbons etc., chalks, paint and a range of brushes and other mark-making tools

Your outdoor space may offer you a number of places to make marks which do not have to be permanent. Your mark could simply be placing an item on the ground or you could take art materials outside. If you would rather use paper to capture marks, bring different colours and types of paper outside; rolls of paper work well in large spaces. Lay out long lines of paper on the ground and experiment with mark making. Find sticks or stones which can be used to make marks or use coloured chalks, tubs of water and tubs of paint or watered-down ink. Use large decorator's brushes, old toothbrushes and other tools such as sponges to make interesting marks.

Ask the children to make small marks, gentle marks, marks that look like rain, wind, snow, marks that are angry, marks that are very big. Invite them to build up a picture of marks, for example using marks that look like water to create a sea, marks that create clouds, splatter marks like the rain coming down. Use certain colours to match the themes of the marks. Leave the marks to dry.

FOLLOW-UP

Add more detail using pencils or crayons to add another dimension in terms of how marks can be made. Put marks straight onto a tarmac surface. Use chalks or place items such as sticks, stones, leaves, petals onto the ground to make a picture.

Muddy Mixtures

Resources: tubs or buckets, mud or soil, heavy paper or card, poster paints, brushes and sand

Mix up some tubs of mud with water, getting to a consistency similar to that of poster paint.
Paint mud pictures onto a piece of card. Combine the mud with poster paints or sand to get different colours and textures. Talk about how people first made their marks with earth colours or by scratching on stone.

FOLLOW-UP

Paint a brighter colour onto your paper. Leave to dry. Paint over this paint with mud. Scrape into the mud to show the bright paint beneath.

Dandelion Patterns and Drawings

Resources: heads of dandelions and sticks

Find a large open space of green grass. Draw on the grass by making a picture made up of dandelion heads only. Find the largest tree in your outdoor space. Draw around the base of the tree with dandelion heads only. Make another circle further away from the base – use sticks this time. Use dandelion heads to draw lines from the sticks and away from the tree. Experiment with sticks, stones, daisies and dandelions to create a carpet of lines and colour at the base of your trees. Photograph the process and the end results for reflection on the activity at a later date.

FOLLOW-UP

Repeat using heads of daisies, celandines or buttercups. Use a mixture of different-coloured, different-sized flower heads to make interesting patterns and pictures.

Filling Outlines

Resources: buckets of different sorts of dry materials that have different colours, for example one of sand, one of dark compost, one of gravel, etc. Find a space in your grounds that has a hard surface such as a paving slab. Draw a frame with chalk. Inside the frame draw a large, simple pattern. Scooping handfuls of the different materials, fill in the pattern to create a textured picture.

FOLLOW-UP

Take photographs of the pictures and experiment with using other natural materials to create other pictures and patterns on the ground.

A Waxy Rub

Learning objective: to explore the texture and pattern of outdoor objects
Resources: several sheets of thin white drawing paper, a chubby wax crayon in a dark colour for each child taking part in the activity, a safe outdoor space with a variety of interesting objects such as bricks, drainage covers, pavement slabs, tree trunks

Take the children outdoors. Give them a wax crayon each and a sheet of white drawing paper. Invite the children to go on a walk around the outdoor play space looking for objects with different patterns and textures. Spend a little time pointing out the different shapes, textures, colours, materials and patterns. Explain that the children are going to make a rubbing to record some of the things they have seen outside. Demonstrate how to make a rubbing by placing the paper on top of the object you want to use. Holding the paper in one hand and using the wax crayon with the other hand, rub the wax crayon over and over the surface of the paper. The texture of the object underneath the paper will create the pattern as some patches of the paper will be left uncoloured. Encourage the children to make several prints of the same object, using different colours and rubbing the wax crayon in different ways across the paper. Compare and contrast the finished results with each other and with the object used to make the rubbing.

QUESTIONS TO ASK

As the children are working, ask them to explain what they are doing. What is the easiest way to use the crayon to make a wax rubbing? Have you noticed anything around you with a pattern made up of lines? Do you know anything else made of wax?

FOR YOUNGER/OLDER CHILDREN

Take younger children out individually to make their wax rubbing. Show them exactly what to do; emphasise that they need to rub the crayon over the paper only. Older children could work cooperatively in pairs to make large wax rubbings. They could go out into the outdoor play area to look for their own objects to use instead of wax, such as mud or stones, and decide where to make their rubbing. They could be given specific tasks, such as to make a rubbing of a tree, a pavement slab, to find a pattern made with curves or straight lines.

FOLLOW-UP ACTIVITIES

- Make a leaf rubbing.
- Find other ways of recording the patterns and textures found in the outdoor environment.

Grow a Scarecrow

Learning objective: to explore three-dimensional shapes and forms using discarded flowerpots
Resources: eight 3in/7.5cm reclaimed flowerpots, two 5in/12.7cm reclaimed flowerpots, a ball of string, 10 or more cotton reels, some strips of brightly coloured parachute material or cotton approximately 2cm wide by 30cm long, a marker pen, a pair of scissors, a blanket or groundsheet, a small patch of garden

Wash the flowerpots if necessary. Take the blanket or groundsheet to a suitable outdoor working area and spread it on the ground. Place all the resources on the groundsheet. Explain to the children the concept of a scarecrow, showing them a picture of one to give them an idea of what a scarecrow looks like. Ask the children to help you join the flowerpots together to make two arms, two legs; separate the flowerpots by threading a cotton reel between them and knotting a piece of parachute material to keep the pots apart. Tie the arms and legs onto one of the large flowerpots to make a body in the same way as you joined the smaller pots to make arms and legs. Using a cotton reel and some parachute material tied between the pots to separate them, fix the head onto the rest of the body. Tie the parachute material all over the string at the top to look like hair. Draw a face on the head flowerpot. Hang the finished model on a fence or in a tree to scare away birds.

QUESTIONS TO ASK

Have you ever seen a scarecrow before? Have you seen a picture of a scarecrow? Why do people put scarecrows in their gardens? What happens to a scarecrow when it is windy? What else could you do to stop the birds eating seeds and plants?

FOR YOUNGER/OLDER CHILDREN

Make individual scarecrows using one flowerpot by drawing a face on one side and tying five or six pieces of parachute material through the drainage holes in the bottom of the pot. Place on the top of empty plastic lemonade bottles standing up in the garden patch. Encourage older children to work cooperatively in small groups to create their own scarecrow from the materials placed on the groundsheet.

FOLLOW-UP ACTIVITIES

- Learn and sing the song 'Dingle, Dangle Scarecrow'.
- Make up a scarecrow dance.
- Use upturned flowerpots to make some stilts by tying long lengths of string onto either side of the pots. Try to balance and walk on them.

Sandy Girl/Boy

Learning objective: to encourage children to express their feelings through movement and dance

Take the children outdoors. Ask them to form a circle by holding hands together. Choose a child to be Sandy, the traditional name for the child in this action song. Sandy is sitting on a stone weeping because there is no one to play with. Explain that they are going to play Sandy girl/boy, a circle game in which the children sing the words: 'Poor little Sandy girl/boy sitting on a stone. Weeping, crying and sitting all alone. Stand up Sandy girl/boy and wipe your tears away. Choose the one you like the most and then go out and play.' The children repeat the verse, singing the sounds 'la la la la la la la la' and clapping their hands as Sandy jumps up to choose a child to dance in the ring with her/him. That child then becomes Sandy sitting in the middle of the ring as the children dance around again. Repeat the activity until all the children have been chosen to dance in the ring with Sandy.

QUESTIONS TO ASK

Why do you think Sandy is weeping? What could you do to cheer her/him up? Why do you sometimes cry? How do you feel when you cry? What cheers you up when you are sad? What makes you happy?

FOR YOUNGER/OLDER CHILDREN

Learn the song and take it in turns to dance around the outdoor play space as the other children sing and clap. Encourage older children to think of a different dance each time they join Sandy in the middle of the ring.

- Play other ring games such as 'Farmer's in the dell', 'There was a Princess Long Ago', 'Ring-a-ring o' Roses' or 'Here We Go Round the Mulberry Bush'.
- Make up actions and dances to other favourite rhymes.
- Discuss feelings. Talk about the importance of being kind and playing with each other.

Outdoor Bands

Learning objective: to encourage children to explore sound and respond imaginatively to what they hear by setting up outdoor music bands

Resources: a frame or similar to hang up pots and pans; several metal pots, pans, jugs and serving spoons, at least two to three for each child taking part in the activity; some string

Check out the availability of a sturdy outdoor frame or a low sturdy tree on which to hang the kitchen implements to make the bandstand. If there is nothing suitable, improvise by using a clothes horse fixed securely to a fence, tree or wall. Place resources on the ground near the frame. Invite the children to handle and explore making sounds with the kitchen implements. When they are ready explain that the implements are going to be tied onto the frame to make a semi-permanent set of band instruments to be used outside. Tie the pots and pans to the frame by threading the string through the handles of the implements. Let them dangle down from the frame on the string so that they will bang together in the wind even when the children are not playing with them. Challenge the children to make noises by banging the pots and pans with serving spoons also tied onto the frame as before. Encourage the children to respond through dance and movement to the sounds they make and hear.

QUESTIONS TO ASK

What will happen when the pots and pans knock together in the wind? Have you ever listened to a live band playing? What instruments do you know or have you seen? Have you seen a marching band? Can you make loud noises with the outdoor band? Can you use the spoons to make quiet noises with the musical frame?

FOR YOUNGER/OLDER CHILDREN

Give younger children their own pots, pans and spoons to play with outdoors. Encourage them to bang them together to make sounds. Encourage older children to create simple tunes or repeated patterns of sound and movement for others to watch or copy.

FOLLOW-UP ACTIVITIES

- Invite musicians to show children how they play real instruments.
- Hang wooden objects from the frame and give the children wooden spoons to create different outdoor sounds.
- Sit down in a quiet, safe spot to listen to the sounds going on all around the outdoor play space.
- Find natural objects to use as instruments.

Spinners

Learning objective: to make a simple spinner to watch splodges of paint spinning in the air
Resources: some sycamore seeds and a variety of light objects such as feathers and dried leaves, some curled, some straight

Collect sycamore seeds with the children when they are in season and store ready to use for this activity. Talk about the way some seeds are transported around in the air by the wind until they drop to the ground and find a growing place. Take the sycamore seeds outdoors and drop from a height if possible, perhaps by standing on a low wall. Watch them spinning to the ground. Experiment by dropping the feathers and leaves and compare what happens when the different objects are dropped from a height.

QUESTIONS TO ASK

Why do sycamore seeds need to fly? What happens to the sycamore seeds, feathers or leaves when they are dropped to the floor? Can you spin around on the spot? How do you feel when you spin?

FOR YOUNGER/OLDER CHILDREN

Let them watch as the adult drops the seeds, feather and leaves from a height. Ask older children to lead the activity.

FOLLOW-UP ACTIVITIES

* Design and make spinners using a variety of materials.
* Ask the children to find different ways of spinning themselves around.
* Encourage the children to spin hula-hoops on the floor and keep them going.

Ice Art

Learning objective: to create three-dimensional pictures by freezing leaves in ice
Resources: freezing weather conditions, leaves, a small recycled food tray, a jug of water

Prepare an example in advance. Place three small, brightly coloured leaves in a tray. Pour water into the tray so that the leaves are fully submerged or until the water in the tray is approximately 2cm deep. Place outdoors in a safe place to freeze overnight. Take the children outdoors to show them the tray of frozen leaves you prepared in advance. Take the ice out of the tray. Let the children handle the frozen ice as you explain how you made it. Make sure that children do not lick the ice or put it into their mouths. Hold up the ice block to the light, pointing out the leaves you have frozen inside it. Invite the children to go off to collect some different sizes, colours and species of leaf to use to make their own ice picture. Ask the children to arrange the leaves in the small food tray. Pour some water on top of the leaves as before. Leave outdoors overnight if the weather permits or place in a freezer until the next day. When the water has frozen, remove from the tray and take the pictures back outdoors. Encourage the children to handle the icy pictures and look at them as they glisten in the light. Place them in a safe outdoor spot to watch them slowly melt away.

QUESTIONS TO ASK

What will happen to the leaves when the ice melts? What patterns have you seen outdoors when it is frosty? What else can you do with ice?

An adult could help younger children to freeze just one leaf in water. Older children could make more complex ice art by freezing an arrangement of several leaves in a tray.

FOLLOW-UP ACTIVITIES

- Make ice balloons to use during outdoor play by filling a balloon with water and freezing it. When frozen, peel off the balloon to reveal the beautifully smooth sphere of ice. Invite children to handle it and talk about its properties.
- Use fruit peel to make funny frozen faces using the same methods as for leaf pictures.
- Freeze arrangements of other small objects to make ice art.
- Make a snowman when it snows.
- Explore the outside area on a frosty day.

Vegetable People

Learning objective: to create characters with vegetables to use outdoors for imaginary play
Resources: a collection of odd-shaped root vegetables such as carrots, potatoes, parsnips, swedes, turnips; pipe cleaners, scooping tools, cocktail sticks, permanent marker pens, a groundsheet. Some of these can be grown in advance by the children.

Make up some examples of vegetable people in advance. Place them outdoors in a suitable place, such as along the top of a low wall or at the bottom of a big tree, depending on what is available. Take all the materials outdoors and place on the groundsheet. Invite the children to look at the vegetable characters. Encourage them to describe the characters and name the vegetables used to make them. Find out what the children already know about vegetables. Allow each child to choose some vegetables to make their own characters. Demonstrate how to scoop out the centre of large vegetables, how to make eye holes, ears and a mouth. Help the children to join some of the vegetables together using small twigs or pipe cleaners. Make sure that the children do not hurt themselves or others with the sticks and that they do not put vegetables in their mouth to eat. Ensure that all sharp ends are safely stuck into the vegetables. Encourage the children to draw funny faces on their vegetable people and use them during imaginative play. Group the vegetable people together as if they are a vegetable family living in the outdoor play space and over a period of weeks watch as they decompose.

QUESTIONS TO ASK

How do things grow? How do you grow? What vegetables have you used to make your character? Is your vegetable person mean, scary, friendly or ugly? What do you think will happen to your vegetable person if it is left out in the outdoor play area?

FOR YOUNGER/OLDER CHILDREN

Younger children will enjoy choosing funny-shaped vegetables for an adult to sculpt and draw a face on. Older children will want to choose and make their own vegetable characters. They might like to draw their design of a character before they make it. They will be able to make up pretend games which involve the characters in the plot.

FOLLOW-UP ACTIVITIES

- Use the vegetables to make vegetable prints.
- Make characters from other food such as fruit, bread or pasta.
- Use the characters to make an outdoor display.
- Encourage the children to grow their own vegetables in the garden patch.
- Use other objects found in the outdoor play space to create play people.

Magic Shoes

Learning objective: to encourage physical control and body awareness by pretending to wear magic shoes

Resources: a safe outdoor play space and a copy of the song 'Put On Your Walking Shoes' by A. Wood and R. Jacques (TRO Essex Music Ltd)

Learn the song 'Put On Your Walking Shoes' as a stimulus for this activity: 'Come Sarah let us go, put on your walking shoes, it's time to move along, so, put on your walking shoes'. Explain that they are going to pretend to wear magic outdoor shoes which make them dance when they hear the words 'put on your walking shoes/your hopping shoes/your skipping shoes/running shoes'. Invite the children to sing the song with you as they dance around the outdoor play area pretending to wear magic shoes. Encourage the children to match their movements to the words of the song and to stop at the end of each verse. Encourage the children to travel in different directions as they dance. Remind them to take care not to bump into each other.

QUESTIONS TO ASK

How can you dance when you wear magic shoes? What are your favourite shoes? Why do you like them? Describe the shoes people wear in winter/summer.

FOR YOUNGER/OLDER CHILDREN

Ask younger children to copy the way you dance around the outdoor area when you pretend to be wearing the magic shoes. Invite them to make up their own dance steps. Encourage older children to include more difficult movements in their dance such as jumping, twisting, tiptoeing, sliding, bouncing, springing or prancing. Encourage them to make contrasting movements, sometimes dancing fast, then slow, or with little light steps or big heavy ones.

FOLLOW-UP ACTIVITIES

- Collect old shoes to set up a shoe shop outdoors.
- Make a collection of shoes to display.

10 Final goodbyes

Introduction

This chapter will discuss the importance of preparing for a satisfactory ending to the programme. It will include ideas for end-of-group celebrations and case studies about how some children handled the end of the programme and looked at what they could do next to continue their healthy, active, outdoor lifestyle. It will include an end-of-group invitation to parents to photocopy, an attendance certificate for the children on completion of the programme and a reward note for the children for special achievements. It will also include ideas of ways for children to record their experience and the final goodbye song (p.167) and will conclude with the group leaders' personal reflections made at the end of one of the programmes.

Final get-together!

It is important to spend some time celebrating the end of the programme with everyone who has taken part, what has been achieved and what fun it has all been. Holding an outdoor celebration to round off the programme of activities is a wonderful opportunity to get everyone together, share experiences and celebrate the feelings and opportunities the outside brings us all. The end celebration can be as big or small as you want to make it as long as there is some kind of celebration to mark the end of the programme and celebrate the children's achievements. The end celebration could be a whole school or setting event, depending on how it has been implemented. The end celebration could be shared with the local community, parents or friends in school or setting so that they can see what has been achieved as a result of implementing the programme. It could just be a small celebration with the children who attended the programme and their parents, a friend of each of the children and the group leaders, or even the just the children and their leaders. Any or all the activities that have been described in previous chapters are suitable for sharing with others on an outdoor open-day event. Below are just a few ideas on how you can involve others in the celebration.

Activities for end-of-programme celebrations

Design invitations for the parents and others from the local community to join you. These could be inspired by some of the artwork done earlier in the programme (in the shape of a muddy splat, leaf or handprint). Consider providing the guests with a lunch prepared by the children from the things they have grown, only food that grows, or have a barbecue and cook sausages over an open fire.

It is the adult's role to establish reasons for having a picnic, going to the shop for supplies and to role-model writing a list of things to do or buy. Whilst out shopping for the picnic food, draw the children's attention to a range of food from other cultures and visit different types of shops such as a delicatessen, fruit and vegetable shop, supermarket and baker's shop. Buy a variety of food to encourage children to try different foods to widen their experiences. Alternatively, just have a picnic and ask all the children to bring a healthy packed lunch to eat outdoors. If there is no grassy area in the setting, cushions, throws, picnic blankets or carpet tiles make the playground more comfortable to sit down on. The event could be a teddy bears' picnic where all the children bring along a teddy bear.

In plenty of time before the actual day of the outdoor celebration the children could make celebration hats and decorate them with messy handprints or natural materials that they have found outdoors. Make invitations, posters, flyers, signs etc. from natural objects to let everyone know about the celebration.

The end celebration is an excellent opportunity to share with everyone some of the outdoor work that has been created throughout the duration of the programme. Many of the activities that have taken place throughout the programme lend themselves well to sharing and displaying. Here are a few examples.

Display the objects collected, grouped according to colours that made up the 'Pick Up a Rainbow' activity, or make a large display or book of the graphs and charts made during the programme. Put photographs taken of the artwork pieces made into an album for visitors to look at during the celebration day and display some of the artwork made during the programme such as the 'dream catchers', drawings or bark rubbings.

Activities for visitors on the day

Some of the activities that visitors can try out on the celebration or open day can be linked to seasonal events such as sitting around a campfire to sing songs in autumn, having a maypole to dance around in springtime, egg hunts at Easter time or multicultural theme days at appropriate times throughout the programme. Get visitors involved in being more active by challenging them to take part in some of the programme activities. Encourage the children to teach the visitors how to play one of the games they played during the programme or take groups of visitors on a treasure hunt around the outside area. Challenge them to work with the children to complete a treasure hunt with prizes for the winners or, in the case of egg hunts, take a basket and find all the eggs to share with everyone during circle time at the end of the celebration.

Arrange for some children to take visitors on minibeast hunts to help them to collect and sort the creatures they find. They could explore the outside area together and the children could take groups of visitors on a tour of the garden patch they have created during the programme and explain how it was made and how to care for the plants. Have a work day where visitors help complete the garden by joining the children in doing some digging and by having some plants, bulbs, trees, vegetables or flowers ready for them to plant.

Many of the activities completed as part of the programme could be photographed or turned into displays and one or two of the activities could be set up on the day for the visitors to try alongside the children. Alternatively, set up a whole range of the activities that the children experienced during the programme as workshops and ask visitors to sign up to just two each. Let the children organise and demonstrate how to take part in a range of different activities from the programme. For example, the visitors could take part in a large-scale survey by setting up one of these activities as a way of involving the visitors and capturing their thoughts on, and attitudes to, some of the issues raised during the programme. Have a start-of-programme survey followed up by an end survey so that two sets of results can be compared and displayed. Alternatively, using the same survey, compare the findings of the adult survey with that of the children.

The visitors could take part in an end-of-programme clean-up of the outside area before joining the picnic as a reward for all their hard work. Sing favourite songs and share poems or thoughts written especially for the occasion before handing out attendance certificates to all the children who took part in the programme (Figure 10.1) and reward notes for special achievements (Figure 10.2).

The goodbye song

The 'goodbye song' is sung at the end of every session to give continuity of structure to the group and a familiar routine which helps to provide security for the children attending. Singing the song also rounds off everything in a satisfactory way and adds closure to the session. It can also be sung by everyone at the end of final celebration for the same reasons.

The goodbye song:
Goodbye everyone
Goodbye everyone
Goodbye everyone, it was good to have you here.

In a small group situation, personalise the song by singing each child's name in turn, instead of the word 'everyone'. This will make each child feel important. Alternatively, if there is not sufficient time to include everyone, choose the name of the child who has been the leader of the group for that week. In this case, ensure the children know what is happening and that it will be their turn another time when they are taking the role of leader.

Personal reflections on the programme

Once all the celebrations are over, it is important to look back and reflect on the programme. You will find the children are naturally interested in what they were doing, which made everything much easier. If you decide to implement the outdoor programme, like us you will find that everyone will have much more fun, laughter and enjoyment, which all naturally lift the spirit of all the people involved. You will find it also makes the teaching and learning processes more effective. The children will have enjoyed learning through physical activity, through first-hand experiences where they were not afraid to make mistakes within the boundaries of safe, non-restrictive routines. They will have experienced the thrills of 'safe' adventure, risks and challenges and the feeling of being successful in a practical rather than academic way. The programme encourages valuing children for what they are rather than the outcomes they achieve. It is rewarding for the facilitators of the programme to see for themselves the benefits and rewards of good healthy exercise, and of getting outdoors to play and work in the natural environment.

Case study – Leader's reflection on the outdoor programme

Although the first outdoor programme took place during the wettest year on record, the group leader's 'shelter-building' and 'fire-lighting' skills are now greatly improved with the help of many tips from the parents and children involved! She has not been so muddy since childhood or had so many scratched knees and is still prone to slipping in the mud lifting the video camera above her head, taking shots of the grey, wet skies instead of catching good video footage of the children involved in activity! The sausages always seem to be burned, and the parents jokingly tell the team members that they are mad when they see them building dens in blizzards – but they do have fun!

To hear a child whoop with glee on discovering something new, or shriek with excitement when they find hidden treasure or a solution to a tricky problem, says it all. Watching a smile spread across a parent's face as she takes pride in her son achieving success when her only previous experiences of school had been negative was a clear indication of the value of this work. Helping to raise the parent's self-esteem in this way will naturally lead to an improvement in the child's life. The added bonus has been the fact that there are video-recordings of this experience to reflect on with the parents and the fact that the whole family will benefit, repeatedly, from the recording of that critical moment.

From observations, the children appeared to be complying because they were naturally interested in what they were doing which also made the teaching and learning processes more effective. And to hear a so-called 'difficult child' whispering, 'I love this' secretly to himself when he forgets he is being video-recorded during a safety game is enough evidence in itself to make the programme worthwhile.

In their own words

During the reflection period of the final celebration session the children were asked what they felt about the outdoor programme. One child who did not want to go outside at all at the start of the programme said:

> I love playing in the woods with you. When can I come again? I can find lots of good things outside to play with, like snails and woodlice, and it is great. I love it. I like building dens most of all and now I want to go outside all the time 'cause it's fun.

Comments from school staff

At the end of the pilot programme teachers were asked to comment on the effects of the programme on the children who attended. Below you will find one teacher's comments about a group of children who were underachieving in all areas at nursery at the start of the programme.

> We noticed the difference in the children going to the outdoor programme after only five weeks. They are much more confident and talking more now. Some are playing with each other now rather than playing alone. We know how well it works because we have seen the results for ourselves; it's a shame more children don't get the chance to go to a similar programme.
>
> We really noticed a difference when the children went to 'Outdoor School' as we could spend more time with the others knowing that they were having individual attention and enjoying themselves.
>
> Now we can see a difference in all the children; they are happier when they come back from playing outside and have a lot more to talk about than usual. Especially ... He didn't say very much at all before and we could not really understand him. Now he always talks excitedly about what he has done at outdoor school. There's the added benefit that his behaviour has really improved too! In fact we have noticed a change for the better in all the children's behaviour. They know the routines well and do what they are told more often as they know how to play outside now. They have much more confidence outside and will try out new things. They are happier playing because they have new ideas from the outdoor programme to bring back to class. The other children are impressed too, especially when they watch the video of their friends.

During the final celebrations teachers commented that the children's language and communication skills had improved as a result of attending the programme and that the difficult behaviour of one particular child had really improved: 'He always talks excitedly about what he has done in the outdoor programme.'

The findings of the research carried out alongside the implementation of the Healthy, Active and Outside programme supported the notion that the whole process of moving outdoors would have a positive influence on the health, behaviour and well-being of the children and adults who took part. The success of the programme was a direct result of children, parents, practitioners and the community working together. At the end of the programme everyone celebrated its success through the reward notes and end-of-programme certificates given to participating children. Final goodbyes were made, and the participants knew that the outside environment had been improved and well used throughout that year and that the whole process would continue to be developed by each new group of children taking part in future programmes.

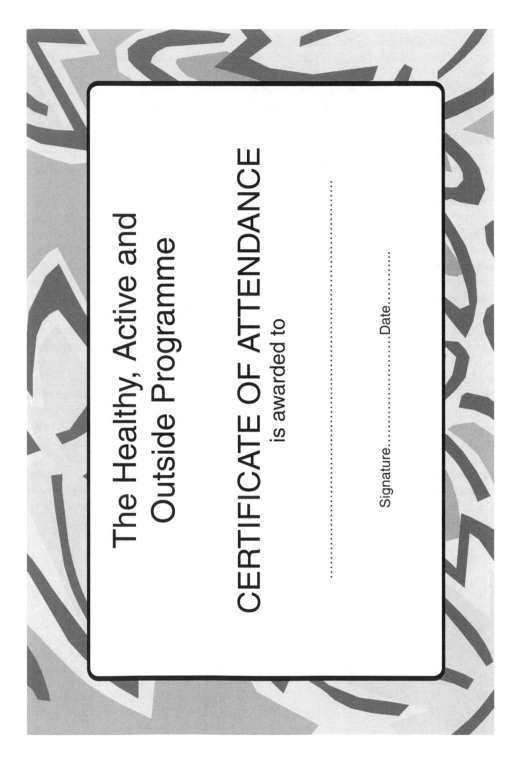

Figure 10.1 Example of certificate of attendance

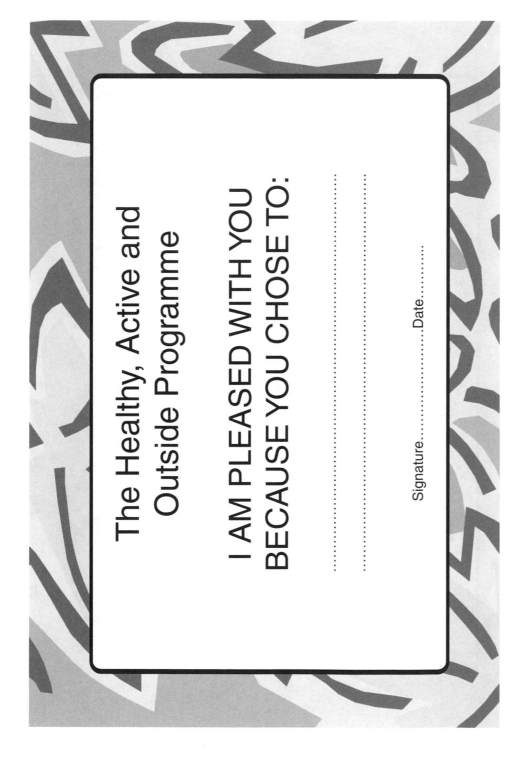

Figure 10.2 Example of reward note

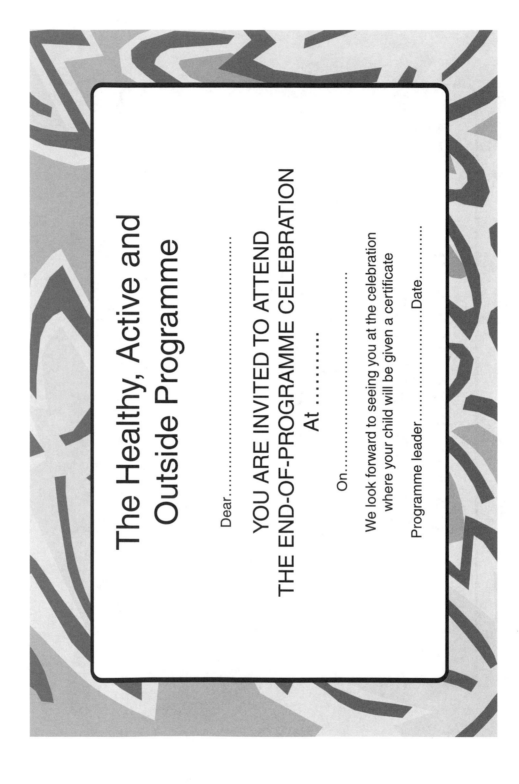

The Healthy, Active and Outside Programme

Dear..............

YOU ARE INVITED TO ATTEND
THE END-OF-PROGRAMME CELEBRATION

At ....

On..............

We look forward to seeing you at the celebration
where your child will be given a certificate

Programme leader..............Date..........

Figure 10.3 Example of invitation to the end-of-programme celebration

References

Ahlberg, J. and Ahlberg, A. (1980) *Funny Bones*. Heinemann Young Books. New York: Greenwillow Books.

Ayres, J. (1972) *Sensory Integration and Learning Disorders*. Los Angeles, CA: Western Psychological Services.

Bandura, A. (1977) *Social Learning Theory*. Englewood Cliffs, NJ: Prentice-Hall.

Bandura, A. (1986) *Social Foundations of Thought and Action: A Social Cognitive Theory*. Englewood Cliffs, NJ: Prentice-Hall.

Bandura, A. and Rosenthal, T.L. (1966) Vicarious classical conditioning as a function of arousal level. *Journal of Personality and Social Psychology* 3: 54–62.

Bandura, A., Ross, D. and Ross, S.A. (1963) Vicarious reinforcement and imitative learning. *Journal of Abnormal and Social Psychology* 67: 601–7.

Benton, W. (1986) (ed.) Montessori System. *Encyclopaedia Britannica*, Vol. 17. Chicago, IL: Britannica UK Ltd.

Bjorklund, D.F. and Brown, R.D. (1998) 'Physical play and cognitive development: Integrating activity, cognition and education'. *Child Development* 69(3): 604–6.

Bronowski, J. (1975) *The Ascent of Man*. London: Little, Brown.

Bruner, J.S. (1985) 'Vygotsky: a historical and conceptual perspective'. In: J.V. Wertsch (ed.) *Culture, Communication and Cognition: Vygotsky Perspectives*, Cambridge: Cambridge University Press.

Bushnell, E. and Boudreau, P. (1993) 'Motor development in the mind: The potential role of motor abilities as a determinant of aspects of perceptual development'. *Child Development* 64(4): 1005–21.

Canter, L. and Canter, M. (1993) *Succeeding with Difficult Students: New Strategies for Reaching Your Most Challenging Students*. Santa Monica, CA: Canter and Associates.

Carmichael, K. and Atchinson, D. (1997) 'Music and play therapy: Playing my feelings'. *International Journal of Play Therapy* 6: 63–72.

Children's Play Council (2002) *Managing Risk in Play Provision: A Position Statement*. London: Play Safety Forum. NCB Publications.

Cranz, G. (1998) *The Chair: Rethinking Body, Culture and Design*. New York, NY: W.W. Norton.

Davies, D. (1999) *Child Development. A Practitioner's Guide*. New York: Guilford Press.

Dennison, P. and Dennison, G. (1989) *Brain Gym: Teacher's Edition*. Ventura, CA.

Department for Education and Skills (2000) *Curriculum Guidance for the Foundation Stage*. DfEE/QCA Publications, London: HMSO.

Department for Education and Skills (2003a) *Every Child Matters*. London: HMSO.

Department for Education and Skills (2003b) *Birth to Three Matters*. DfES Publications.

Department for Education and Skills (2004) *Building for Sure Start: A Client Guide. Integrated Provision for Under-Fives*. CABE/DfES Publications.

Department for Education and Skills (2006a) *National Framework for Sustainable Schools*. London: HMSO.

Department for Education and Skills.(2006b) *Learning outside the Classroom Manifesto*. London: DfES.

Department for Education and Skills (2007) *Statutory Framework for the Early Years Foundation Stage: Setting the Standards for Learning, Development and Care for Children from Birth to Five*. London: HMSO.

Department for Education and Employment and QCA (1999) *The National Curriculum: Handbook for Primary Teachers in England: Key Stages 1 and 2*. London: HMSO.

Department for Education and Skills and QCA (1999) *Aims for the School Curriculum*. The National Curriculum. London: HMSO.

Department for Environment, Food and Rural Affairs (1999) *A Better Quality of Life: Strategy for Sustainable Development*. London: Defra Publications.

Dhyan, S. (1995) 'The transforming force of laughter with the focus on laughing meditation'. *Patient Education and Counseling* 26(1–3): 367–371.

Douglas, J.W.B. (1964) *The Home and the School: A Study of Ability and Attainment in the Primary School.* London: MacGibbon & Kee.

Easterbrook, J.A. (1959) 'The effect of emotion on cue utilization and the organization of behavior'. *Psychological Review* 66(3): 183–201.

Edgington, M. (2002) *The Great Outdoors: Developing Children's Learning through Outdoor Provision.* London: British Association for Early Childhood Education.

Education for Sustainable Development (ESD) (2002). London: HMSO.

Filer, J. (1998) *Outdoor Play: Learning through Play.* London: Scolastic.

Filer, J. (2002) 'Outdoor School Report'. End-of-year report to the commissioning body, The Children's Fund. December 2002. Unpublished.

Fordyce, D.E. and Wehner, J.M. (1993) 'Physical activity enhances spatial learning performance with an associated alteration in hippocampal protein kinase C activity in C57BL/6 and DBA/2 mice'. *Brain Research* 619(1–2): 111–19.

Gardner, H. (1999) *The Disciplined Mind.* New York, NY: Simon & Schuster.

Goddard Blythe, S. (2000) 'Early learning in the balance: priming the first ABC'. *Support for Learning* 15 (4): 154–8.

Goleman, D. (1995) *Emotional Intelligence.* New York, NY: Bantam Books.

Haley, J. (1955) 'Paradoxes in play, fantasy, and psychotherapy'. *Psychiatric Research Reports* (American Psychiatric Association), 2 (December), 52–8.

Hannaford, C. (1995) *Smart Moves: Why Learning Is Not All in Your Head*, Arlington, VA: Great Ocean Publishing.

HASPEV (2002) 'Standards for Adventure', Part 2 of *Health and Safety of Pupils on Educational Visits: A Good Practice Guide.* Also: 'Health and Safety: Responsibilities and Powers', 'Standards for LEAs in Overseeing Educational Visits', 'A Handbook for Group Leaders' 4: 155–69.

Hawkins, (1987) Hawkins' integrated model for outdoor education, HORIZONS Practical Outdoor Learning, 2003 Institute for Outdoor Learning, 2003. 24: 4. Outdoor Learning Services, Penrith, Cumbria.

Hayes, D. (1999) *Foundations of Primary Teaching* (2nd edition). London: David Fulton.

Henning, R., Jacques, P., Kissel, G. and Sullivan, A. (1997) 'Frequent short breaks from computer work: Effects on productivity and well-being at two field sites'. *Ergonomics* 40(1): 78–91.

Hobcraft, J. (1998) 'Childhood experience and the risk of social exclusion in adulthood'. CASE Briefing Nov 1998.

Jensen, E. (2000) *Learning with the Body in Mind.* San Diego, CA: The Brain Store.

Karmiloff-Smith, A. (1994) *Baby It's You.* London: Ebury Press.

Khalsa, G.C. (1988) 'Effect of educational kinesiology on static balance of learning disabled students'. *Perceptual and Motor Skills* 67: 51–4.

Learning Through Landscapes (2003) *National School Grounds Survey.* Crediton, Devon: Southgate Publishers.

Learning Through Landscapes (2005) *Outdoors for Everyone: enjoying outdoor play in the Early Years.* Crediton, Devon: Southgate Publishers.

Milne, A.A. (1926) *Winnie-the-Pooh.* London: Methuen.

Morris, N. (1982) *Where's My Hat?* London: Hodder & Stoughton.

Nuttall, W. (1999) 'The effects of posture on learning: insights from the Alexander Technique'. *Early Years* 20(1): 65–76.

Ofsted (2003) 'Taking the first step forward, towards an education for sustainable development', HMI 1658.

Ouvry, M. (2000) *Exercising Muscles and Minds: Outdoor Play and the Early Years Curriculum.* London: National Children's Bureau.

Palmer, L. (1980) 'Auditory discrimination development through vestibule–cochlear stimulation'. *Academic Therapy.* 16(1): 55–68.

Palmer, S. (2007) *Toxic Childhood: How the Modern World Is Damaging Our Children and What We Can Do about It.* London: Orion Publishing.

Pestalozzi, J.H. (1894) *How Gertrude Teaches her Children.* Trans. by Lucy E. Holland and Frances C. Turner. London: Swan Sonnenschein.

Piaget, J. (1952) *The Origin of Intelligence in Children.* Trans. M. Cook. New York, NY: International University Press.

Pintrich, P.R. and Schunk, E.H. (1996) *Motivation in Education: Theory, Research and Application.* Englewood Cliffs, NJ: Prentice-Hall.

Plowman, L. and Stephen, C. (2006) *InterActive Education: Teaching and Learning in the* Information Age. Stirling: University of Stirling.

Reilly, J., Dorosty, A.R. and Emmett, P.M. (1999) 'Prevalence of overweight and obesity in British children: Cohort study', *British Medical Journal* 319: 1039.

Rittel, H. and Webber, M. (1973) 'Dilemmas in general theory of planning'. *Policy Sciences* 4(2): 155–69.

Rogers, C. (1967) 'The interpersonal relationship in the facilitation of learning', reprinted in H. Kirschenbaum and V. L. Henderson (eds) (1990) *The Carl Rogers Reader*, London: Constable, pp. 304–11.

Rosen, M. and Oxenbury, H. (1993) *We're Going on a Bear Hunt*. Walker.

Sifft, J. and Khalsa, G. (1991) 'Effects of educational kinesiology upon simple response times and choice response times'. *Perceptional Motor Skills* 73: 1011–15.

Sigman, A. (2005) *Remotely Controlled: How Television Is Damaging Our Lives*. London: Vermilion.

Silva, K., Melhuish, E., Sammons, P. and Siraj-Blatchford, L. (1999) *The Effective Provision of Pre-School Education (EPPE) Project – A Longitudinal Study funded by the DFEE / 1997–2003*. University of London: Institute of Education.

Siraj-Blatchford, I., Sylva, K., Muttock, S., Gilden, R. and Bell, D. (2003) *Researching Effective Pedagogy in the Early Years*. Department for Education and Skills, Research Report RR356.

Thayer, R. (1996) *The Origin of Everyday Moods*. New York, NY: Oxford University Press.

Titman, W. (1999) *Special Places, Special People: The Hidden Curriculum of School Grounds*. Learning Through Landscapes. Crediton, Devon: Southgate Publishers.

Tomporowski, P.D. and Ellis, N.R. (1986) 'Effects of exercise on cognitive processes: A review'. *Psychological Bulletin* 99(3): 338–46.

Top Outdoors Hand Book (2000) TOP Outdoors Advisory Group. Youth Sport Trust.

US Department of Health and Human Services (2000) *Healthy People 2010*, 2nd edition. With *Understanding and Improving Health* and *Objectives for Improving Health* (2 vols). Washington, DC: US Department of Health and Human Services.

Vygotsky, L.S. (1978) *Mind in Society: The Development of Higher Psychological Processes*. Cambridge, MA: Harvard University Press.

White, V. (2004) *Sure Start, Building for Sure Start Integrated Provision for Under-fives*. London: HMSO.

Williams, B., Williams, J. and Ullman, A. (2002) *Parental Involvement in Education*. London: Department for Education and Skills.

Websites

A better quality of life: http://www.environment.detr.gov.uk.

Adventure Activities Industry Advisory Committee (AAIAC): Statement of Risk Perception in Adventure and Outdoor Activities: http://www.hse.gov.uk

A Guide to Risk Assessment Requirements: http://www.hse.gov.uk

Department for Education and Skills Health & Safety: *Health and Safety of Pupils on Educational Visits (HASPEV)* http://www.teachernet.gov.uk/visits

Department for Education and Skills Health & Safety: Responsibilities & Powers: www.teachernet.gov.uk

Early Learning Goals and Stepping Stones: www.tlfe.org.uk

Early Years Experience from 'Big Eyed Owl' – http://www.ictadvice.org.uk

Five Steps to Risk Assessment: http://www.hse.gov.uk

Foundation Stage (Early Years) websites: http://www.early-education.org.uk

Guidance on First Aid for Schools: http://www.teachernet.gov.uk/firstaid

Health and Safety: Responsibilities and Powers: http://www.teachernet.gov.uk/visits

http://curriculum.becta.org.uk/docserver.php?docid=2666

http://www.hitchams.suffolk.sch.uk/foundation/D

http://www.bristol-cyps.org.uk/services/outdoor_ed.html

http://www.mape.org.uk/curriculum/earlyyears/earlyyears.htm

http://www.outdoor-learning.org

http://www.sparklebox.co.uk/ie.html

http://www.teachernet.gov.uk/responsibilities

Learning Through Landscapes website: http://www.ltl.co.uk

Safegard website: Policy of Safety and Guidance – Outdoor Education: http://www.dorsetforyou.com

Safe Kids Campaign Report 2000, Child Accident Prevention Trust: http://www.evc-childsafe.gov.uk

Safety Education Guidance Leaflet Adventure activities centres; five steps to risk assessment http://www.teachernet.gov.uk/safetyeducationguidance

Supporting Pupils with Medical Needs: A Good Practice Guide: http://www.teachernet.gov.uk/medical
Teachers and the Law Booklet – The Professional Association of Teachers (2002): http://www.hse.gov.uk
The Incredible Years website: http://www.incredibleyears
The Department for Education and Science website: http://www.standards.dfes.gov.uk
The Quality and Curriculum Authority website: http://www.qca.org.uk
The Teacher Training Agency website: http://www.canteach.gov.uk

Index

Healthy, Active and Outside!